DUCKWORTH ARCHAEOLOGICAL HISTORIES

Tarquinia

AN ETRUSCAN CITY

Robert Leighton

Duckworth

First published in 2004 by
Gerald Duckworth & Co. Ltd.
90-93 Cowcross Street
London EC1M 6BF
Tel: 020 7490 7300
Fax: 020 7490 0080
inquiries@duckworth-publishers.co.uk
www.ducknet.co.uk

A catalogue record for this book is available
from the British Library

ISBN 0 7156 3162 4

Typeset by Ray Davies
Printed and bound in Great Britain by
Biddles Ltd, King's Lynn, Norfolk

To Jane

All'uomo che cavalca lungamente per terreni selvatici viene desiderio d'una città.

Italo Calvino, *Le Città Invisibili*

Contents

Contents

Preface

There are many good books about the Etruscans, but a general survey of one major site is a comparatively unusual, and I hope welcome, departure. Etruscan cities differed from each other in character and appearance, and sometimes in their historical development. I have concentrated, therefore, on themes and features specific to Tarquinia, but with reference to the regional setting and, where helpful, to the wider stage of Mediterranean archaeology. The intention was to provide an introduction not only to this key site but to a range of topics in Etruscan archaeology.

To gain familiarity with the primary sources on Tarquinia would require considerable time and commitment on the part of any interested reader. Apart from the literary references of antiquity and antiquarian writings pre-dating the late nineteenth century, the list of publications is dauntingly long and continually expanding. My bibliography cannot pretend to be comprehensive, although it includes most of the more recent work. Those who wish to see more images of the site and the finds in colour, notably the tomb paintings, must consult some of the books cited in my text or search the increasing number of relevant internet web pages.

A book of this nature is obviously indebted to primary research by many people, especially those dedicated Etruscologists who have laboured long and hard at Tarquinia, and whose works I have read and sometimes plundered with relish. I can only seek their indulgence for my often summary treatment of their discoveries and cherished theories, and for the compression or neglect of other detailed information.

*

My thanks go to several individuals for their advice and help: Claudia Pritchard and Tom Harrison for comments on the manuscript; Francesca Serra Ridgway and Nigel Spivey for bibliographic information; Allan Hood for Latin translations; Maria Lidia Perotti and Sylvia Diebner for documentation respectively from the Comune di Tarquinia and the German Archaeological Institute in Rome; and Deborah Blake at Duckworth for seeing the book through to publication. The sources of illustrations and photographs are listed in the text. The poem 'To the Etruscan Poets' cited in Chapter 5 is from *The Mind-Reader*, © 1975 by Richard Wilbur, reprinted by permission of Harcourt, Inc.

List of Illustrations

Plates (between pages 116 and 117) with sources

DAI = Deutsches Archäologisches Institut, Rome

List of Illustrations

Figures

1. Discovery and Loss

The discovery of ancient Tarquinia (*Tarch(u)na* in Etruscan, *Tarquinii* in Latin) followed trends in Italian or, more broadly, European scholarship from the age of Humanism through the Enlightenment, the Romantic and modern eras.[1] Like many histories of archaeological exploration that largely pre-date the modern practice of archaeology, it was driven by conflicting interests – mercenary as well as historical and artistic – but with little concern for preservation, resulting in both gains and losses. In the last 50 years, it has also reflected new techniques of archaeological investigation.[2] Tarquinia has contributed more than any other site, with the possible exception of Cerveteri (Caere in Latin), to an understanding of the genesis of Etruscan civilisation from its prehistoric roots to Romanisation, and it continues to feature prominently in Etruscan studies (*Etruscologia* in Italian).

The exploration of the archaeological remains is also bound up with the history of the modern town on the edge of the Monterozzi plateau. Formerly known as Corneto, this new centre of population was the medieval successor of the ancient city on the adjacent promontory of Civita (see Figs 1, 12, 57, and Chapter 2 for a topographical description). As a reminder of its illustrious ancestry, it was renamed Corneto-Tarquinia in 1872, but the conjoined name did not last long. In 1922, at a time of growing nationalism and pride in classical antiquities, Corneto was officially dropped from the title and the town reverted to the ancient name, Tarquinia.

Thanks to Greek and Roman writers, it had always been known that Tarquinia was a major Etruscan city, prominent in the fourth-century BC struggles against Rome, and perhaps the most prestigious of the dodecapolis or 'League of Twelve' mentioned by the written sources. For antiquarian scholarship it was not entirely surprising to learn of buried treasures, despite the scarcity of surface remains. Aside from the more fanciful lucubrations, the earliest research at the site provides some valuable records of finds and monuments subsequently damaged or lost, especially in the case of tomb paintings. It was the discovery of these brightly painted frescos in subterranean chambers within vast burial grounds that brought Tarquinia to the attention of a wide public. The tomb paintings are still the principal attraction for visitors.

There were several phases in the process of recovery, outlined in this chapter; its origins are obscure but it was well under way by the Renaissance. A growing interest in Etruscan antiquities in the eighteenth century stimulated periodic bursts of frenetic and chaotic exploration, while news of exciting finds brought the first visitors, mainly wealthy gentlemen initially, or clergy, collectors, scholars and artists, curious to see at first hand the surviving works of an as yet little-known civilisation. They were succeeded by increasing numbers from further afield, culminating in the mass tourism of modern times (around 140,000 people visited the site in 1984). Writers and travellers, including Stendhal, George Dennis, D.H. Lawrence and Corneto's native son, Vincenzo Cardarelli, have also contributed to what one might call a Tarquinian literary archive.

In the course of the twentieth century, state-sponsored or public archaeology began to supersede private interests, while new aims and methods came to the fore. A growing awareness of the fragility of the site and of the erosion of its finite endowment prompted a crisis of conscience, stimulating better planned research and conservation work. Nevertheless, spread over an area of at least 25 square kilometres, much of it farmland, Tarquinia poses daunting challenges for the local authorities. Looting is a constant affliction. At the same time, the scientific quest has always been shadowed by popular perceptions – fashions, fantasies and fixations – about the supposed identity and nature of the Etruscans.

Sepulchral treasures

Tomb-robbing is possibly the oldest profession in the world. Graves have been stripped of valuables at Tarquinia and sometimes re-used since at least Roman times (p. 175). The same must apply to buildings, demolished, dismantled or adapted over time. Cities feed off themselves sooner or later. Like many abandoned sites of antiquity, Tarquinia was a tempting quarry for its medieval descendant. Old Corneto, dotted with churches and crowned with an imposing circuit of walls and towers dating from the ninth/tenth centuries, bears mute witness to various episodes of recycling: ancient sarcophagi make decorative door lintels in the façade of San Giovanni Gerosolimitano, while Etruscan inscriptions, including one of Larth Velchas (probably one of the illustrious family buried in the Shields tomb; p. 167) are embedded in the Cosmatesque floor of Santa Maria di Castello (1121-1208), the town's foremost shrine. Churches in this area habitually cannibalised useful building materials, undoubtedly because it was often convenient and cheap to do so. In some cases, however, this suggests an assertion of ownership and of a certain pride in a venerable past, which any self-respecting civic authority might wish to appropriate and utilise.[3]

The name of Civita for the abandoned promontory across the valley,

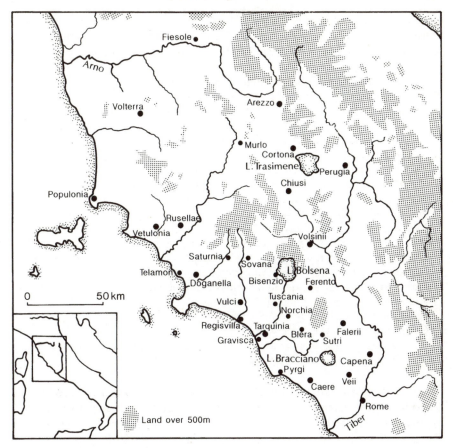

1. Regional map with principal sites.

used since at least the fourteenth century, when it was largely given over to vineyards and agriculture, preserves the memory of an urban past. Petrarch and his fellow humanist, Domenico Bandini of Arezzo, associated Corneto with Tarquinia and its remains:

> Next [is] Cornetum, a remarkable town with towers, surrounded by a double wall and looking down over distant seas from a high hill. In its territory was Tarquinii, once a city, now nothing but a bare name and ruins; from it issued the Tarquins who ruled in Rome.[4]

By contrast, a fifteenth-century Latin ode by a local poet, L. Vitelli, in praise of his native town, flatteringly assumes Corneto to be derived from mythical King Coritus, the father of Dardanus, founder of Troy, and

3

alludes to underground chambers with carved benches and ceilings. Confusing tombs with palaces, archaeology and myth, Vitelli's poetic encomium recalls the archaeological *mirabilia* of medieval scholarship:

> That mount is Coritus, ancestral to ancient Troy,
> on which the wealthy city of Cornetum now sits.
> The city was not girt with a wall; the mount is extraordinary;
> Its founder had no need of dusty lime.
> No people of Italy is older. Very important monuments survive,
> and more have been found in deep soil.
> There are vast palaces hewn from white stone:
> there was many a dwelling of an exceedingly great people.
> And where there are springs and seats cut from the rock around them,
> vents allow daylight to enter.
> In one there is a carved ceiling, beautiful to behold:
> that was, I believe, the palace of king Coritus.
> Eyes have scanned those memorable carvings,
> but the passage of time has diminished that original work.
> Moreover, there are statues and tombs of men of old,
> and there are images of demigods and gods.
> However, no letter has been inscribed there as a witness;
> Carmenta had not yet come to Italy.
> A large number are filled up; if care had been taken to explore the entrances,
> many things would have been discovered in several of them.[5]

A fabulous foundation myth for Corneto is also delineated in the seventeenth-century frescos of the Palazzo Comunale, featuring a genealogical tree with famous ancestors, including Dardanus and the child seer, Tages (p. 75), as well as excerpts from local history. While the etymology of Corneto was always problematic, civic pride doubtless steered the poetic imagination away from more prosaic, but likely, suggestions, such as a derivation from the Latin *cornus* (cornel tree), which has periodically served as the emblem of the town.

In the sixteenth century, Annius of Viterbo, a notorious forger but nonetheless influential concocter of bogus histories, believed that the antiquities around Corneto were to be identified with ancient Tarquinia. Tombs with paintings and inscriptions were undoubtedly known; some were probably only rediscovered in the eighteenth and nineteenth centuries, having already been opened and then forgotten centuries before. For example, Christian graffiti of about the fifteenth century scar the Bartoccini tomb, while the Mercareccia tomb (Fig. 2), remarkable for its carvings (p. 145), may well have inspired Vitelli's fantasy (above) about the palace of Coritus. By the thirteenth century, local artists must have been familiar with a range of antiquities. It is possible that some of the imagery of

4

2. Mercareccia tomb, upper chamber, late fourth/early third century BC, from
Antient Hypogaei (1842) by J. Byres.

medieval and Renaissance art was influenced by Etruscan motifs, notably
on sarcophagi and urns. A drawing of Hades by Michelangelo, resembling
a figure in the Orco tomb (Fig. 64B), is even thought by some scholars to
have been based on a tomb painting, although this is questionable; it more
likely follows a Roman model.[6]

Drawings of Etruscan monuments from this time are rare, yet the
sixteenth-century architect, Antonio da Sangallo the Younger, sketched
the foundations of a building on Civita, possibly part of the Roman baths
or a water reservoir (p. 175).[7] Venal interests were also roused by the
prospect of easy lucre. Digging is already documented in 1489 by the
arrival of an emissary from Pope Innocent VIII, charged with obtaining
items from a tomb which had contained a quantity of gold used by the
townsfolk to pay for repairs to local buildings. In 1546, Cardinal Farnese
tried to persuade the town council to supply Rome with 6,000 libbra in
metal objects (nearly 2,000 kilos), to be melted down and used to embellish
the basilica of St. John Lateran. Further papal involvement transpires
from a licence to dig issued by Gregory XIII in 1573, allowing some finds
(gold, marble and statues) to be retained locally.

In the seventeenth century, a local cleric, Muzio Polidori, recorded
Etruscan inscriptions in Corneto. A painted Hellenistic tomb (Tartaglia)
with sarcophagi was entered in 1699 and published in engravings accom-

panying *De Etruria Regali*, the landmark monograph in Etruscan studies by Thomas Dempster (1579-1625).[8] This book was commissioned by Cosimo II de' Medici and intended to buttress the prestige of the Florentine family by highlighting their prestigious 'Etruscan' past, although it was only published a century later (1724) owing to Dempster's fall from favour at court. Nevertheless, it did much to foster the fashion for Etruscan studies, or *Etruscheria*, which had an enthusiastic following in learned societies and academies, notably that of Cortona founded in 1726.

In the same year, a widely travelled French cleric, J.B. Labat, visited Tarquinia, where he saw fast fading tomb frescos and obtained ancient vases.[9] The collection of old coins, curiosities or *anticaglie* (antiquities of no particular aesthetic significance) was quite common at this time. Illustrations and more detailed descriptions of the Mercareccia tomb were published by A.F. Gori in 1743, thanks to the efforts of an Agostinian monk of Corneto, G. Forlivesi, who provided information about recent discoveries to scholars of the day and acted as the local guide. Scipione Maffei, a pioneer of eighteenth-century Etruscology, was shown tombs with painted inscriptions and banquet scenes during his visit of 1739 and recorded his concern about their deterioration, a problem that has preoccupied conservation science ever since:

> It is rare to enjoy so much, because the paintings appear lovely and fresh on first opening the grottoes, but after the air enters freely, in a few years all is lost and the plaster on which they are painted becomes wet and crumbles.[10]

Nonetheless, Etruscan sites remained marginal to the more predictable interests and itineraries of eighteenth-century Grand Tourists, mostly bound for the Eternal City, the Bay of Naples and, in the case of the more adventurous, the Greek temples of Sicily.[11] Once opened, tombs would likely become sheepfolds or hen coops, or be closed to prevent their use as hideouts by *malviventi*. It was only with the opening of the Biclinium, Ceisinie, Tapestry and Cardinal tombs in the later eighteenth century that the existence of the 'Corneto grottoes' became relatively well known and began to attract visitors. Winckelmann mentions them in correspondence (e.g. in 1758), while the Comte de Caylus published a letter of 1760 from the Italian antiquary, Paolo Maria Paciaudi, who had spent three days at Tarquinia digging, copying inscriptions and observing tombs and frescos, which he associated with 'the passage of souls to the Elysian Fields'.[12] Thomas Jenkins, an Englishman who combined such profitable activities as antiquary and banker while resident in Rome, participated in the excavation of three tombs in 1761, one of which was the Cardinal (Fig. 3; p. 166), and sent information about them to the Royal Society of London, which published a short description of 'Civita Turchino' in 1763.[13]

1. Discovery and Loss

The unearthing of a fine Hellenistic sculpture, the bronze 'putto Carrara' (Fig. 4; p. 160), in 1770, probably on Civita, indicates that digging was not confined to tombs. Donated to Clement XIV, its transfer to the Vatican stimulated an outburst of propagandistic rhetoric by Gioacchino Pizzi. Poets of the papal court were always keen to extol the role of the Church as the true guardian of Italy's cultural treasures. The poem (1771) fancifully surmises that even the Etruscans would have approved of this:

> Oh youth, who in ancient bronze
> preserve the art and valor of an Etruscan hand,
> do not complain if for a long age
> you lay hidden in the proud Tarquinian plain:
> The splendid gift of a gentle heart,
> you go now to the Sovereign Ruler of august Rome,
> and in the shelter of the famous Museum
> you lift your smiling face in the Vatican.
> Perhaps long ago the soothsayers
> already envisioned
> your luminous new destiny;
> and they wished the immortal work concealed
> from the ancient Tyrrhenian wave nearby,
> to allow the fate of your greatness to ripen.[14]

Interest in the site was soon spreading amid artists and cognoscenti in Rome, who included antiquarians, dealers and erudite guides (*ciceroni*), such as James Byres (1734-1817), a Scot, like Dempster, whose Etruscan work (*Hypogaei or Sepulchral Caverns of Tarquinia, the Capital of Antient Etruria*, London 1842) was published posthumously.[15] This is notable for

3. Cardinal tomb, probably third century BC, from *Antient Hypogaei* (1842) by J. Byres.

7

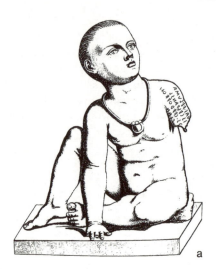

a b

4. Hellenistic bronzes, prized by collectors: (a) the 'putto Carrara', found in 1770 (H 33 cm; after Micali 1832, pl. 44); (b) mirror with Scylla, relief decoration, found in 1866 (D 11.5 cm; after Lambrechts 1978, 32).

illustrations of the Cardinal, Biclinium, Ceisinie, Mercareccia and Tapestry tombs in a rather mannered style, reminiscent of Piranesi, and based largely on the work of a young Polish painter, Franciszek Smuglewicz, who accompanied Byres to Tarquinia between 1763 and 1766 (Figs 2-3). The need for subscriptions in order to promote and publish the projected book doubtless encouraged Byres to enhance the appearance of the tombs with dramatic lighting and false human scales, making them look larger and better preserved than they were, while exaggerating the expressions and poses of some painted figures (p. 166). He may equally have been interested in exciting interest in the frescos with a view to detaching them for potential sale.

Piranesi also visited Tarquinia together with Byres, drawing artefacts and part of the Cardinal tomb in 1763-64. His writings on Roman architecture were to fuel a debate on the primacy of Roman versus Greek art in which he asserted the essential independence of Roman architecture through its Etruscan, not Greek, antecedents. Like most of his erudite colleagues, Piranesi believed, wrongly, that the finest painted pottery from the tombs was Etruscan.[16] Thus Josiah Wedgwood named his famous Staffordshire factory of neoclassical ceramics 'Etruria' and his own home 'Etruria Hall', while Robert Adam designed elegant 'Etruscan' rooms for English stately homes from a pastiche of Graeco-Roman motifs; in fact, there was nothing very Etruscan in any of their creations. Contemporary scholarship had only just begun to grapple with the thorny issues (linguis-

8

tic, racial, cultural, artistic) of Etruscan identity, although some scholars were more wary than others of facile equivalences. Already in 1717, for example, Maffei had warned that not all Etruscan finds in private collections should be credited as such:

> I suspect that everything they have not understood they have called Etruscan.[17]

A capricious flirtation with Tarquinia and the Etruscans persisted for the rest of the century. The early nineteenth-century works of Micali and Inghirami abandoned some of the wilder theories and excesses of *Etruscheria*, while introducing some new prejudices of their own, but added little to existing information. Meanwhile, the trade in antiquities flourished. A Parisian dealer, Dunand, was probably just one of many to embark on a profitable trip around Etruria in 1792, buying vases for a fraction of their sale value in the Paris and London markets, although local people were fast becoming wise to their potential worth.[18]

With the realisation early in the nineteenth century that the figured vases (or at least their models) were Greek, the Etruscans undoubtedly lost status. By now they were also having to compete for attention not just with Roman remains but with a growing international interest in Greece, Egypt and the East. In the absence of Etruscan literature, moreover, there was no rich vein of popular heroes and myths, like those of Greece and Rome, to be tapped by contemporary artists. When Etruscans occasionally did feature in Renaissance and later art, the viewing public were inevitably reminded that the only vaguely familiar characters, the Tarquin rulers of Rome, comprised several tyrants and Sextus Tarquinius, that infamous defiler of female virtue (p. 132). Even the chapel of Palazzo Vitelleschi (now the National Museum of Tarquinia) has fifteenth-century frescos of the rape of Lucretia and the death of Tarquinius at Gabii; the story, popularised by writers and poets, helped to keep alive an ancient cliché of Etruscan immorality (p. 159).

On the other hand, the Etruscans had certain claims to fame and a mystique which the Romans lacked, including chronological priority. Strabo, for example, acknowledged Roman debts to Etruria and specifically to Tarquinia (p. 132), an admission readily exploited by Dempster and the anti-Roman or more politically motivated eighteenth-century devotees of *Etruscheria*. The Etruscans also occupied a literary twilight zone, illuminated, albeit dimly, by increasing numbers of puzzling inscriptions, presenting philologists, linguists, translators and a few cranks from all over Europe with the irresistible challenge of decipherment. From Dempster onward, the nature and origins of the Etruscan language were major issues for debate, subsequently stimulated by the publication of encyclopaedic corpora of inscriptions. The care taken in their recording, already exemplified by the work of Byres (Ceisinie tomb inscriptions), contrasts strikingly with the rough handling or destruction of so much else. In addition, the tomb paintings were fostering a new and seductive image of Etruscan life to which connoisseurs and the literary world would quickly succumb.

The lucrative adventure

A second phase of discovery in the post-Napoleonic years was partly inspired by the opening of an intact tomb by a municipal official of Corneto, Carlo Avvolta (p. 64). In 1823, stone was being taken from a large tumulus in order to mend a road when the chamber roof appeared; a slab was removed and Avvolta found himself peering into a dark time capsule. His description reflects the thrill of the moment and the idea, ever potent in the popular imagination, of revisiting an inviolate past by the light of a flickering torch:

> ... almost in ecstasy I stopped to look at everything visible from that position and, above all, fixed my gaze on the warrior lying before me on the bed; in a few minutes I watched him almost vanish before my eyes, as the more air entered the tomb, the more his oxidised armour crumbled into tiny particles, leaving ... scarcely a vestige of what I had seen. Widening the aperture ... I had a workman help me descend, which I did forthwith and forbade anyone else to enter without permission. Thus, taking my time, I looked, examined and noted everything that was placed in the tomb and which I am sure the reader would like to hear described ... such was my astonishment, that I cannot express the effect upon me produced by this sight; but I can safely assert that it was the happiest moment of my life.[19]

Eager hands then set about dismantling the once careful arrangements, some finds were stolen and others given to landowners or sold; only Avvolta's sketch and a few artefacts eventually stored in the Berlin museum remain (Fig. 5). Thanks largely to its citation by Hamilton Gray (p. 20), this account was almost as famous in Victorian England as that of Howard Carter, 99 years later, on entering the tomb of Tutankhamun. It inspired several poems (below), as well as the description of the François tomb at Vulci in 1857, where warriors also turned to dust:

> It was an evocation of the past that lasted no longer than a dream, and disappeared as though to punish us for our foolhardy curiosity.[20]

Yet the Vulci report arguably lacks the more genuine feelings and enthusiasm of Avvolta, despite the reverential sentiments of the excavators.

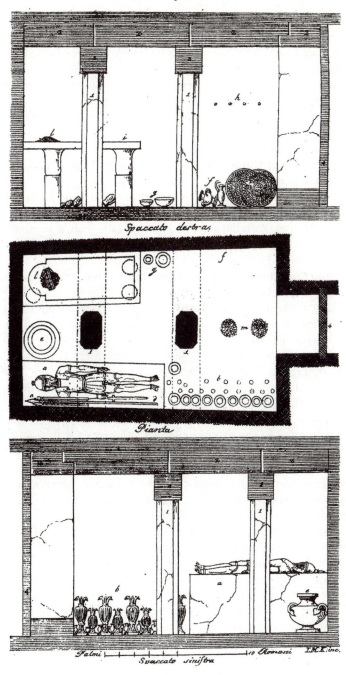

5. Plan of the Avvolta tomb (after Avvolta 1829).

From a slightly cynical modern perspective, they also have a hollow ring, coming from persons engaged in what was ultimately little more than depredation and self-enrichment. When George Dennis visited Vulci some years later, he was appalled to find that the workmen were under orders to smash all the unpainted pots, perhaps in order to keep the prices high.[21]

Over the next decade, until 1833, painted tombs came to light almost annually at Tarquinia. Some information can be gleaned from reports of the *Instituto di Corrispondenza Archeologica*, founded in 1829 by the Hyperboreans, a circle of German scholars in Rome, inspired by Eduard Gerhard.[22] The great tumuli on Monterozzi were prime targets, but rich burials were also opened on outlying Monte Quaglieri, and mosaics, columns, statues and inscriptions plucked from the Roman baths on Civita. Wealthy foreigners, such as the Hanoverian minister, August Kestner, and Lord Kinnaird, collaborated in excavations with a local workforce, obtaining and selling most of the finds, especially the painted vases, often illegally.

Staggering quantities of Etruscan antiquities were now being dispersed throughout Italy and Europe, whetting the appetite of national museums. Like wealthy individuals, they could be aggressively competitive collectors. In the case of private collections it is often impossible to identify the source of objects. Nevertheless, outside Italy, antiquities from Tarquinia have migrated to collections in Berlin, Frankfurt, Hanover, Munich, Stuttgart, Würzburg, Brussels, Copenhagen, Leiden, Geneva, Paris (Louvre), Madrid, London (British Museum), New York (Metropolitan), Boston, Philadelphia, and Toronto.

One may be wary of glibly romanticising this period; in fact, it was more like a holocaust for Etruscan archaeology.[23] Gangs of workmen 50-strong picked over the site like ants on a carcass. The Roman authorities suspected that frescos were being removed from painted tombs and the tombs being dynamited in order to obliterate the evidence. Excavation licences issued by the papal government imposed certain restrictions, but did little to encourage any recording; they were more concerned with asserting a kind of *droit de seigneur* over the pick of the crop. Even the restoration of fine vases was often spoilt by filing down sherds from different vessels and joining them to produce hybrid reconstructions. Attitudes were largely conditioned by mercenary interests and by the fact that much was destined for private enjoyment and profit. While the renowned goldwork and jewellery of the Castellani craftsmen promoted the fashion for Etruscan replicas throughout eighteenth-century Europe, the princess of Canino (the wife of Lucien Bonaparte, Napoleon's brother, and plunderer of Vulci) wore the real thing at Roman soirées.[24]

Amid the frenetic and essentially destructive activity on site, the *Instituto* merits some credit for a concern with recording and publishing. One of the few enduring contributions stemmed from its interest in tomb paintings. In 1827, Baron Otto von Stackelberg (whence the 'Stackelberg', or Biga tomb), who had excavated at the Temple of Apollo at Bassae in 1812, made illustrations *in situ* of several Tarquinian frescos, together with Kestner and the architect Jospeh Thürmer; these were intended for a lavish book, which never materialised, although the bound specimen sheets survive in Rome. They were followed in 1829 by Henri Labrouste, a French architect resident in Rome, who included sections and measurements in some illustrations of tombs and tumuli.[25] Much more was done by an otherwise little-known Roman artist-cum-craftsman, Carlo Ruspi, sent to Tarquinia by Gerhard in 1831 with the specific task of illustrating the Querciola tomb on behalf of the *Instituto*, which feared that the papal authorities might soon forbid copies to be made, or that frescos might be detached and sold. As it turned out, Ruspi also produced watercolours of the Triclinium tomb (Plates VII-IX), the source of analytical descriptions published in 1831.[26]

Fortunately, Ruspi then had the excellent idea of making tracings (*lucidi*) of other painted tombs (Fig. 6; Plate X), which would provide an accurate basis for coloured facsimiles destined for the Vatican library, thereby preserving them for posterity: 'the said cartoons conjoined will form the entire chamber'.[27] By a remarkable coincidence, while visiting Tarquinia, probably in 1834, Stendhal (below) saw the conscientious Ruspi at work:

> We had occasion, three years ago, to see M. Ruspi at work on new copies of these singular paintings .... We are assured that M. Ruspi added nothing to the truly sublime drawing and brilliant colours of the originals. Not once, for example, did he wish to correct hands which nonetheless resemble frogs' feet. But we learned that, over three years, the colours of these frescos are much changed. A wolf-like dog, placed at the foot of one of the tables, in one of the pictures showing a funerary ceremony, with admirable realism and feeling, has disappeared completely.[28]

Against the odds, many of these tracings have survived; they are valuable documents, held in the German archaeological institute in Rome, although – despite Stendhal's asssurances – there are occasional signs of minor elaborations and 'corrections'. Ruspi acted as a guide for Ludwig I of Bavaria who visited Tarquinia in 1834 and commissioned another set of copies for the gallery walls of the Alte Pinakothek in Munich, where they provided a thematic backdrop for the vase collection until their destruction in 1943. Likewise, in 1834, a copy of the frieze from the recently discovered Baron tomb (Plate VI) was incorporated by the architect F.P. Palagi into the ceiling decorations of Racconigi castle, near Turin, probably following the illustrations of Labrouste.[29]

6. Deceased tomb, *c.* 510 BC (after an illustration of 1835 by Carlo Ruspi: *MonInst* 2, 1834-38).

The Vatican versions of Ruspi's original copies also helped to inspire a kind of virtual reality exhibition mounted by the Campanari brothers in London's Pall Mall in 1836-37, where artefacts and sarcophagi were placed inside reconstructions of painted tombs (Biga, Triclinium, Deceased, Inscriptions), seen by candlelight in a stagey attempt to create an eerie atmosphere of the kind recorded by Avvolta. It was a great success, confirming the popular notion of archaeology, especially in the Mediterranean, as a romantic adventure in picturesque settings, an alluring idea for the city-dwellers of industrial England. The aim was also commercial, however: to encourage the British Museum to purchase the artefacts, which it duly did, if only to display them subsequently in a comparatively dull fashion, in a rather nondescript area somewhere between the Elgin marbles and Egyptology. Not surprisingly, they were now '... passed by with but little, if any, attention ... so much has arrangement to do with exciting public interest'.[30]

By 1838, a set of Ruspi facsimiles was on show in the newly founded Etruscan Gregorian musem in the Vatican, albeit with the tactful omission of immodest figures in the Biga tomb (Plate X; p. 120). Other museums later followed suit.[31] By 1881, the main hall of the Museo Civico di Bologna was richly adorned with a rather inaccurate set of reproductions, partly for didactic purposes but doubtless also as a way of enlivening the galleries. In 1899, Carl Jacobsen, the founder of the Ny Carlsberg Glyptothek in Copenhagen, inspired by the Munich museum and working in close collaboration with Wilhelm Helbig, an agent for foreign dealers and institutions, sponsored the creation of new copies, based partly on Ruspi drawings and others done afresh. Finally, in 1912, the Etruscan museum in Florence commissioned Etruscan tomb murals for the galleries which opened in 1932. As fashions subsequently changed and museums came to scorn the notion of displaying copies, these works were consigned to the store-rooms, although interest in them has recently revived, resulting in exhibitions in Italy and abroad (1985-87); perhaps one day they will be rehabilitated, or succeeded by computerised recreations.

Of the French nineteenth-century writers who occasionally refer to the Etruscans, Stendhal had more than a passing interest in ancient Etruria and a personal knowledge of Tarquinia, thanks to his years as consul at Civitavecchia (1831-36, 1840). This transpires from several letters and works, notably an essay of 1837 entitled *Les tombeaux de Corneto*, an engaging mixture of local news and description, more concerned with the price of vases than with Etruscan scholarship – not surprisingly perhaps, since he himself was a buyer and joined in the digging.[32] For all its potential to stir the emotions and challenge the intellect, archaeology was basically a good sport, like a hunting or fishing trip, and often remarkably profitable. In Etruria it was also a flourishing industry, in which private fortunes could be made.

Like many writers, Stendhal was attracted by the Etruscans, to whom he ascribed one of Italy's three golden ages, along with the Augustan and the Renaissance. At times, he is mischievously and inconsistently anti-

Roman, in a manner reminiscent of the old rhetoric of Etruscheria. He also foreshadows the sporadic anti-Roman outbursts of D.H. Lawrence a century later (p. 22):

> I feel indignant about these Romans who came to disrupt, with no justification other than ferocious courage, these republics of Etruria which were so superior to them in their arts, riches and in the art of being happy .... It is as if twenty regiments of cossacks came to ransack and destroy Paris .... The Romans have been a great ill for humanity, a baneful malady which retarded the civilisation of the world.[33]

Coincidentally, while Stendhal likens Romans to cossacks, D.H. Lawrence thought of them as the 'Prussians' of antiquity (*Sketches of Etruscan Palaces* [*EP*], 9.24).[34] What troubled them both in particular was their perception that the all-conquering upstarts destroyed something especially precious in Etruria: not so much Etruscan art *per se* (for the Romans had their own artistic achievements, which could hardly be ignored), as that elusive 'art of being happy' or, for Lawrence, their art of living, even a 'religion of life' (*EP*, 56.35). The Tarquinia tomb paintings, with their dancing and banquets, were largely responsible for the popular notion, or myth, of Etruscan happiness, which persists to this day, and finds another pleasing corollary in the proverbial 'Etruscan smile' – in fact a somewhat stylised convention of Archaic art. Even if they were not masterpieces, as artistic revelations of an extinct civilisation the frescos were ready icons of a paradise lost, especially potent in the Romantic imagination and in the minds of travellers from northern Europe, some of whom were on personal quests, seeking inspiration or solace in antiquity; or else, like Goethe, on an intellectual journey back to the supposed roots of western culture. Stendhal, however, retained some reservations about the Etruscans, whose main or only fault, he suspected – thus revealing a strain of anti-clericalism and the influence of Micali – was to have let themselves be dominated by a caste of religious leaders.

Two redoubtable Victorians did much to familiarise English readers with Tarquinia and the Etruscans. The first was Mrs E.C. Hamilton Gray, who attended the London show of 1837 and, as a result, became rapidly enamoured with all things Etruscan, and went on to record her experiences and impressions in a lively account of a *Tour to the Sepulchres of Etruria in 1839*. Published in three editions (1840-43) it was a popular success, despite a harsh review, and deservedly so. Her genial enthusiasm, albeit lacking in scholarly depth, undoubtedly encouraged growing numbers of English visitors to include Etruscan antiquities in their tours of central Italy.[35] Having befriended Kestner, and with Avvolta as her guide at Tarquinia, Hamilton Gray is also a useful source of information and

7. Painted Vases tomb, *c.* 500 BC (after an illustration of 1869 by L. Schulz: *MonInst* 9, 1869-73).

gossip. For example, she reports that the Rome antique shops were full of Etruscan antiquities, and confirms other sources (including Stendhal) when she writes that ' ... all the principal dealers had bought or hired land for themselves in the burying places or on the sites of such Etruscan cities ... the hospital of the Borgo di Santo Spirito had more possessions in these newly discovered treasuries than all the rest put together' – including the Tarquinia cemetery, which it ' ... let out for excavations and for sheep-feeding'.[36]

8. Monterozzi tumulus base (the 'Mausoleum'; after Dennis 1878, 387).

In 1848, another Etruscan book was published, with an improved edition in 1878, entitled *The Cities and Cemeteries of Etruria*, by George Dennis, a rather unlikely employee of the London Excise Office, who was inspired by Hamilton Gray's work, but also goaded by its shortcomings. This was a fuller, meditated study, carefully observed and free of the partisan Etruscomania of some earlier scholarship. Dedicated to Henry Layard (the excavator of Nineveh), it was also the fruit of extensive travel in Etruria from 1842-47.[37] Tarquinia was the first base for Dennis and his painter friend, Samuel Ainsley, where they lodged from 7 June to 9 July 1842. Ainsley produced illustrations and views of Etruscan tombs and landscapes. They also met Carlo Avvolta, almost 80 years old, whose main hobbies were still hunting and excavating.[38] At this time, 19 painted tombs were visitable, unlocked by a custodian, including the recently discovered Orco and Painted Vases tombs, which had been illustrated by two artists (G. Mariani and L. Schulz; Fig. 7). The stone drums of some tumuli could still be seen (Fig. 8).

Tarquinia also features in the lavishly illustrated folio by Luigi Canina, *L'antica Etruria marittima* (Rome, 1846-51), an expensive and finely crafted successor of Byres' *Antient Hypogaei*, and a luxurious precursor of

9. Monterozzi necropolis, reconstruction hypothesis (after Canina 1846-51, pl. LXXIX).

the modern 'coffee-table' genre. It has a topographical plan and imaginative, but flawed, reconstructions of grand conical tumuli on Monterozzi and a city-scape on Civita (Fig. 9; p. 90).

A lull in digging around the mid-nineteenth century was followed by a string of major discoveries: the painted Orco tomb (1868), the late Villanovan Warrior tomb (1869), the Hunting and Fishing tomb (1873) and the 'Amazon' sarcophagus (Plate XXII).[39] The collections of the Bruschi family of Corneto continued to grow, while local landowners, such as the Marzi, went on digging untroubled by any notions of scientific method. Some of the finest painted tombs came to light in the later nineteenth century: the Lionesses (1874), Leopards (1875), Augurs (1878) and Bulls (1892), as well as the older Bocchoris tomb (1895) and the later Hellenistic vaults of the Partunu (1876) and Pulena (1878) families, containing respectively 14 and 21 sarcophagi.

Literary encounters

The relationship between archaeology and landscape, and the juxtaposition of past and present, elicited responses that varied according to changing aesthetics, individual personalities and perceptions. The natural or architectural beauty spots of Tuscany and Umbria were a regular source of inspiration for nineteenth-century poets and painters. Tarquinia, however, was little more than a series of grain fields in a landscape that was certainly not unattractive but nevertheless unrenowned. The Roman Campagna to the south and the sparsely populated Maremma to the north, with its scruffy heathland, malarial coast and impoverished peasants, were worlds away from the famous cities, centres of art, and the mountains, lakes and vistas of the Grand Tour. Dante (*Inferno*, 12.137; 13.9) refers to the Maremma as a wild place of notorious brigands. Brigandage was indeed still rife in the nineteenth century. To some visitors, Corneto, with its down-at-heel hostelry incongruously housed in a dilapidated Renaissance palace (il 'palazzaccio', later the museum), reinforced a sense of decay, prompting predictable comparisons between 'then' and 'now'. Dennis, surveying Civita and Monterozzi, goes on to say:

> The one was the city of the living; the other the city of the dead. Formerly, how different! Now, but too similar – rivals in desolation! It is a wild and dreary scene.[40]

Nineteenth-century writers, nurtured by a Greek and Latin education, were perhaps unlikely to find the same inspiration in Etruria as, for instance, in classical Campania. Carducci, for all his Maremman boyhood, passion for antiquity and use of classical myth and allusion, only mentions the Etruscans occasionally, although Tarchon (p. 75) has a cameo role in 'To Friends in the Tiber Valley' (1867). Yet writers and poets were not unmoved by the mystique of Etruscan archaeology or by the riches flowing from the tombs. The 'Etruscan vase' is a recurrent motif in nineteenth-century poetry and prose.[41] Above all, it was the Avvolta tomb and its ghostly mirage which captured the imagination, inspiring, for example, the opening stanza of 'Aylmer's Field', a major poem by Tennyson, written in 1862-63:

> Dust are our frames; and, gilded dust, our pride
> Looks only for a moment whole and sound;
> Like that long-buried body of the king,
> Found lying with his urns and ornaments,
> Which at a touch of light, an air of heaven,
> Slipt into ashes, and was found no more.[42]

Tennyson knew of the discovery from Hamilton Gray and from another poem, 'The Etrurian King' (1842) by his friend, the Archbishop of Dublin, eminent theologian and writer, Richard Chenevix Trench (whose source is also Hamilton Gray):

> One only eye beheld him in his pride,
> The old Etrurian monarch, as he died;
> And as they laid him on his bier of stone,
> Shield, spear, and arrows laying at his side;
> In golden armour with his crown of gold,
> One only eye the kingly warrior spied;
> Nor that eye long – for in the common air
> The wondrous pageant might not now abide,
> Which had in sealèd sepulchre the wrongs

Of time for thirty centuries defied.
That eye beheld it melt and disappear,
As down an hour-glass the last sand-drops glide.
A few short moments – and a shrunken heap
Of common dust survived, of all that pride:
And so that gorgeous vision has remained
For evermore to other eye denied:
And he who saw must oftentimes believe
That him his waking senses had belied,
Since what if all the pageants of the earth
Melt soon away, and may not long abide,
Yet when did ever doom *so* swift before
Even to the glories of the earth betide?[43]

This poetic sermon has a counterpart in the Pre-Raphaelite imagery and once popular sentimentality of 'Mimma Bella. In Memory of a Little Life' (XXVII), by Eugene J. Lee-Hamilton (1845-1907), half-brother of the writer Vernon Lee:

Once, breaking open an Etruscan tomb,
Man came upon a figure, lying there
In seeming sleep, pale, young, and very fair,
Wearing a small gold locket in the gloom.

But scarce the breeze had filled the buried room,
The form fell in: robe, pallid cheek, and hair
Turned to white ash beneath the newer air;
And on that ash they saw the gold still loom.[44]

By the early twentieth century, both the poetry of burial and percep-tions of landscape were becoming less predictable. D.H. Lawrence arrived in Etruria in the spring of 1927 and devoted nearly half of his *Sketches of Etruscan Places* to Tarquinia.[45] A late work, published posthumously in 1932, it is a rather poignant personal memoir, with reflections on art, religion, sex and the human condition, incorporating several of his cher-ished themes, especially that of lost innocence. Lawrence, however, was enchanted by the 'soft and swooping' wheat-green hills around Tarquinia (*EP*, 33.20) and was drawn to the idea of cultural and even ethnic continu-ity, which he sought in the landscape and in the facial geography of its inhabitants, whose eyes, lineaments and expressions spurred some strange flights of fantasy (such as the faun-faced shepherd). There is a tendency amongst Etruscan scholars, perhaps not entirely justified, to dismiss Lawrence's Etruscans as the product of wishful thinking, a pretext for proselytising, overly influenced by personal frustrations and failing health.[46] Yet, aside from issues of literary merit, the book is in many ways relevant and challenging for archaeology, unlike the merely amusing anecdotes or somewhat faded Etruscan vignettes of E.M. Forster and Aldous Huxley.[47]

A troubled genius Lawrence undoubtedly was, but he was also well read, widely travelled and deeply interested in non-western societies. Despite encroaching tuberculosis, he had not lost his sense of humour. He plays Etruscans off against Romans in a slightly naïve and stereotypical manner, although this is partly tongue-in-cheek, a provocative game fuelled by his desire to challenge the more entrenched puritanical values of contemporary society and its admiration for Imperial Rome. Lawrence saw himself as a champion of the Etruscans, which may seem an unnecessary and slightly eccentric role today, but one which is comprehensible when set against the prevailing conventions of the time. In part it represents an extension of his own battles with current social mores and censorship, brought to a head by the furore surrounding *Lady Chatterley's Lover*, which is also a late work. However, his interest in Etruria was of long standing and he had read or at least dipped into several ponderous tomes by Mommsen, MacIver, Weege and Ducati, as well as Dennis. Without any pretensions to scholarship himself, he betrays a good grasp of the limitations and conundrums of contemporary Etruscology: the elusiveness of the aboriginal people ('now ridiculously called Villanovans'; *EP*, 27.15), the poor quality of excavations, the lack of settlements, the distorting lens of Greece and Rome, and the interplay of internal and external forces in shaping Etruscan society.

Responsibility for his occasional erroneous statements often lies with his academic sources ('most of them contradicting one another'; *EP*, 28.3), whereas some of his own attitudes and approaches now seem commendable, or even ahead of their time: he challenges the ancient literary sources, he uses archaeology and the content of the art itself (rather than analogies with Greek art) in order to discuss Etruscan identity, is prepared to grapple with symbolic meanings in funerary art and the links between art, religion, ideology and culture, conscious all the while, like a modern archaeologist, that the past is indeed 'foreign'. Less interested in objects (with an understandable aversion to decontextualised museum displays) than in the philosophy or thought system that produced them, he shares some of the current concerns of cognitive archaeology and phenomenology. Moreover, Lawrence wrote with a powerful sense of empathy and engagement, for example, on the strength of religious belief in antiquity and haruspicy (the study of entrails for the purposes of divination).

Aldous Huxley, a good friend and admirer of Lawrence, often resided in Tuscany and must have visited Tarquinia in the early 1920s. His description of the site in *Point Counter Point* (1928) also suggests a knowledge of the work of George Dennis. The chief characteristic of the relevant passage is the witty banter of the English 'house party' at the cemetery. They are soon onto the subject (becoming a little tiresome now) of Etruscans versus Romans:

> But in these Etruscan vaults … one gets no such impression of organised and efficient beastliness as one gets from the Roman mosaic. There's a freshness, as you say, Mr. Cardan, a certain jolly schoolboyishness about all the fun they represent. But I have no doubt, of course, that the impression is entirely fallacious.[48]

Vincenzo Cardarelli (1884-1959), the native poet, provides an interesting contrast with foreign visitors. He is ambivalent about Corneto, the town of his childhood. In an early work (*Il sole a picco*, 1929), its atmosphere of melancholy provincialism is intensified by the 'sadness' of antiquity and archaeological remains, which he recalls the townsfolk regarding with disdain. The ancient sarcophagi become grotesque, with their fleshy, staring lid figures '… almost in the act of getting up and preparing to speak, as if they had had enough of being dead'.[49] In some of his poems, Tarquinia is a place of ghosts, but Cardarelli is nevertheless drawn to the necropolis, with its long tradition of burial, linking past and present, Christian and pagan:

Alto su rupe	High on a rock
battuto dai venti	battered by winds
un cimitero frondeggia:	a cemetery bears leaves:
cristianá oasi nel Tartaro etrusco.	Christian oasis in the Etruscan Tartarus.
Là sotto è la fanciulla	There below is the most beautiful
bellissima dei Velcha,	girl of the Velcha,
che vive ancora nella Tomba dell'Orco.	who lives on in the Orco tomb.
È il giaciglio gentile	The gracious resting place
della Pulzella	of the Pulcella
poco discosto.	is not far away.
Legioni di morti calarono	Legions of the dead were lowered
in quell'antica terra over sperai	into that ancient ground where I hoped
dormire un giorno e rimetter radici.	to sleep one day and put back roots.[50]

In prose works, such as *Il cielo sulle città* (1939), Cardarelli also asserts historical continuity, vaunting ancestral connections to the Etruscans through the very earth of the fields in what today sound like oddly rhetorical passages, tinged with the slightly giddy nationalism of the period.

Etruscan and especially Tarquinian motifs occur in the work of other modern poets: for example, the Spaniard, Antonio Colinas (*Sepulcro en*

Tarquinia, 1975), the American, Richard Wilbur ('The Etruscan Poets' in *The Mind-Reader: New Poems*, 1976, cited in Chapter 5), and in a collection of poems by Rika Lesser, which looks closely at objects, appropriately entitled *Etruscan Things* (1983).[51] Death and loss are only some of the concerns in these works. D.H. Lawrence's famous poem, 'Cypresses', quoted in part below, is also about recovery and reinterpretation; a poem for archaeologists, it foreshadows many of the ideas subsequently elaborated in *Etruscan Places*:

> For oh, I know, in the dust where we have buried
> The silenced races and all their abominations,
> We have buried so much of the delicate magic of life.
>
> There in the deeps
> That churn the frankincense and ooze the myrrh,
> Such an aroma of lost human life!
>
> They say the fit survive,
> But I invoke the spirits of the lost.
> Those that have not survived, the darkly lost,
> To bring their meaning back into life again,
> Which they have taken away
> And wrapt inviolable in soft cypress-trees,
> Etruscan cypresses.

It is perhaps slightly surprising that none of these visitors express discomfort that the 'legions of the dead' should have been so unremittingly and unceremoniously dismembered while their intended resting places were ransacked. Even churchmen and the Vatican authorities seem to have been unconcerned; pagan bones evidently merited no respect and only the uneducated feared curses or divine retribution. Defunct civilisations cannot launch lawsuits or demand restitution. Today, the *clandestini* may be fined or incarcerated if caught, although theirs is regarded as a crime against science or property, not one of profanation, while archaeologists excavate tombs unchallenged, as long as it is done scientifically. On this apparently sentimental point, no one has ventured a word on behalf of the long dead Etruscans.

New aims and methods

Italian Unification fostered new initiatives and attitudes to excavation, archaeological monuments and the national heritage, curtailing the power of wealthy aristocrats and landowners, and substituting the old papal administration with the officialdom of a new state. The first Mayor of

Corneto, Luigi Dasti, promoted excavations energetically on municipal land from 1881-96 in order to enrich the local museum.[52] Founded in 1874 and initially housed in a former ecclesiastical prison, it grew rapidly. Most of the Bruschi collection was obtained by the State in 1913 and the elegant Renaissance Palazzo Vitelleschi, cleaned and restored, opened as the new premises in 1916. The occasion was marred, however, by a theft of about 650 objects, mainly jewellery and coins (including goldwork from the Bocchoris tomb), a further setback in the struggle to build up the local collection after the long history of dispersion and loss. Many years later another blow was sustained, literally, by the museum during an aerial bombardment on 17 January 1944 when the building was badly damaged and several objects destroyed.[53]

The late nineteenth-century excavations also opened a new chapter in the history of the site, represented by Iron Age graves, identified with the Villanovan culture, known from pioneering work at Bologna. Hundreds of these tombs, especially the shaft graves (*pozzi*) on the Monterozzi plateau, had remained largely undisturbed since antiquity (Figs 10, 19, 21-23).[54] Unfortunately, however, there was only limited supervision of workmen by Dasti or a local foreman, whose reports formed the basis of the schematic accounts by Helbig, Ghirardini and Pasqui in the *Notizie degli Scavi*, the new national journal. The lack of skill and care in excavation is obvious, and the integrity of most tomb-groups, essential for proper study, has been lost. The documentation for the rich cemeteries on the nearby hillocks (*poggi orientali*), investigated from 1904-07, is better and the preserved tomb-groups, mostly housed in the Florence museum, later provided the basis for a major study of the Tarquinian Iron Age by Hugh Hencken (1968).

A fine monograph of 1937 by Massimo Pallottino (1909-95), Italy's foremost Etruscologist, provided the first comprehensive synthesis of the archaeology of Tarquinia.[55] Meanwhile, work on the city wall by Romanelli (1934-38) uncovered complex sequences of architectural development (never fully understood) around the north gate and at the great Ara della Regina temple, which brought to light the famous winged horses.[56] Further discoveries and clarifications also came about in tandem with more general advances in Etruscan scholarship, as reflected, for example, in every volume of *Studi Etruschi* published annually since 1927. Certain developments, however, stand out.

Geophysical prospection pioneered by the Lerici Foundation was designed to elucidate the layout and extent of the city and to map burial and residential zones, known only from inadequate old records.[57] In 1955, Carlo Lerici initiated at Tarquinia one of the most extensive and successful programmes of resistivity surveying in archaeology, with more or less annual campaigns until 1980, documenting the presence of several thousand

10. Villanovan grave goods. Pottery: (a-c) hut urns; (d-f) jar urns; (g) triple bowl with human handle; (h) 'candelabrum'. Bronze: (i) wheeled animal; (j) crested helmet, urn cover (various scales; after Montelius 1904).

tombs on Monterozzi. Electrodes driven into the ground measured variations in electrical resistance, betraying potential cavities or tombs; a long drill hole (7 cm wide) was then made down into the putative underlying chamber through which a small camera or a specially designed periscope was inserted in order to view any contents or paintings (Fig. 11). The residential site on Civita was also first surveyed in the 1960s and indications obtained of regularly spaced thoroughfares, buildings and open spaces. In 2000, ground penetrating radar provided some further information.[58]

Most of the tombs recorded in this way had been stripped ages ago, but the method at least compensated for the lack of massive area excavations, made almost impossible by the vast extent of the cemeteries, one of the largest burial grounds of antiquity. Thanks to Lerici, more painted tombs came to light, while others whose location had been lost were rediscovered; about 180 are now known, although some have only limited decoration (p. 100). The most recent (Blue Demons tomb, in 1985) came to light as a result of road works. Technical advances in 1967 permitted better tomb plans to be made by use of an electronic measuring device, without actually excavating. A considerable databank therefore exists, which could shed further light on the development and layout of the cemetery. Nevertheless, we still lack a complete plan of Monterozzi. The need for some form of computerised recording (such as Geographical Information Systems) seems increasingly obvious.

By 1943, John Bradford, an RAF pilot, was using air photography to interpret ancient landscapes; he was the first to map the Monterozzi burial mounds from wartime air photographs.[59] Interest has also grown in the relationship between the city and surrounding territory. Air photo

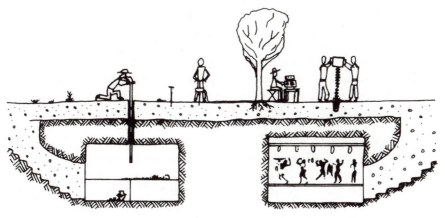

11. Lerici prospecting techniques: resistivity surveying, drilling and using a periscope.

interpretation backed up by research on the ground, promoted by Schmiedt, Adamesteanu and Castagnoli, has helped to identify ancient roads and the nearby port at Gravisca, first excavated by M. Torelli in 1969 (see Chapter 4). The location of many other sites in the vicinity of Tarquinia is known from ad hoc explorations. On Civita, however, a systematic collection of surface finds by A. Mandolesi has revealed an unexpectedly wide scatter of Iron Age material (p. 41), another reminder that comparatively unglamorous research, even without excavation, can provide new insights.

The Lerici explorations also identified a large Hellenistic cemetery in the adjacent Scataglini estate, excavated (1963-66) by R.E. Linington (p. 147).[60] Trial trenches opened in 1975 on Monterozzi (Calvario) revealed Iron Age house foundations beneath Archaic tombs. Two more Villanovan cemeteries have come to light: 62 tombs at Le Rose, excavated in 1953-54, and over 100 at Villa Bruschi-Falgari, excavated in 1998. The Iron Age graves provide a good basis for new approaches to the social structure, ideology and evolution of early Tarquinia (see Chapter 2). A series of volumes cataloguing material in the Tarquinia museum has further clarified past discoveries.[61]

Legislation was passed in 1966 forbidding ploughing or construction on Civita where, since 1982, regular campaigns of excavation and study have been undertaken by a team from the University of Milan, led by M. Bonghi Jovino and C. Chiaramonte Treré, inspired by the desire to investigate the residential area. The gradual extension of trenches has revealed complex sequences of walls, pits, wells, kiln, trackways and a remarkable subterranean drainage network, all compressed within relatively shallow deposits dating from the Iron Age to the Hellenistic period. The seventh to fifth centuries BC are represented by puzzling structures, votive deposits and child burials, interpreted as a sanctuary. Lacking obvious parallels elsewhere, this shows how much we still have to learn about Etruscan civic and religious life. The Archaic ancestry of the Ara della Regina temple has been illuminated by recent soundings, and more fragmentary Latin inscriptions (the *elogia Tarquiniensia*; p. 133) have been fitted together and studied along with a growing body of epigraphic evidence.[62] New research is also opening up another chapter in the history of Tarquinia between late Roman and medieval times.[63]

On a gloomier note, despite these advances, Tarquinia retains a certain notoriety as a place of clandestine digs, which fuel an international traffic in plundered antiquities. As the value of ancient vases has soared in recent years, the site has been under sustained attack. The countless items sequestered by the police are but a fraction of the vast quantities involved. International legislation and the state have been slow to confront the matter and rather ineffective in dealing with it. The problem stems in part from a kind of counter-culture encompassing a range of more or less complicit individuals, from the semi-professional gangs who work doggedly by night, to the casual looters and thieves, sometimes abetted by corrupt officials, and their many and varied clients: unscrupulous visitors who are willing to pay for a 'real' souvenir, shady dealers working for wealthy private collectors, and even museums, although the latter are generally unwilling to buy illegally exported items. In southern Italy and Sicily the criminal underworld also encourages and manages the trade.

The activities of an infamous freelance *tombarolo* of Tarquinia, Luigi Perticarari, who has spent most of his adulthood, minus eleven years in prison, looting the local tombs, have been vividly recounted.[64] His tawdry memoirs, pieced together from tape-recorded interviews, are a mixture of bragging, self-justification, apology and denial. He has confessed to the destruction of painted tombs on Monterozzi by cutting out blocks of frescos with an electric saw on the orders of clients. Spurred on by a mania for finding things, by the potential profits (although he denies this is much of an incentive) and by the satisfaction of outwitting the authorities, Perticarari resents professional archaeologists and Superintendency officials who he believes are interested solely in their own careers and in denying public access to archaeology. Yet he represents only one link in a sophisticated network of criminality and greed, most of which, especially in its 'upper' echelons, has managed to cover its tracks and evade any form of punishment. To some extent, he also implicates a wider section of society, which stands accused of indifference.

In the world of scholarship, the literature on the painted tombs has burgeoned in recent years. Etruscan art still raises problems of evaluation and definition. Lack of associated grave goods has always hindered interpretation, focussing attention on stylistic evolution and foreign connections, notably with Greek art and painted pottery, and the date of certain tombs, especially in the Hellenistic period, is controversial. However, leaving aside some dogmatic value judgments, exemplified by the contempt of H. Brunn ('What is good is Greek: what is poor, Etruscan'), studies of iconography and symbolism have blossomed with a widening range of approaches and interpretations.[65] Detailed monographs have been dedicated to individual tombs and much care taken to improve the quality of the documentation and photographic reproduction.

This has also helped to fix these images in the consciousness of contemporary culture and to maintain their role in the world of marketing and advertising. The Triclinium tomb figures, for instance, are among the most popular images of ancient art and – aside from their prominence on postcards and site souvenirs – have for decades been promoting wines, foodstuffs, restaurants, bars, shops, holidays, calendars, aftershave and even lottery tickets.[66] At the risk of sounding pedantic, this can make it more difficult to challenge or shift popular perceptions of ancient Etruria, often narrowly focussed or out-dated, and to encourage interest in the less glamorous but not necessarily less significant findings of field archaeology. Some Etruscan museums have moved away from older forms of display in which *objets d'art* dominate the scene, and given visitors more help in the understanding and appreciation of daily (and non-funerary) life, based on recent research – a welcome trend.[67]

Meanwhile, the precarious state of some tomb paintings is still a cause for concern for all those who aspire to an enlightened policy of cultural resource management. With the help of modern conservation technologies, several complete tomb frescos were uplifted between 1949 and 1960 (Biga, Triclinium, Olympics, Ship, Funeral Bed, Bruschi and Black Sow tombs) and re-assembled (the first four) in a room with special temperature and humidity controls in the Tarquinia museum. However, this rather desperate measure, undertaken with some reluctance and only in the case of tombs seriously threatened, is unlikely to be repeated. Recent conservation, mostly limited to consolidation with resins, the removal of salts, incrustations and any metal hooks or fillers from old restorations, has greatly improved the appearance of many tombs.

Scientific investigation during the 1970s illuminated the processes of deterioration, proving that the abrupt temperature and humidity changes caused by the entry of visitors were resulting in the formation of saline or fungal deposits and causing other adverse reactions.[68] Plainly, with the growing public interest in archaeology, encouraged by television and the media, bringing more people to the site every year, the authorities were faced with a mounting problem. In fact, the number of visitors more than doubled between 1969 and 1984, from 60,000 to 140,000 per year, with sudden seasonal surges caused by springtime school visits and peak summer tourism. The question of public access to painted tombs has been much debated therefore since the 1950s.[69]

The situation has parallels, for example, in the international concern over the deterioration of fragile Palaeolithic cave paintings, like those at Lascaux in the Dordogne or Altamira in Spain, which have had to be closed or opened on a very restricted basis. At Tarquinia, one must be grateful for a less drastic solution. It is possible to see a reasonable number of tombs during a visit, opened on a rota system, while others are shut for lengthy periods. At the time of writing, the cemetery areas open to the public are those in state ownership near the town (Calvario and Scataglini), where about 12-15 painted tombs can usually be seen during a single visit. The tombs are accessed by modern steps following the ancient passageways down as far as the original chamber entrance, where sealed doors with windows (first installed in 1987) allow most of the frescos to be viewed without actually entering. About 30 painted tombs can be viewed in this way, and others may eventually be provided with similar visitor facilities; seven tombs are in the museum, about 50 are permanently closed or known only from the Lerici prospections, and about two dozen are lost, possibly destroyed.

By contrast, comparatively few visitors venture on to Civita, doubtless deterred by the distance from the tombs and by the bumpy farm tracks. Much of the surrounding land is privately owned and worked, the terrain is rougher, and there are few signposts. Our nineteenth-century predecessors were often more intrepid, despite having to go on foot. Mrs. Hamilton Gray ascended the 'citadel', where she found just a few incomprehensible vestiges of old masonry, but was far from disappointed:

> Such are the pleasures which belong to one who travels with some knowledge
> of the past, and sufficient imagination to use that knowledge in the repro-
> duction of beautiful and mighty things long departed and forgotten.[70]

Today, in fact, the uncovered basement of the Ara della Regina is a mighty landmark, quite unlike the dainty wooden structure that D.H. Lawrence imagined would typify an Etruscan temple (*EP*, 32.38). The north gate and adjacent fortifications are also unexpectedly well preserved and partly restored. Elsewhere on Civita, one is likely to encounter the eroded remains of the perimeter wall, the spoil heaps of a recent excavation and a dusty topsoil sprinkled with potsherds and spent cartridges, but traces of antiquity grow dimmer and the pleasure of ruins is superseded by that of landscape and nature. Exploring the wind-swept plateau, one might well feel torn '... between the pleasure of finding so much and the disappointment that so little remains' (*EP*, 54.31).

2. Origins and Growth

Site and setting

Tarquinia lies about 70 km north-west of Rome and 6 km from the Tyrrhenian coast in the province of Viterbo. This was the south-western zone of ancient Etruria, the heartland of Etruscan civilisation between the Tiber and the Arno, covering parts of modern Latium, Umbria and Tuscany (Fig. 1). The ancient city occupied a system of plateaux, hillocks and valleys flanking the river Marta at its confluence with the coastal plain (Fig. 12); the Arrone and Mignone chart a roughly parallel course to north

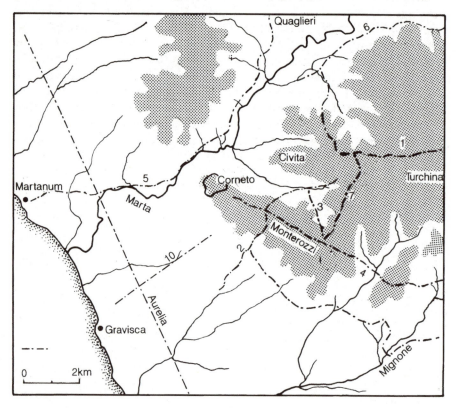

12. Area map with ancient roads or tracks (after *Tarquinia 1*, pl. 3).

and south. Lake Bolsena, 30 km inland, is a major landmark (p. 136), while Monte Argentario and the Tuscan islands of Giglio and Giannutri frame the seaward view. Further south lie the once metal-rich Tolfa hills. Ancient Vulci, Caere (Cerveteri) and Volsinii (Orvieto) were the main neighbouring rivals.

The core of the Etruscan city was Civita (Fig. 13; Plate XXI). Its western end is a fairly level promontory (the Pian di Civita), 1.2 km long and 300-500 m wide, ringed by a steep but undramatic escarpment overlooking the shallow Albucci and San Savino valleys. It abuts on the Pian della Regina, which is more of a hillock (up to 177 m above sea level), crowned by the Ara della Regina temple. Civitucola, a little platform, and Castellina, a narrow prominence, mark respectively the western and north-eastern tips of the unit. By the fourth century BC, if not earlier, this urban area of about 130 hectares was delimited by a long city wall.[1]

A longer ridge with a craggy northern flank runs parallel to Civita about 1.5 km to the south; this is called Monterozzi ('rough hillocks') after the artificial mounds, or tumuli, erected over just some of the several thousand tombs in its vast burial grounds (Fig. 35). About 600 of these grassy humps were still visible in 1830, and 800 or more are indicated by crop marks on air photographs, but stone-robbing and subsequent land use have taken their toll. Only a handful are identifiable at ground level today. Local place names, such as Primi Archi, Arcatelle and Secondi Archi, denote intermittent but still conspicuous ruins of an eighteenth-century aqueduct, which line the Viterbo road. Monterozzi and Civita – two plateaux 'inseparable as life and death' (*EP*, 34.1) – are linked by hillocks (*poggi*) to the east, where there were several cemeteries: Poggio Quarto degli Archi, Selciatello, sopra Selciatello, Impiccato and Sorgente. Poggio Cretoncini, Gallinaro and Cavalluccio have patchy evidence of Iron Age or later occupation, while Roman remains lie further north, across the Marta on Monte Quaglieri, attesting the outer limits of ancient settlement.

Each promontory afforded good views over a surrounding territory with easy access to coastal and inland communications, marine resources, fresh water, agricultural land, copper sources to the south (Tolfa) and, probably, more extensive woodland to the east. The choice of location is easy to appreciate and paralleled elsewhere: spacious plateaux at Caere, Veii and Vulci were also occupied in later prehistory and developed into prominent Etruscan cities. In late antiquity, however, Civita must have been increasingly depopulated, while Corneto, on the steeper western edge of Monterozzi, grew into the main inhabited centre of the Middle Ages (see Chapter 5).[2]

Etruscan sites inland typically occupy picturesque tufa crests, created by recurrent bursts of Quaternary volcanism, responsible for shaping much of the varied landscape of southern Etruria. By contrast, Tarquinia

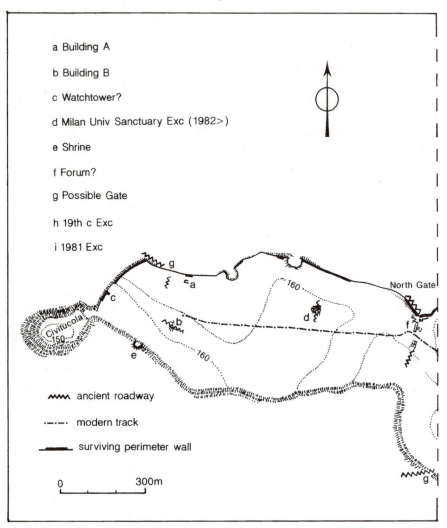

a Building A

b Building B

c Watchtower?

d Milan Univ Sanctuary Exc (1982>)

e Shrine

f Forum?

g Possible Gate

h 19th c Exc

i 1981 Exc

ᴧᴧᴧ ancient roadway

---·- modern track

▬▬ surviving perimeter wall

0   300m

13. Civita plan (after *ET*, fig. 1).

is characterised by pliocene sedimentary formations, making for a flatter, gentler relief. Dark tufaceous rocks (popularly known as *nenfro* and *peperino*) were sometimes imported for architectural elements, but limestone predominates, conspicuous in the city wall and temple basement; often fossiliferous, it is locally called *macco*. Sporadic sandstones, conglomerates, clays and marls also occur in the area. Long sandy beaches fringe the flat coastal belt, its monotony broken – and more so in antiquity – by Holocene fluvial deposits and marshes. Before the nineteenth century,

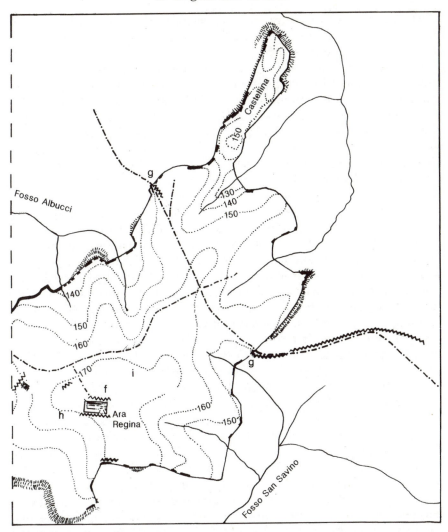

there were at least four lagoons between Gravisca and the Mignone, forerunners of now defunct salt-works (*saline*), which provide sanctuary for flamingoes and water fowl.[3] The shoreline seems to have changed little between the Etruscan and Roman periods, although eroded subsequently in places.

The vegetation has altered since antiquity. Today's open scenery of rolling fields and sparse woodland reflects comparatively recent trends in a long history of land use, but not easy to reconstruct. The timeless landscape dear to painters and poets is a pleasant myth. Abandoned and robbed of building stone, the picturesque ruins of Civita must have gradually turned to scruffy pasture, eventually ploughed, strewn with asphodel, broom, ferula, lentisk, myrtle and thistles; thicker undergrowth and bushes cling only to the scarp.

Botanical remains provide some clues to former habitats, but excavated samples are small and derive from varied activities: wood burning, cult offerings and food discard among others.[4] Charcoal remains of the ninth to fifth centuries BC are mainly from deciduous and evergreen oaks (holm oak/ilex), perhaps used for building. Rarer hornbeam and silver fir, non-existent locally today, may have come from cooler hilly zones inland. Cereal grains include emmer, barley, spelt and oats. A solitary grape pip (morphologically more like a cultivated than a wild variety) from an Iron Age context suggests viticulture in some form, though not necessarily wine-production. Millet, possibly pea, lentil, beans and vetches, fig, olive, mulberry, plums, apples and possibly melon and cherries, as well as a range of herbs and other potentially edible plants (parsley, celery, rosemary, gold-of-pleasure) date from at least the sixth/fifth century BC, by which time Etruscan subsistence had embraced a wide range of cultivars (cereals, legumes, olive, grape) characteristic of Mediterranean polyculture. Pollen analysis from Cretoncini attests cereal growing, arboriculture, including walnut, and some open pasture land in the Iron Age. Livy (28.45) mentions that Tarquinia provided sails for Scipio's fleet in 205 BC; perhaps, then, linen (flax) production was a local speciality at the time. Grain fields, olives, vines, orchards, pasture and woodlands must have occupied surrounding land, though their extent and evolution are unknown.

The maritime as well as the agricultural vocation of Tarquinia was central to her development. Villanovan potsherds from the salt-pans may denote an Iron Age precursor of the main Etruscan harbour at Gravisca, which existed by at least 600 BC (Chapter 4), possibly covering an area greater than the six hectares of the Roman site (Fig.14). Vulci and Caere also had dependent *emporia* at Regisvilla and Pyrgi. The Roman *colonia* founded in 181 BC at Gravisca was probably succeeded by a medieval harbour and then by porto Clementino (now Tarquinia Lido), which served eighteenth-century Corneto. Another docking place could have been the mouth of the Marta, which was probably navigable across the plain. Just beyond the present-day estuary are remains of a Roman pier, probably ancient Martanum, while another Roman port seems to have existed further up the coast at Quintiana.[5]

Reclamation projects last century transformed once feverish coastal lowlands, now peppered with residential zones. How serious was the drainage problem in antiquity? Roman writers, including Vergil (*Aeneid* 10.184), imply that Gravisca was not the most salubrious place in summer, more especially so in late antiquity, as noted by C. Rutilius Namatianus (p. 181). Although firm evidence of malaria is lacking, stagnant pools may

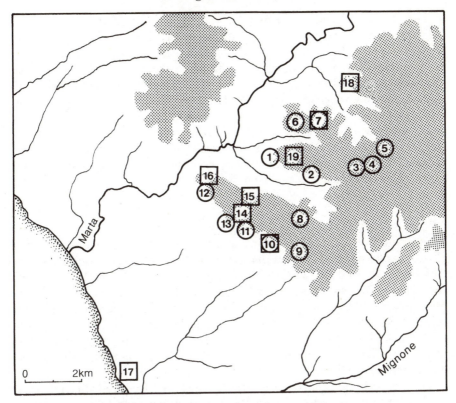

14. Early Iron Age findspots (circle = tombs, square = habitation): 1 Civitucola,
2 San Savino, 3 Selciatello, 4 Poggio dell'Impiccato, 5 Poggio della Sorgente, 6
Gallinaro, 7 Cretoncini, 8 Arcatelle, 9 Fontanaccia, 10 Acquetta, 11 Castagno,
12 Le Rose, 13 Villa Bruschi-Falgari, 14 Infernaccio, 15 Calvario, 16 Santa Maria in
Castello, 17 Saline, 18 Vignaccia, 19 Civita (after Mandolesi 1999, figs 63-4).

help to explain why major Etruscan sites generally avoided the coastal
plain, where exposure to attack was also greater. Yet they were close
enough to enjoy access to its good communications, commercial potential
and natural resources, such as fish and salt.[6] The biodiversity of coastal
wetlands might also have been attractive, if birdlife, lagoon fish and
molluscs supplemented the more traditional products of an agro-pastoral
diet. Pliny (*Natural History* 9.173) refers to a *coclearum vivaria* (a pond
for raising molluscs) near Tarquinia in the first century BC.

Ancient trackways linked Civita, the San Savino valley and Monterozzi;
some are still visible, passing through natural gaps in the scarp, and aerial
photographs show further traces of an evolving regional road network
(Fig. 12).[7] Most obvious is the Roman Via Aurelia, dating from the third
century BC, which follows the coast like a ruler, trailed by its modern

successor. Other roads are undated except by general inference. One from Monterozzi to Gravisca (no. 10), could be an Etruscan artery, renewed in Roman times, linking metropolis and port, while another (no. 2) may have reached the Mignone estuary at Rapinium; yet another (no. 4) led onto Monterozzi, probably from Allumiere or ultimately Caere. Unlike the Aurelia, Etruscan roads generally followed natural, even meandering patterns in the landscape, avoiding the coastal plain. Tracks (nos 5 and 6) shadow the Marta for some distance towards Vulci, Tuscania and Lake Bolsena. A road (no. 1) from Civita towards Blera, skirting the cemeteries, must have been a useful link between the Roman Aurelia and Via Clodia, but probably had a much earlier history.

Prehistory

The environs of Tarquinia were inhabited for thousands of years before the Etruscan city emerged.[8] Farming (Neolithic) societies took hold in central Italy around 5500 BC. Their Copper Age successors (3500-2500 BC) are represented by two oven-shaped rock-cut tombs amid Etruscan graves on Monterozzi and by scattered finds in the territory. Another subterranean tomb at Bandita di San Pantaleo, near the Marta, held five individuals, flint arrowheads and a pottery flagon. Bronze Age occupation (2000-1300 BC) is identifiable at several locations, especially along river valleys, and on Castellina di Civita.

During the Final Bronze Age or Protovillanovan period (1200-900 BC), local settlement patterns crystallised around promontories and hilltops, presumably exploited for natural defences and communications through adjacent valleys.[9] Near Tarquinia were at least eight such sites (tombs or surface finds), more or less regularly spaced and potentially allied in order to control the wider territory of the lower Marta basin. They are ancestral to the various nuclei of Villanovan occupation (900-750 BC, Fig. 14) that subsequently coalesced into Etruscan Tarquinia. Proximity, interaction and interdependence probably helped forge their common cultural tradition.[10]

Elliptical stone and timber houses of a Protovillanovan settlement are encountered on the Torrionaccio hill, 8 km north-east of Tarquinia.[11] Similar dwellings and smaller quadrangular structures occur at San Giovenale, Sorgenti della Nova and Luni sul Mignone, probably small villages without elaborate urban layouts. One may infer a subsistence regime of crop-growing and stock-rearing, perhaps requiring seasonal movements from lowland to upland pastures (transhumance). Domestic sheep, goat, cattle and pig are well represented, with a few dogs, horses or donkeys, as well as cheese-making and milk-boiling devices, in keeping with an old Bronze Age tradition. Wild boar and deer were hunted.

Following an earlier tradition of inhumation burial, cremation was now predominant, as in much of central Europe. This has sometimes been thought to reflect the arrival of immigrants from over the Alps or the Balkans, although no specific migration is readily identifiable and other possible explanations include a change in ideology or a gradual process of cultural convergence over a wide area, perhaps encouraged by trade links. In fact, despite its more localised regional traits, the Protovillanovan culture seems related to a very widespread European Late Bronze Age complex (known as 'Urnfield' after the burials), with which it shares certain aspects of material culture, a comparable level of technological development, social organisation and probably ideology.

A large cemetery at Pianello di Genga (Marche) had 650 tombs, while Crostoletto di Lamone had a few inhumations and cremations, occasionally covered with large mounds. Poggio la Pozza (Allumiere) had at least 100 tombs, but elsewhere only groups of a dozen or less have been found, consisting of just a pottery urn. A minority, often dated later in the period, also include a few pots or personal ornaments, such as a bronze fibula (brooch).

Pottery was not wheel-turned; it has a homely appearance, like buffed leather, despite some incised decoration. Metalwork was obviously more desirable and effective as an expression of prestige and wealth and more abundant than before. It best illustrates the technological and socioeconomic advances of the time and the prominence of Etruria in production and distribution. New or more efficient versions of tools and weapons were developed: saws, sickles, spears, axes and chisels, linked with the elaboration of craft activities and warfare. Skills of engraving and embossing are demonstrated by bronze daggers, swords, cups and items of adornment, such as large ornate fibulae. Many artefacts come from hoards, perhaps destined for recycling, while some intentional but unrecoverable depositions, from lake beds for example, must have been ritual offerings.

In terms of social structure, burials suggest only limited divisions by rank. Some fine bronzes may be the work of expert craftsmen and the property of more eminent individuals, but there is not much evidence of advanced divisions of labour or of urban or 'proto-urban' complexity. Since regional settlement hierarchies seem little developed, the main impression is of relatively numerous but small-scale communities, unable or unwilling to create and institutionalise power structures extending much beyond neighbouring sites or their local territories.

A Villanovan township

Early Iron Age or Villanovan Tarquinia (ninth/eighth century BC) sprang from these earlier traditions but witnessed certain changes, including more varied and sophisticated craft production, greater social differences, territorial control and more elaborate burials. While funerary evidence predominates, recent work has begun to correct the imbalance. Excavations on Civita have uncovered patches of lime plaster or clay and pebble flooring, post-holes, pits, an oven and two hut floors, which had escaped destruction by later building. One small, perhaps ancillary, structure (6.8 x 2.8 m) with a sunken floor, was still in use around 700 BC. Associated finds include cooking stands, thread-spools and pottery, sometimes decorated with incisions and impressions. This earliest phase has been dated (though more precisely than the evidence really allows) to the late tenth century BC and was followed by a series of thin levels of the ninth/eighth centuries.[12]

Near the centre of the excavated zone (*alpha*) was a bedrock cavity or pit (263) about a metre across, possibly natural, surrounded by tracts of plastered floor (Fig. 31). A few metres away, a child's skeleton (293) with a bronze pendant, pin and two lead fragments, lay in a shallow grave, roughly dated to the late ninth century.[13] Skeletal examination suggested a seven/eight-year old, possibly male, with cranial abnormalities (arteriovenous malformations) that might have impeded physical coordination, causing epilepsy or even premature death. Four other infants were buried nearby in the late eighth/early seventh century and, a little further away, a Euboean jug of about 750-725 BC was placed in a narrow trench with an adult male, perhaps killed by a blow to the head.[14] In the excavators' opinion, the entire zone was for burial rituals; the mysterious pit (263) was the object of veneration, while other finds, such as worked horn, antler, pits, charcoal and burnt patches of flooring, represent cult activity, votive food offerings and animal sacrifices (mainly sheep, goat, pig and cattle). It has also been ventured, though real proof is lacking, that the burials could represent human sacrifices.[15]

Nevertheless, the presence of child burials within residential zones is not unknown in this period. The fragmented nature of the deposits makes it difficult to specify 'grave-side' rituals or to distinguish cult areas (more likely in the case of adjacent hearths and finds) from others, with post-holes, pits and an oven (about 10 m away), that might represent domestic contexts. The artefacts consist mainly of coarse pottery, some finer wares, a few Greek imported sherds (750-700 BC) and occasional bronze fragments, such as pins from broken fibulae, which could come from domestic contexts. The emphasis placed by the excavators on a 'ritual' interpretation is avowedly influenced by the elaboration of cult activities in the subsequent period. They suggest continuity in ritual practice from the Villanovan phase, which began with burials. However, the architectural development of the area in the seventh century BC seems to mark a new departure, with changes in layout and building technique (see Chapter 3).[16]

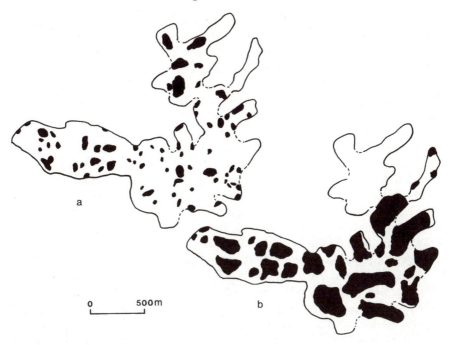

15. Ploughsoil finds: (a) Early Iron Age; (b) Orientalising (after Mandolesi 1999, figs 63-4).

More evidence of Villanovan occupation comes from the edge of Civita, near the north gate, where part of a hut was revealed in 1985, and from pottery in pits and cavities at the Ara della Regina and Tullian baths. Clusters of Villanovan potsherds, collected as surface finds, are widespread on the plateau (Fig. 15), but are hard to date accurately and, without test excavation, reveal little about putative underlying buildings. Nor is it certain that they all denote contemporary buildings. Only on Cretoncini have soundings revealed patchy floors and pits with domestic pottery, daub from hut walls and animal bones (mainly sheep and goat, followed by cattle and pig). Nevertheless, the ploughsoil finds are often used to postulate the presence of numerous clusters of dwellings all over Civita and Cretoncini, or even a single continuous settlement associated with surrounding burials on Cretoncini, Gallinaro, Civitucola, San Savino and the nearby *poggi* cemeteries (Selciatello and others).[17]

Surface finds also suggest that there were at least three habitation areas on the Monterozzi plateau: under the modern town, associated with the Le Rose cemetery; at Infernaccio, linked with the Villa Bruschi-Falgari tombs; and at Acquetta, with tombs nearby (Fig. 14). A clearer picture of Villanovan buildings comes from a fourth site, at Calvario, where thin

41

deposits on bedrock survive in places beneath Etruscan burial mounds.[18] Parts of at least 20 structures were uncovered here, over about 200 x 100 m, although the original extent of the built area is unclear; the blank spaces on the plan (Fig. 16) reflect lack of excavation or destruction due to the superimposition of tombs. Most imposing are elongated elliptical buildings (up to 16 x 9 m) delineated by narrow rock-cut channels (foundation trenches for walls now gone) and post-holes for supporting wooden frameworks, thatched roofing and occasional internal partitions. They are fairly regularly spaced and juxtaposed with smaller rectangular and quadrangular huts. These 'longhouses' stem from an ancient tradition in western Europe of timber-framed architecture; their heavy posts and beams, decorated finials and protruding eaves, must have projected an impression of hand-crafted monumentality. Parallels are inevitably drawn with hut urns (Fig. 10: a-c), though the latter were perhaps only schematically modelled on the elliptical buildings, since they are not always elongated like the excavated houses.

Were contrasts in size and shape determined by the number or status of occupants, different uses, chronological or other factors? Complementary functions seem likely, but no special-purpose structures (for storage, or shrines, for example) are readily identifiable, and the poorly preserved contents, including some domestic pottery from the few surviving patches of stratigraphically intact deposits, provide no clear answer. A general lack of alteration and overlap hints at a single phase of occupation, although it has been suggested on rather flimsy grounds that the larger elliptical huts could be earlier. Many elliptical huts were aligned roughly east-west in what was no doubt a planned unit, perhaps associated with the Arcatelle cemetery.[19]

The overall layout and development of Villanovan Tarquinia, therefore, is not easily reconstructed. There are at least two possibilities: that there was a single, essentially continuous sprawling township; or that there were several detached constellations of houses (and burials) scattered over Monterozzi, Civita and Cretoncini. The latter is perhaps more likely. In either case, if all or most of the known or putative residential zones were coeval – a theory slightly favoured since the various cemeteries seem contemporary – the overall occupation area must have been as large as that of the later Etruscan city, or even slightly larger since Cretoncini was not enclosed by the later city wall. However, the relative extent of built and unbuilt zones, or the density of habitation, remains uncertain, but was probably less than in later periods, when the population was undoubtedly much larger.

A settlement system of this kind, occupying such a broad expanse of ground, could have helped to consolidate territorial controls and communication routes, while perhaps buttressing a core community on Civita.

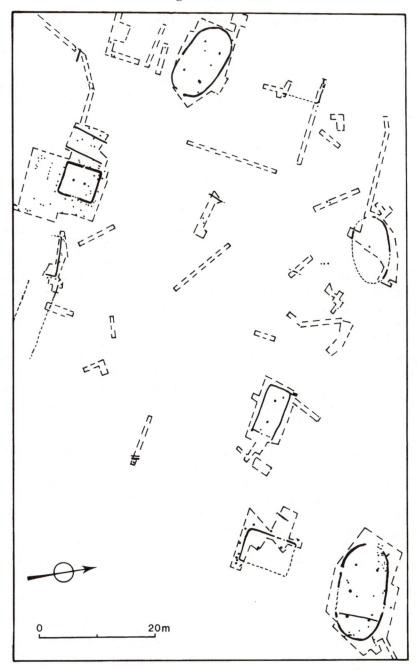

16. Early Iron Age trenches and structures at Calvario (superimposed tumuli omitted; after Linington 1982, pl. 1).

The arrangement might also reflect an organisation of semi-independent units, such as clan-like or kinship groupings with only limited needs for a centralised administration or hierarchy, albeit sufficiently coordinated and organised for certain purposes (religious, political or economic); their spatial distribution might also have adapted in order to cater for the rights and ease of access of each group to respective tracts of nearby agricultural land. Large but loosely aggregated settlement structures certainly existed in prehistoric Europe; one should not necessarily anticipate a simple or direct prototype within a predictable evolutionary continuum for the more tightly knit urban geometry of the classical Greek or Roman city. Nonetheless, it is also possible that the earliest social and administrative divisions (*curiae*) of Rome into essentially horizontal units, are rooted in a segmented Iron Age pattern of the kind seen here.[20]

At some stage, however, prior to the late eighth/early seventh century BC, the Calvario site was abandoned and given over to burial, while Civita either continued as, or turned into, the main centre of habitation. Why and when did this happen? Civita plainly had practical and scenographic advantages over surrounding hills, being fairly level, clearly delimited and most easily defensible. A natural focal point nearest the centre of the residential system, it may always have been a place for periodic gatherings. Moreover, during the eighth century, its changing character and growing prestige were perhaps increasingly defined not just by residential functions but by cult activities, favouring its growing hegemony. An internal dialectic, therefore, perhaps even rivalry between the various groups, could have provoked the rearrangement, making for more centralised coordination and control, drawing in the outlying communities, voluntarily or forcibly.

This probably occurred in the eighth century BC; the crucial moment would be the abandonment of Calvario and peripheral groupings. It is unfortunate that the date is not fixed more precisely, because if it did occur earlier – say in the ninth century – it would strengthen the case for viewing this early stage in the development of the Etruscan city in terms of an endogenous process, peculiar to the Villanovan culture. This would then weaken the idea that external influences (Greek and Phoenician contacts) provided the main impetus for local change in the eighth century BC; we will return to this question in the next chapter.[21] In any case, however, outside stimuli and broader regional processes of interaction are undoubtedly also relevant. Vulci, Caere and Veii seem to have been expanding and consolidating concurrently in similar settings, and there are parallels too with Rome, where the Palatine hill would emerge as a prestigious focal point. Tarquinia is not unique, therefore, but fits with a wider pattern.

44

Regional and trade links

Regional settlement patterns suggest that increasingly polarised centres of population formed in the Iron Age, with control over larger geographical areas than before.[22] The size of their territories has been estimated in various ways, some of which would credit Villanovan Tarquinia with an extensive zone of control (up to 200 km²), equal to that of the later Etruscan city, matched only by that of other Iron Age centres at Vulci, Caere and Veii (Fig. 17). If boundaries coincided with geographical features, a proximal territory between the Marta and Mignone rivers may well have been dominated by this time, perhaps with an outer arc of looser control extending roughly half-way to Vulci and Caere, delimited by the Arrone and Capo Linaro. No other sites on this scale are known within this zone.

Coastal Villanovan findspots around the salt-pans (Fig. 14), and perhaps also further south near Civitavecchia, could represent subordinate or affiliated settlements exploiting seashore environments, prior to the later appearance of dependent emporia, such as Gravisca, which served the Etruscan city.[23] The latest theory about these coastal sites, based on their high concentrations of reddish impasto jars and fire pits, is that they were engaged in some kind of industrial activity, possibly the extraction of salt, or fishing.[24] The point, however, is that major centres were already emerging in the ninth/eighth century BC, and probably defining themselves partly in response to each others' growth, through emulation and competition. On the other hand, what the eventual outcome of the process might have been is unclear since, in the course of the eighth century, this indigenous regional system became increasingly subsumed within a broader sphere of cross-cultural interaction, stimulated by Greek and Phoenician colonisation and trade in the western Mediterranean.

Long-distance trade was intensifying throughout the western Mediterranean during the Iron Age. Widely diffused types of artefacts and metal hoards signal multiple contacts across Italy, Sicily and Sardinia, and interaction between major centres, such as Tarquinia, Vetulonia, Populonia, Vulci and Caere (Fig. 18).[25] The growing power and prestige of sites like Tarquinia in the ninth/eighth century BC is already indicated by large cemeteries and metal production, especially weaponry, ornaments and sheet-bronze. Metal sources in the Tolfa region were probably exploited, perhaps necessitating some agreement with Caere, while prominent Villanovan sites probably already functioned as regional market centres.[26] Links with northern Italy (notably Emilia-Romagna) and Campania (Pontecagnano, Capua, Sala Consilina) can be traced by artefacts and burials like those of southern Etruria and by the placement of new sites geared to the control of natural communication routes, suggesting an expansion of

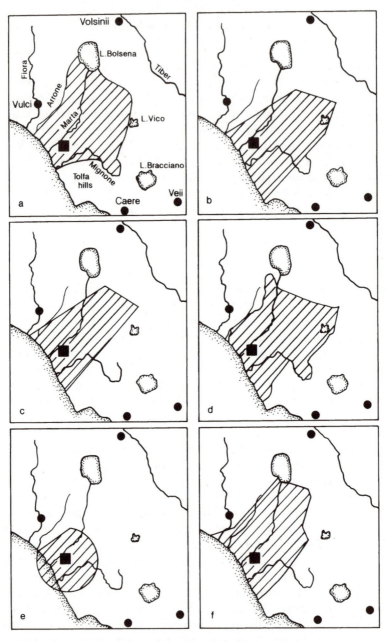

17. Hypothetical zones of territorial control: (a) after Pallottino (1937);
(b) Thiessen polygon; (c) simple weighted Thiessen polygon; (d) Thiessen
polygon modified to take account of geography; (e) Xtent model, undeveloped;
(f) Xtent model, developed (after Spivey and Stoddart 1990, fig. 17).

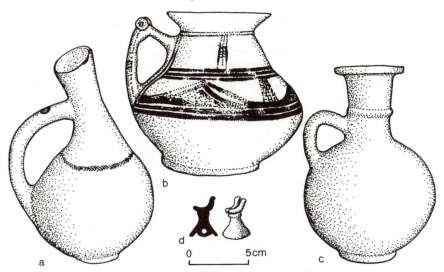

18. (a) Sardinian-Vetulonian type jug; (b) South Italian jug; (c) Phoenician jug; (d) Sardinian bronze pommel (after *ET*, figs 60, 66; *EM*, n. 98; Hencken 1968a, fig. 450).

Villanovan influence (more evident in Campania than in neighbouring Latium), or even movements of settlers.

Several bronze objects, such as buckets and urns, with bird and disk motifs, wheeled animal figures, some weaponry, armour and dress items (Figs 10, 21, 23), have parallels in Urnfield or Hallstatt Europe.[27] Etruria was evidently still part of this extended European cultural province. Some of these items may have been disseminated by trade, although periodic movements of people cannot be excluded, perhaps encouraged by changes in settlement and demography. Later literary sources preserve memories of splinter groups moving within Italy, generally from north to south, notably of Italic peoples entering Sicily prior to Greek colonisation in the eighth century BC. Sporadic incursions from northern areas possibly occurred prior to the historically documented movements of Celtic people into Italy during the later Etruscan period.

From about the mid-eighth century, external relations are also vividly attested by Greek geometric pottery (p. 68), inspired by, or obtained from, Euboean craftsmen resident in western colonies such as Pithecusae and Cumae (Fig. 22: r,s).[28] Local potters could have adopted their techniques of production, although the presence of Greek-style vessels made locally at Tarquinia and Veii raises the possibility of foreign craftsmen at these Etruscan sites. Greek settlers in the Naples region might also have promoted links between Tarquinia and local 'Villanovan' communities in Campania. Tarquinia in turn was well placed to mediate between Greek colonists and metal-rich northern Etruria, where sites like Vetulonia and Populonia seem to have favoured trading links with Sardinia, Iberia and a western Phoenician sphere of activity. Phoenician or eastern Mediterranean goods also reached Tarquinia during the eighth century BC (Fig. 18: c), prior to the full flourish of Orientalising fashions in the seventh century.[29] The complex web of maritime connections, crucial for subsequent developments, was already taking shape.

Cemeteries and symbols (900-750 BC)

Rituals of death and burial, steeped in ceremony and symbolism, account for much of what remains from this period. The graves have invited a range of interpretations despite certain drawbacks, notably the lack of good plans and human bone analyses.[30] Cremation was prevalent in Villanovan Etruria, though inhumation was concurrent at certain sites, such as Caere, Populonia and, less often, at Tarquinia, becoming more common towards the end of the period and predominant thereafter.

Most Villanovan graves from the Tarquinia cemeteries consisted of cylindrical shafts (*pozzi*) up to 1.5 m deep, with a smaller shaft (*pozzetto*) holding the pottery urn at the bottom, usually covered by a slab (Fig. 19: A). Some urns (17 = 15% at Villa Bruschi) were inside cylindrical stone containers (mainly *nenfro*) with a domed lid (Plate XIX); in one case (Villa Bruschi 73) the lid was cut to resemble a hut roof. During the eighth century, these capsules appear to have been superseded by large jars (*dolia*). Large stone chests with lids (up to 150 x 90 cm) are less common (2-3%), while trench graves (*fosse*), mostly covered or lined with stone slabs and used for single inhumations, are a small minority.

Our mainly old and schematic records shed limited light on the organisation and layout of burial grounds.[31]. Some of the 300 or so tombs excavated in the late nineteenth century on Monterozzi formed roughly concentric groupings, while one particular zone had densely clustered shafts about 0.5 m apart, linked by horizontal channels, perhaps affiliated by family or kinship (Fig. 19: B). Another cluster of about 80 shafts, covering around 100 m², was interspersed with occasional trench graves. Certain trench graves at Impiccato and stone chests at Arcatelle also formed little clusters, possibly prescribed by age, social or family group. By contrast, Villa Bruschi had shafts with stone capsules in rows. Evidence of probably extended family groupings comes from Le Rose, one of the earlier cemeteries, in which the tombs seem to have been arranged in more or less analogous social groups, possibly consanguineous, each dominated by a distinguished male and female burial (respectively with helmet cover, various ornaments and a spindle whorl), suggesting a dominant

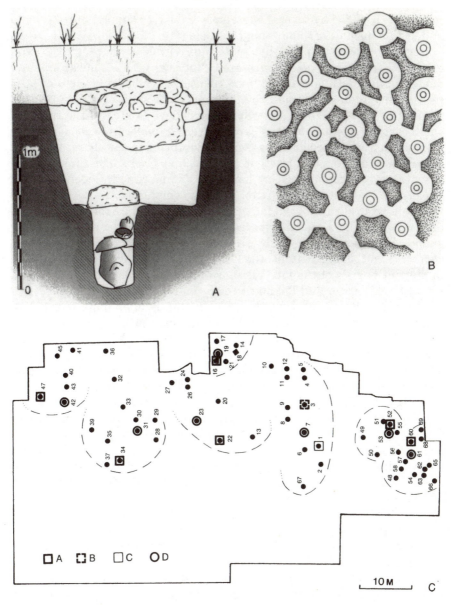

19. Iron Age burials: (A) shaft with cremation urn; (B) interconnected shafts; (C) Le Rose tombs: A, male with helmet; B, probable male with helmet; C, male with razor; D, prominent female (after *TE*, fig. 101; Hencken 1968a, fig. 11; Pacciarelli 2000, fig. 133).

couple, surrounded by several apparently 'minor' or simpler burials, male and female, including some younger people (Fig. 19: C).

Regular spacing implies that plots were visible or marked at ground level. Two putative grave stones are cylindrical with a conical top, and quadrangular with a pitched 'roof', perhaps symbolising circular and rectilinear buildings. A small boulder topped the shaft of a Villa Bruschi tomb (Fig. 19: A).[32] Wooden markers might have existed, while traces of small earthen mounds or stone cairns covering tombs and even a circular emplacement of stones are occasionally mentioned in the old records, and sporadically documented at other sites, such as Caere. The tumuli of the seventh century could therefore have had Villanovan antecedents.

Certain contrasts between the various cemeteries are not obviously attributable to chronological factors. For instance, the somewhat peripheral tombs of Le Rose are spaced further apart and have few richly endowed graves, which could suggest a slightly marginal grouping, weaker than that of Arcatelle; the latter are more likely ancestral to some prominent burials of the late Villanovan and early Orientalising period, such as the Warrior and Bocchoris tombs on Monterozzi.

Nothing is known of such obsequies as the lying-in-state (*prothesis*), banquets or games of later Etruscan and Roman practice. In one or two cases, bones of a second individual have been identified in an urn, perhaps the result of joint or multiple cremations in which the remains got mixed. The deceased probably wore fibulae when cremated; some burnt examples were found. Ashes and charred bone were then gathered, perhaps in a special cloth, and placed in the urn. Other items may have been entirely destroyed on the pyre (p. 65). However, small unburnt objects, such as fibulae, spindle-whorls, razors and cups, were sometimes added to the urn contents, while larger pots went into the shaft, or occasionally into a special niche. A bowl containing pyre remains, food offerings (meat, fruit) or small objects was sometimes balanced on the mouth of the urn, but more often positioned upside-down like a cap. Another typical urn cover is a bronze helmet, or a pottery imitation, which can be crested or dome-shaped and surmounted by a knob or a roof-like motif (Fig. 10: e, f, j). The grave was subsequently back-filled with earth and stones, although pyre remains have also been found in them.

The different burial types may well be socially significant in that the stone cylinders, apparently used for males and females, required more effort to produce and generally held more numerous or impressive objects. By contrast, the many simple urn burials without artefacts (about 40-50%) are hard to attribute and date. Sometimes they occurred in groups near wealthier ones. It is tempting to rank them lower on the social scale, although we can only guess at the significance of their austerity. Notwithstanding some unusual combinations, one senses that the prevailing ethos permitted only limited variations and specific selections of artefacts for deposition. Both sexes were evidently buried in the same general manner, though sometimes with gender-specific objects. However, some of the more recurrently articulated artefact combinations seem to be from male burials, and all three stone chests from Villa Bruschi are thought to have held males, including tomb 58, a double burial.

Recent analyses have examined the covariant associations of the grave-offerings, shedding light on aspects of ritual, status and gender.[33] For example, spinning and weaving items, known from about 140 tombs (33%), hardly ever occur with weaponry or helmets, found in about 49 tombs (12%). Razors seem to have been male objects, the elegant serpentine fibula usually (but not exclusively) male, whereas fine sheet-bronze belts, pendants, spiral hair ornaments and beads were more likely female. Arched fibulae may be prevalently for females, but perhaps also for young males, while pottery vessels mostly lack obvious gender implications. Certain distinctions are discernible, therefore, from tombs with grave goods (about 40%). Some combinations hint at the possibility of a small minority of tombs containing two persons, as occasionally documented in other Villanovan and later cemeteries (below).[34]

To what extent and in what way do the offerings characterise an individual? Do helmets literally signify warriors, and spindle-whorls women who spun? Quite possibly, yet they may also symbolise a social condition, a concept of manhood, womanhood, maturity or even marital status, related to role and rank, albeit obliquely. Certain items are rather banal, unlikely prestige markers in themselves, such as spindle-whorls, which are recurrently associated, almost as a formality, with girls and women at some other cemeteries (notably Osteria dell'Osa in Latium).[35] Perhaps the razors too were conventional tokens for post-pubescent males. Not all items were necessarily personal possessions of the deceased. Models or pottery surrogates (of helmets, for example) imply a purely symbolic funerary purpose. They may not always denote the real persona, but rather certain aspirations and conventions. For instance, in one Villa Bruschi tomb, the pottery helmet was with an 8- to 14-year-old male – too young to be a real warrior.[36] This might imply status ascribed by family affiliation, or inherited, but the liturgical processes and beliefs dictating the use of such tokens and their role in funerals, or the afterlife, remain obscure. Some graves (such as Villa Bruschi 64, probably a female, four to eight years old, with numerous beads) may have been well endowed for sentimental reasons.

Distinctions between funerary and everyday items are also evinced by the standard pottery urn, with conical neck.[37] Those from domestic sites had two handles, whereas the burial jars nearly always had one, which sometimes required breaking one off. In daily life this was perhaps a water

20. Incised panel and anthropomorphic motifs on jar urns (after Hencken 1968a, 31-2; Buranelli 1983, fig. 106).

jar, while the standard cover-bowl, occasionally replaced by another vessel, was probably for food, alluding, then, to the basic but often socially important activities of drinking and eating. The accompanying crockery (cups, bowls, jugs, plates and stands) also suggests dining or a funerary meal, which is a favourite motif of later tomb painting. Since some of these are probably female burials, it has been ventured that the presence of high-ranking women at banquets, which is a well-known feature of Etruscan social custom, dates back to the Iron Age.[38]

Later Etruscan urns with modelled heads from Chiusi are clearly humanised. Another, though less overt, form of anthropomorphism, possibly with animistic implications, is also implied by some Villanovan examples: notably the helmeted urns, which are a speciality of Tarquinia, and by the 'dressing' of urns with a necklace of spindle-whorls, rings, a bronze girdle or a cloth wrapping. Most urns had incised decoration of meanders, triangles, swastikas, geometric panels (metopes) or metal appliqués, motifs perhaps with ritual or funerary connotations (Fig. 20). A Tarquinian decorative style, with an emphasis, for example, on 'N' motifs, highly schematised versions of bird, disk and boat motifs, is to some extent distinguishable from that of other sites, at least from statistical analysis. At the same time, the shared distribution of certain motifs suggests links with Vulci and other smaller neighbouring sites.[39] A few urns were undecorated, another possible sign of social inferiority. However, we can only guess at the significance of what look like schematised human figures, often shown near the handles, facing each other or holding hands (Fig. 20; below).

The seven hut urns clearly stand out (Fig. 10: a-c). Their frequent associations with stone chests and numerous grave goods (often male items) suggest special status burials, possibly dominant males or *patres-familias*, although females can be inferred at other sites, and one example from Tarquinia might have held a couple.[40] Moulded structural and decorative details (beams, windows, doors, eaves, flues), traces of paint, incised geometric designs or schematic human figures, sometimes linked as in a procession or dance, and bird-head roof finials, might also suggest rather more than ordinary dwellings, perhaps shrines or houses whose occupants had special powers.

Horse-bits and models of horses and wheels (the carts have probably perished) occur mainly in well-endowed graves and doubtless signified social eminence, foreshadowing the appearance of real chariots in later rich tombs. However, cart or boat models, occasionally found together, might also allude to an afterlife journey, as in later funerary iconography (Fig. 21). One boat contains a human figure, and one cart (Le Rose 49) comes from a probable female tomb. Other special items, such as vases with human figures, so-called candelabra, incense burners and a wheeled animal vase, also suggest ritual or ceremonial functions, rather than just high rank (Fig. 10: g-i). Incense burners are also known in later Etruscan tombs, a further sign that the antecedents of Etruscan funeral practice, and doubtless many religious beliefs, are rooted in the Villanovan period.[41] A bronze tripod from a tomb of about 700 BC shows mounted warriors wearing Villanovan crested helmets.

Thus, while graves and grave goods may not represent the status and

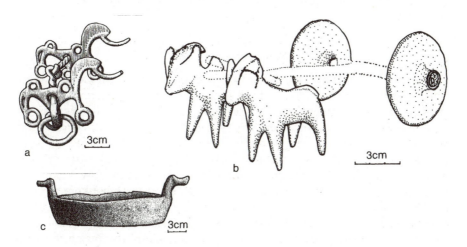

21. Villanovan grave goods: (a) bronze horse-bits; (b) pottery horse and wheel models (yoke hypothetical); (c) pottery boat model (after Montelius 1904; *CE*, 56).

persona of the living in an absolutely literal way, a structured ritual syntax (rather than a haphazard or idiosyncratic melange) plainly existed and is to some extent comprehensible. At one end of the scale are tombs without grave goods, while a recurrent 'middle' category seems to be represented by tombs with a cover-bowl and only one or two personal items, partly determined by gender, role and ritual. Helmet covers (about 16% of cremations) predominate in the iconography of fighting or warrior imagery, whereas real weapons are uncommon, evidently deemed inappropriate for inclusion, as was the case in other contemporary cemeteries. There are just a few burials with a dagger, or dagger and spear, perhaps differing in rank, as well as the odd outstanding tomb, such as Impiccato I, which contained bronze equipment (sword, spear, helmet, razor, vessels), pottery and personal ornaments, including a small amount of goldwork, probably of about 800-750 BC.[42] This rich tomb anticipates the more conspicuous warrior burials of the late eighth/early seventh century. The aristocratic connotations of hunting and banqueting in later funerary iconography may also be foreshadowed by a hunting scene on the sword-sheath from this tomb and by miniature sheet-bronze table-stands or a pottery plate-stand with a human figure.

The complexity of the ritual, the quantity of tomb goods and the differences between burials grew during the Villanovan period. In part, this may reflect a general increase in the range of material possessions and in the ability of some to acquire more unusual or prestigious artefacts; but it also denotes the increasing importance of funerary ceremonies as an occasion for display. During the later eighth and seventh centuries, the trend continued as burial wealth and architecture reached new heights of ostentation.

Illustrious corpses (750-700 BC)

The second half of the eighth century was a time of continuity and change. The eastern cemeteries were already prominent, those on Monterozzi were growing, while Civita assumed a more central role in a unified settlement complex. Traditional cremation urns were undoubtedly still current and shafts with large jars were becoming more common. Trench graves were also spreading, lined and covered with slabs or provided with roughly hewn sarcophagi. Some held inhumations, but others may have had cremations too. In certain cases, the slabs leaned together like a pitched roof, thereby creating a house-like space beneath, from which may have developed the small corridor tombs with a narrow rock-cut bench and the more elaborate rock-cut chambers of the Orientalising period (see Chapter 3).[43]

The growing popularity of inhumation at Tarquinia is consistent with

22. Items from a rich late Villanovan tomb, probably female. Bronze: (a-e) fibulae (a-d with amber attachments); (f) spindle; (g) girdle; (i) armlet; (j) coil bead; (k-l) axes; (m) flask; (n-o) jars. Iron: (h) knife. Pottery: (p-s) (scales various; after Montelius 1904, pl. 282).

a regional trend. Although a simpler practice than cremation, it was accompanied by an increase in richly furnished graves, requiring larger plots and, arguably therefore, preserving a more tangible point of contact with the deceased than was the case with the old urnfield rite. This may again be linked with more articulated social structures and elitist or aristocratic values – claims to fame being helped or determined by conspicuous ancestral tombs.

The proliferation of grave goods (a dozen objects or more is not unusual) characterises this period, while more prominent burials have sheet-bronze items, including urns, cups, buckets, jars, splendid lenticular flasks and weaponry (Figs 22-3). Engraved waist-bands were still worn and a growing range of jewellery: serpentine and thickened arched fibulae, pendants, beads, spirals and bracelets, mostly of bronze or glass, silver and gold. Children also had grave goods, including gold pendant amulets, perhaps a sign of status ascribed by birth.[44] The old rites were not followed so rigidly, at least not by the wealthy. For example, jar urns could be substituted by different vessels: fine bronze urns and, in one case, a painted water jug (hydria) of Greek type, but probably a local product, with one handle removed in adherence with local tradition.

However, despite the greater range and numbers of tomb goods, their associations and symbolism seem little altered. Polished cups with elegantly modelled handles appear as part of 'table sets' (with little bowls, jugs and jars), a persistent allusion to eating and drinking. Helmets, weaponry and spindles are still gender-related. Females may have numerous items of adornment, bronze axes and iron knives, perhaps denoting sacrificial activities or simply food preparation, and both sexes can have fine metal vessels. One rich, probably female, cremation consisted of a large jar, holding a decorated bronze urn and cover bowl and several other bronze items: flask, girdle, bucket, cup, two axes, chain, bracelet, beads, pendants (with gold leaf), a distaff with spindle-whorl and thread attached, about 16 ornamented bronze fibulae, one of silver, a bone-handled iron knife, glass beads, wheel-made pots with geometric painted decoration and a few hazelnuts (Fig. 22).[45]

An outstanding tomb of about 700 BC is that of the warrior, found in a large stone box (3.4 m long) near Primi Archi in 1869 (Fig. 23). The documentation is minimal and the full list of finds is of debated reliability, but there is little reason to doubt that the dazzling array of items published in 1874 came from this tomb (some are now in Berlin, but most lost).[46] The burial heralds the very rich depositions of fine craft items and exotic paraphernalia of the full Orientalising period, yet is still very much in the local tradition. Aside from Villanovan vessels, there were at least 15 vases in Greek Late Geometric (mostly local Italo-Geometric) style, evidently prestigious items. The weaponry and body armour, some of it with re-

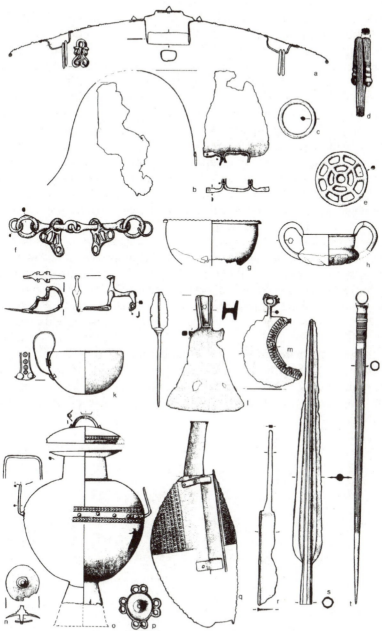

23. Warrior tomb, select metal items: (a) shield; (b) shoulder-guard; (c) ring; (d) armlet; (e) wheel ornament; (f) horse bits; (g) bowl, (h) cup; (i-j) fibulae; (k) cup; (l) axe; (m) razor; (n) stud; (o) jar; (p) ring-button; (q) flask; (r) knife; (s) spear; (t) shaft point (scales various; after Kilian 1977).

poussé (hammered) decoration, included: a bronze spear and spear butt; a bronze knife with bone, amber and perhaps gold handle inlay; a bronze shoulder-guard with linen lining; a bronze shield (on leather), and gold-plated pectoral. At one side was a bronze flask and, nearer the feet, two bronze vessels and wooden bowls with bronze studs. There were also several other bronze vessels, wooden containers, two silver cups, an iron rod with bronze discs, two axes, two horse bits, various probable chariot trappings (discs, strap-holders, hooks, rings and a cross-tube), a lunate razor, carved or plain wooden rods, and a hazelnut. Items of dress and adornment included numerous fibulae (bronze, silver, possibly gold or electrum, with various bone, amber and iron attachments), bronze rings, chains, globular pendants, bracelets, a spiral, a scarab swivel-ring, glass and amber beads, bone or possibly ivory rings, and other fragments of bronze-studded leather and cloth.

Here evoked is a knight of the Iron Age in parade regalia, complete with chariot, reminiscent of the flashy heroes of Homeric poetry. The majority can hardly have been so well equipped as this leader. Elite showmanship doubtless characterised late Villanovan warfare. Prior to the development of more standardised weaponry and infantry formations (p. 68), war was probably waged by bands led by charismatic chieftains, skilled combatants and duellers. However, burial weaponry and the proliferation of arms, so prominent in the iconography of status, is unlikely to be purely symbolic. Territorial expansion and hierarchies, foreign competitors, the increasingly high stakes of trade in valuable luxuries and burgeoning social inequalities must have sparked some rivalry and conflict, periodically resolved by force.

3. The Rise of the City State

Social dynamics

The wealth and ostentation of this period are highlighted by spectacular burials endowed with luxury and exotic goods (a mere fraction of those lost to looters since antiquity), attesting rapid economic growth and social transformations central to the emergence of the Etruscan city. Nonetheless, detailed tomb plans are few, spatial relationships poorly understood and ordinary graves under-recorded by comparison with more impressive ones.[1] As a result, we cannot easily compare the lower ranks (the majority) with an elite, who dominate museum displays and the archaeological literature, and so assess the distribution of wealth across a wider social spectrum. This was a time of transferable technologies and ideologies. Yet innovation and change, in craft production for example, need to be weighed against the strength of local tradition, which has been underestimated. New work on Civita, however, is gradually broadening our horizons, and we can now begin to see more clearly the links between archaeological and written evidence.

The deceased, like their Iron Age predecessors, were still interred at various locations around Civita (Fig. 24), although burial rites were changing.[2] Inhumation in slab-lined trenches is common. Status differences are suggested at Turchina, where some simple graves have few or no inclusions, whereas others are bigger (2 m long), lined with *nenfro* slabs and rich in offerings; one such was set apart within a circular emplacement of stones originally covered by a mound, a design also encountered in northern Etruria (Vetulonia and Marsiliana). Two large contiguous graves (nos 65/5-6) of about 700 BC with fine local pottery and bronzes probably held an adult male and female, perhaps a married couple.[3] Wine-drinking, weaponry and wheeled transport still designated men of influence. This is exemplified by cremation tomb 65/1 (about 675 BC), which was provided with imported and local vessels, some imitating Greek and Phoenician shapes. The weapons and metal goods were probably removed in Roman times, but iron chariot wheel-rims survived. Even a little bronze grater has elitist connotations: known from several prominent graves of the period, such items also occur in Iron Age Greece and fit Homer's description (*Iliad* 11.628-43) of heroic warriors drinking wine mixed with grated goat's cheese and barley.[4]

An intriguing burial (Rogani 6337) came to light recently on Mon-

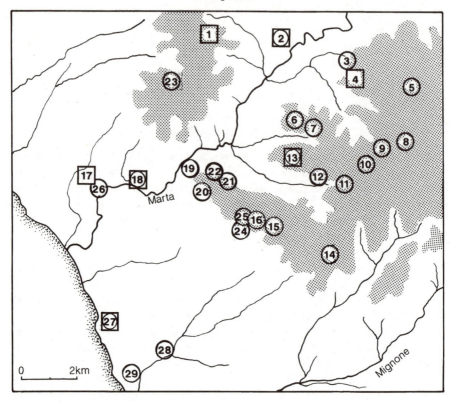

24. Location of seventh-century BC finds (circle = tombs, square = habitation):
1 Fontanile dell'Olmo, 2 Quagliere, 3 Cavaluccio, 4 Vignaccia, 5 Forno,
6 Gallinaro, 7 Cretoncini, 8 Turchina, 9 Sorgente, 10 Impiccato, 11 Quarto degli
Archi, 12 San Savino, 13 Civita, 14 Pisciarello, 15 Doganaccia, 16 Madonna del
Pianto, 17 Pian di Spille, 18 Grottelle, 19 Cartiera, 20 Le Rose, 21 Ortaccio,
22 Porta Nuova, 23 Macchia del Ritiro, 24 Villa Bruschi-Falgari, 25 Infernaccio,
26 San Nicola, 27 Gravisca, 28 Fontanile delle Serpi, 29 Saline (after *TE*, fig. 12).

terozzi: a large rectangular trench (250 x 175 cm) was set above a smaller
one (110 x 220 cm) containing two young men (13-20 years old) side by side
(Fig. 25). Each was flanked by an iron-tipped spear and provided with a
set of fine burnished vessels and geometric painted pottery (typical drinking forms), placed around the feet; a bronze basin and an iron knife (dining
equipment) were perhaps meant to be shared. An unusual detail is that
each wore a silver anklet. Buried simultaneously, they may well have died
together, and were presumably twinned in death because they had been
partnered, somehow, in life.[5]

Tombs undoubtedly provide only a limited sample of the growing range
and number of imported goods and exotic luxuries in circulation. We can

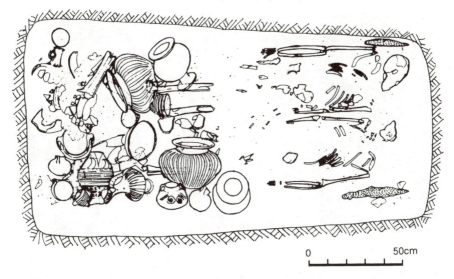

25. Monterozzi, Rogani tomb 6337, a double inhumation (after *TE*, fig. 113).

only imagine the perishables: furs, skins, leather and wooden items, textiles, clothing, dyes, herbs, foods, perfumes, even animals and pets. The western Phoenicians would have been ideally placed to delight their trading partners with trophies, dead or alive, of African fauna. Ivory and ostrich shells were widely traded, and wild animals, frequently depicted in Tarquinian tomb painting, permeate the art of the seventh century BC.

Most tombs have a set of vessels and personal items. A rich female burial on Gallinaro (*fossa* 8, 700-690 BC) had a Rhodian perfume flask (aryballos), Protocorinthian cup (skyphos), Italo-geometric pottery, local red-burnished vessels, several bronze items (beaded bowl, fibulae, chains, tubes, rings,) a glass bead and faience pendant. The adjacent tomb, possibly of her consort, had numerous bronzes (canteen, cups, fibulae, a pendant figurine), an iron spear, knife and ring. An early seventh-century female burial (Monterozzi 2879) contained five bronze fibulae, a hair spiral, sheet-bronze basin, eight pedestal bowls, jars, cups and a late eighth-century Protocorinthian skyphos inscribed with the Greek pronoun *mi* ('I'), one of the earliest examples of writing at Tarquinia (Fig. 34: a). Earrings, bracelets and jewellery were worn, and pottery placed by the legs and feet.[6]

The first chamber tombs also date to around the end of the eighth century. These were small rectangular rock-cut rooms (2-3.5 m long, 1.5 m high) with a pitched roof and one or two benches for the deceased, sometimes a couple, entered from a corridor and a doorway blocked with slabs. The walls often curved inward and were completed with cut slabs (Fig. 26).

61

26. Monterozzi, rock-cut chamber tomb, with a Protocorinthian-style oinochoe (700-650 BC), probably made locally (attributed to the so-called 'Palm painter'; after Marchese 1944-45, fig. 2).

In one case (Rispoli 1888) a female inhumation lay on the bench, while a cremation urn had a pottery helmet cover and an iron spear nearby, undoubtedly for a male, in the Villanovan tradition. Such tombs were possibly once covered by mounds, as at Caere, which are no longer visible today.[7]

A famous rock-cut tomb with a pitched roof and bench, found in 1895, contained a faience vase bearing a cartouche of the pharaoh Bokenranf (Greek Bocchoris), who reigned from about 720-715 BC, a useful chronological peg, although the burial need not have occurred until later, perhaps between 700 and 675 BC.[8] The rich and rather eclectic finds (Fig. 27), partly rifled before excavation, suggest someone, probably female, who liked Egyptian knick-knacks, faience unguentaria and necklace beads (two of the god Bes are in silver mounts). In addition, there were gold foil plaques, probably sewn onto clothing, Italo-geometric vases, bronze vessels, fibulae, and bronze-studded wooden cups. The red or brown polished wares, which anticipate the production of black bucchero pottery (below), and tall pedestals (holmoi) surmounted by painted or ribbed bowls, must have been prominent at banquets, helping to create and define the occasion; inspired, at least in part, by Near Eastern metal counterparts, they show how local craftsmen incorporated foreign motifs within an increasingly sophisticated repertoire of Etruscan prestige goods.

Tomb 55, a rock-cut chamber of about 640 BC held two deceased on side benches: one (probably female) wearing a gold necklace and the other

27. Select items from the Bocchoris tomb (a-c and k could be from a different tomb): (a-d) gold plaques; (e-f) faience pendants; (g) bronze fibula; (h) bronze jar handle; (i-k) burnished jugs; (l) jar with incised decoration; (m) cup (kotyle); (n) red burnished bowl on pot stand (holmos); (o) faience situla, the 'Bocchoris vase'; (p) jug (oinochoe). (Scales various; after Montelius 1904, pl. 295).

(probably male), a gold pectoral decorated with interlaced coils, palmettes, rosettes and lions. Painted ostrich eggs, lion figurines, a scarab, fine bucchero and red wares had also been left by the looters.[9] Tomb 6118 (625-600 BC), reminiscent of the Avvolta tomb, had a solid rock-cut bench, a stone table with elegantly carved legs, and the remains of iron weapons and a chariot (Fig. 28). Despite looting, it preserved sufficient pottery to set a banquet for about ten: nine Etrusco-Corinthian jugs (olpai; Fig. 30: g), nine bucchero jugs, seven kantharoi (Fig. 30: a), ten chalices (Fig. 30: b), an East Greek wine cup (kylix), seven local amphorae, a large storage jar (pithos), storage vessels, pedestal bowls, a bronze basin, iron firedogs and a knife, as well as Corinthian forms generally used for perfumed oils (pyxis, aryballos and alabastra).[10]

Such people must have ranked highly, but been surpassed nevertheless by those in the grandest chambers of the 'princely tombs', the circular pyramids of the day, up to 38 m in diameter and 10 m in height. They were often spaced around the edge of the settlement (notably at Doganaccia, Infernaccio, Poggio del Forno and Gallinaro), dominating surrounding terrain and lesser burials (Fig. 29).[11] Their earth and rubble domes, girt by a wall of polygonal or ashlar masonry, were probably ascended by steps or ramps (see p. 88). The sunken rock-cut chambers, occasionally a double room, were partly built of large stones, with carved architraves, door-posts, benches and even roof-bearing pilasters. Several have ample quadrangular vestibules before the entrance, reached by a broad ramp or staircase, a useful place for gatherings or commemorative ceremonies; they suggest a continuing form of devotion, perhaps for hero cults or communing with the ancestors. There may even have been open-air venues in the cemetery, like that at Grotta Porcina (a few miles away), where it has been postulated that grand funerals with theatrical performances or funeral games in the Homeric tradition took place.[12] Later Roman funerals could also involve elaborate proceedings (see p. 114).

All these tombs had been robbed, not surprisingly, although pieces of fine pottery were left behind in the Gallinaro mound (675-625 BC) as well as ivory plectra, little pottery figurines, perhaps symbolising mourners, and pottery axes, suggesting status symbols or badges of office ancestral to those carried by later Etruscan and Roman magistrates (see p. 167). Scraps of bronze, gold plate and iron chariot fittings came out of the Doganaccia tumulus.

Regrettably, the contents of many famously rich tombs found in the nineteenth century disappeared into private collections. In the case of the Avvolta tomb, its location now unknown, the chamber with its contents *in situ* was sketched (see p. 10; Fig. 5).[13] It was unusually large and elaborate, with bevelled pilasters bearing stone ceiling slabs. Five more rooms with separate entrances, largely robbed, are reputed to have lain under the same mound, an arrangement also encountered at Caere, where the chambers may be sequentially dated. In the Avvolta chamber, the famous warrior resting on the stone bench, flanked by his spears and sword, wore a helmet, tunic, cuirass and greaves. On a stone table opposite lay a gold diadem and 'fine black soil'. In between, a large bronze vessel held parts of a burnt chariot, a sign that some items were still offered on a pyre in the old Villanovan way.[14] Against the walls were a bronze vessel, jug and two basins with ashy offerings, two decorated shields, originally hung from iron nails, and two rows of vases, including eight big red-burnished pedestals, one bearing a griffin-handled cauldron, of a type also known in bronze (see p. 98). In the middle were small objects and piles of pottery, including bucchero and painted ware (perhaps geometric), some also burnt.

Overall, therefore, burials became more overt statements of power and status between the late eighth and seventh century: most notably those in well-furnished trench graves, followed by the likes of the Bocchoris and gold pectoral chambers, and culminating in the great tumuli, more characteristic of the mid/late seventh century BC. The latter were well designed to promote status claims through ancestry and, in the possible cases of multiple chambers sharing a mound (Avvolta tomb), to serve aristocratic dynasties. They project power in a manner typical of early states in a phase of growth: that is by sheer ostentation, or an assertion by an elect

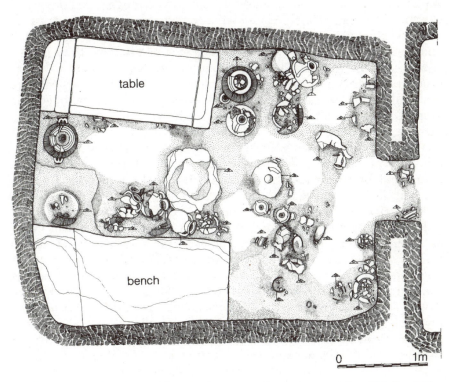

28. Monterozzi, chamber tomb 6118, late seventh century BC (after *ET*, fig. 271).

few of their ability to command the labour of many in pursuit of their own glorification.

They also show Etruscan society promoting itself on an international stage, using symbols readily understood both at home and abroad. With ancient precedents in European prehistory, and now also widely scattered in the eastern Mediterranean, mound burials were an ideal, archetypal medium in the visual lingua franca of aristocratic display. The Etruscan ones have many original features but may owe something to North Syrian, Cypriot and more especially Anatolian (Lydian) influences.[15] It is also noteworthy that a large contemporary tumulus at Lavinium became the focus of a hero cult of the legendary Aeneas, providing a powerful symbol for a propagandistic linkage between heroic ancestry, the gens and the origins of the city. As we shall see, Aeneas has a kind of parallel at Tarquinia in the figure of Tarchon.

Presumably these burials represent the affluent successors of a Villano-van elite and the ancestors of those later Etruscan aristocrats whose wealth must have derived largely from land holdings, trade and, perhaps occasionally, warfare. By the mid-seventh century, expanding trade networks would have required more complex wide-ranging relationships. Certain luxuries probably circulated through gift exchange, incurring obligations, while cementing familial or marital bonds. Mutual recognition and solidarity between a widely dispersed elite of different ethnic groups is suggested by the almost universal appeal of similar kinds of luxury goods; membership of an exclusive club generally requires a degree of conformity and possession of certain badges and material credentials. This kind of ideology underpins the Orientalising phenomenon, spurred on through freelance activity by middlemen and wealthy entrepreneurs. In fact, this must have been a time of important socio-economic transformations, even if the main effect initially was to extol and entrench aristocratic values and forms of leadership, heralding the ideologies of typically mon-archical or tyrannical regimes in the sixth century BC.

With reference to early Roman tradition, it can be argued that the social order was based not just on familial power structures, dominated by heads of families (*patresfamilias*), but on the more extensive powers of certain leaders or *principes*, a Latin term used to describe Etruscan aristocrats and heads of clans.[16] This enlarged structure, if organised along the clannish lines of the Roman gens system, would have co-opted and bound blood relations and other associates (*clientes*) to act in the interests of the *princeps gentis*. Roman writers refer to the priestly duties and powers of Etruscan leaders or *lucumones* and the literary sources (below) hint at their control of religious authority. Growing numbers of skilled artisans might also make for increasing social articulation during the seventh century, a trend that would be consistent in Etruria and Latium with

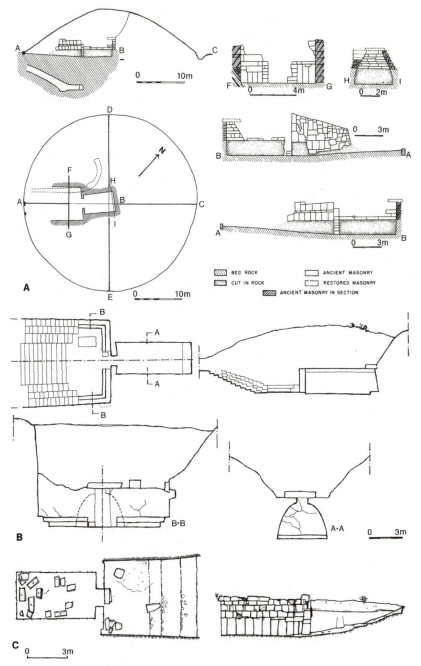

29. Tumuli and chamber tombs: (A) Doganaccia Tumulus I; (B) Infernaccio;
(C) Gallinaro (after Hencken 1968a, fig. 370; Cataldi 1993, fig. 107; *ET*, fig. 168).

double nomenclature: a personal name (*praenomen*) was now more frequently followed by a gens name (*gentilicium*), gradually superseding an earlier system of single names (see p. 80).

More elaborate power structures require servicing and staff. There were presumably slaves, albeit practically invisible archaeologically and only sporadically mentioned in later written sources. Their position possibly varied from that of humble serfs working the fields of landowners (like Latin *servi*) to a less disadvantaged class, likened by Dionysius of Halicarnassus (2.44.7) to Thessalian *penestai*, who had more rights and independence.[17] With greater social complexity and urbanisation, we might also hypothesise the emergence of intermediate classes, perhaps ancestral to a group of *gentes minores*, townsfolk or an urban *plebs*.

From the mid-seventh century there is some evidence for Greek hoplite (foot-soldier) equipment at Etruscan sites, such as the round shield, spear and helmet (see p. 90). This does not necessarily imply phalanx warfare, far less the democratic orientation of classical Greek citizen armies, and yet this century probably saw larger and more efficient fighting forces develop in Etruria and perhaps an adoption of hoplite tactics.[18] Real weaponry, moreover, is now quite common in graves. In early Roman tradition, ascribable to the monarchical or Archaic period, if not earlier, there was a direct link between a man's ability to bear arms (which were his own property and therefore dependent on his wealth) and his social status. One of the first recorded administrative divisions of the Roman male *populus* into associations (the Latin *curia* and *tribus*) was intended partly as a basis for the recruitment of differentially equipped and ranked classes of foot soldiers and cavalry.

East meets West: arts and crafts

Pottery is a useful indicator of trade contacts. By the late eighth century BC, local potters had adopted several new production techniques – the potter's wheel, better firing and surface treatments – probably stimulated by the demands of local clients, their appetites whetted by fine imports from Greece or Greek colonies in Italy (see p. 56). Vessels of Euboean derivation occur from the mid-eighth century at Tarquinia. Corinthian (notably Protocorinthian) production strongly influenced Greek-style 'Italo-geometric' ware and, to a lesser extent, some black bucchero, one of the most distinctive Etruscan craft products. Copies or local versions were also occasionally made of East Greek, Phoenician and Cypriot wares (Fig. 30: f).[19] The first Attic and Corinthian imports (skyphoi and kotylai) date from about 700 BC (Fig. 34: a-b); these forms, as well as trefoil-lipped jugs (oinochoai), are probably linked with the spread of wine-drinking and their use was perhaps initially confined to a privileged class. A number of

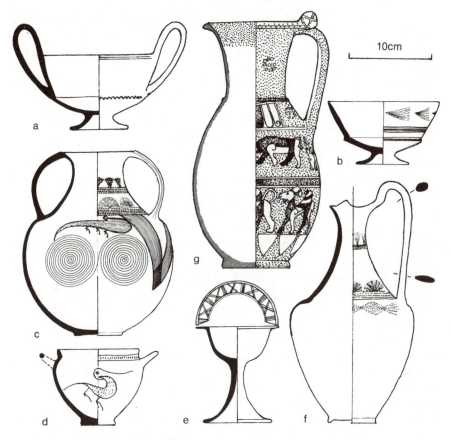

10cm

30. (a-f) Seventh-century BC bucchero pottery; (g) Etrusco-Corinthian jug (olpe), *c.* 600 BC (after *ET*, figs 28, 245, 299).

Early-Middle Protocorinthian imports, of a type also encountered at other Etruscan sites, consist of small luxury items, like containers for unguents and perfumes (aryballoi and pyxides), probably obtained from Greek sites, such as Pithecusae or Cumae in the Bay of Naples area. A few forms with red and black geometric decoration (around 700 BC) may be of Cypriot origin, although East Greek imports, mostly of about 700-670 BC, are uncommon.

Euboean potters may have helped to initiate local production by offering their services at Etruscan sites; they have sometimes been associated with a putative 'Painter of elongated horses' at Tarquinia, represented by oinochoai betraying Euboean, Attic and Corinthian traits. Another potentially local potter, or workshop, is the so-called 'Palm painter' (about 700-675 BC; Fig. 26), evidently keen on large tuna-like fish and maritime

69

scenes, as well as palms. Manufacture of Italo-geometric vessels persisted through the first half of the seventh century at Tarquinia, although they occur in much smaller quantities than traditional local ware, especially in domestic contexts.

Villanovan traditions were steadily transformed. New grades of old-fashioned coarse ware (*impasto*) were developed with a superior glossy finish to make traditional vessels as well as imitations of foreign imports, while shiny red and black wares betray the old love of metalwork.[20] Handsome ribbed jugs, bowls on stands and bucchero testify to local skill and a reinvigorated local tradition. Bucchero was in use by about 670 BC, perhaps as early as Caere, and followed the usual pattern of development from a more refined bucchero *sottile* (thin-walled, 675-625 BC), with elegant graffito decoration, to the *transizionale* (625-575 BC) and *pesante* (heavy) varieties, which persisted into the early fifth century.[21] Fine chalices and kantharoi (two-handled cups) typify richer tombs of about 625-550 BC.

The Bocchoris tomb (above) illustrates the popularity of luxury items of eastern Mediterranean and Egyptian type, which link Etruria with western Greek and Phoenician trading centres (such as Pithecusae, Carthage, Motya and undoubtedly the nearer Sardinian colonies). In this category also belongs a glass juglet of possible Syrian manufacture from a Monterozzi trench grave and an Egyptian alabaster canopic jar of the later seventh century BC, attributed to the reign of Psammetichus I. Local metalwork shows greater continuity, while adopting some Orientalising motifs, for example on fibulae and sheet-bronze vessels. New techniques of jewellery decoration, notably granulation and filigree, were inspired by growing familiarity with Near Eastern craft traditions, and perhaps learnt directly from Phoenician craftsmen. The sheet-gold pectoral of tomb 55 and gold versions of traditional leech and boat (*navicella*) fibulae are generally regarded as local products.[22] Casting by the lost wax technique is exemplified by a small human pendant from Gallinaro tomb 9; although rather schematised, it reflects a growing interest in a more naturalistic rendition of human and animal figures.[23] It is also possible that some of the earliest stone relief carving from the cemetery (see Chapter 4), which makes use of both Greek and Near Eastern motifs, dates from the end of the seventh century BC.[24]

Settlement and territory

The later levels in the Civita excavations are better preserved than the Villanovan (Fig. 31).[25] In the early seventh century, area alpha, the site of child burials (see p. 40), was reorganised and covered with a tough lime-plaster floor (107), flanked by stone walls, creating a quadrangular structure or precinct, probably unroofed, with an adjacent room (23) to the south. Directly across a narrow passage containing the pit (263) was a larger complex (beta), consisting of a smaller central chamber and two adjacent precincts. The chamber, perhaps subdivided (by wall 94), had a raised bench in one corner (387) delimited by large stone blocks. Two nearby conduits (616, 228) led outside towards the pit (263). An area to the south, probably open but not well preserved, extended to a hearth (330), while a larger room to the north (8.5 x 14 m), perhaps added around the mid-seventh century, may have been an open court, with an alcove in one corner (302). Against the wall of room beta was a pit (349) containing a small jar, sherds, charcoal, seeds and one or two sheep and pig bones, perhaps votive offerings.

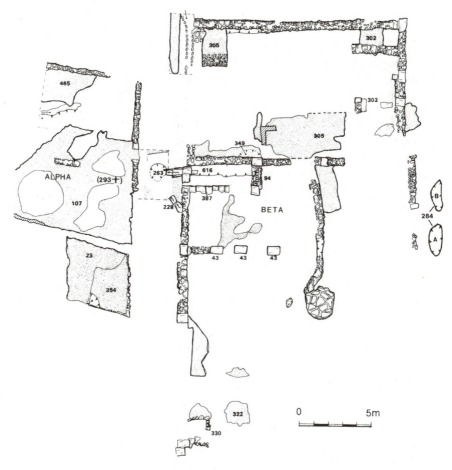

31. Civita excavations, seventh-century BC features (after *Tarquinia 1*, plan 9).

Tarquinia

Two shallow pits (284A-B; about 1.8 x 0.8 m) a short distance away support the idea of a cult place. One contained goat and pig bones, fragments of flat dishes, little jars, a bucchero chalice and three remarkable bronzes: a trumpet (or *lituus*) 1.45 m long, with a curved end, which had been folded; a round shield with spiral, animal and geometric motifs, also folded; and a decorated shaft-hole axe (Fig. 32).[26] The adjacent pit had fragments of a jar and cups. The deposits seem votive in nature, perhaps derived from a ceremony involving music, animal sacrifice, or feasting and drinking, with the axe (a sacrificial implement?) and shield as ritual symbols and offerings. The same general area produced a variety of pottery types and even tortoise carapaces.

The entire complex is regarded by the excavators as a sanctuary enclosing a cult chamber in which the corner bench (387) served as an altar for sacrifices whose blood drained into the pit (263). This is an intriguing reconstruction, not easily proven, although more convincing alternatives are not obvious. The scale and layout suggest public or religious buildings. With reference to early Roman traditions, however, others have suggested a king or priest's residence (like a *regia*), an official meeting-place (like a *curia*, ancestral to the senate) or some sort of political and religious building.[27] Uncertainties persist, particularly as parallels are lacking at other sites in Etruria, where few settlements have yet been excavated.

Nor are the burials easy to interpret: they comprise four children (late eighth/early seventh century), one adult male (see p. 40) and an adult female (seventh century). Comparisons are hardly justified with Phoenician tophets (cemeteries with hundreds or thousands of urns holding the remains of sacrificed children), since we are dealing here with just occasional depositions over a long period, the last in the sixth century (see Chapter 4). A single designation for the entire area is further complicated by the presence nearby, at least from the sixth century, of installations with industrial or other possible functions (kilns, wells, a cistern, conduits and drains). If the central part of the complex is a kind of sanctuary, the nature or identity of any presiding deity also arises. Uni is a possible candidate in view of one bucchero inscription (Fig. 34: d; see p. 80). She is generally regarded as an Etruscan deity akin to Juno and Hera, though in this case affinities have also been proposed with an Aphrodite/Astarte of Near Eastern origin.[28] The pits and animal sacrifices might, however, suggest some form of chthonic ritual (directed to the subterranean sphere), perhaps of Villanovan origin.

From an architectural standpoint, one can see a new concern with monumentality, urban geometry and stone construction, which set the pattern for the next century. Noteworthy too is the sturdy pilaster wall (43), linked by sections of smaller stones, which is reminiscent of masonry styles used in the eastern Mediterranean and in western Phoenician

72

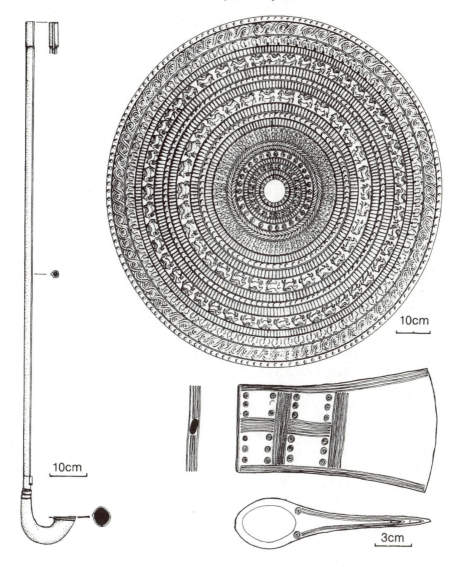

10cm

10cm

3cm

32. Bronzes from pits on Civita: trumpet, shield, axe (after *Tarquinia 1*, pl. 125).

colonies (known as *opus africanum* in the Roman period); so far it is not documented at other Etruscan sites.[29] While ordinary dwellings at Tarquinia in the seventh century no doubt still employed timber, wattle, daub and thatching, certain buildings were roofed with terracotta tiles by about 650 BC. Roof-tiles in Greece date from about 680 BC, so Tarquinia was in the vanguard of this development in central Italy. Traces of late seventh-century occupation occur on Cretoncini, although the earliest roof-tiles here seem to be later.[30] At other Etruscan sites, such as San Giovenale, rectilinear multi-roomed dwellings with ashlar masonry foundations appeared around the end of the seventh century.

The excavations also provide new faunal and floral evidence. Most of the animal bones of the ninth/seventh century BC come from area alpha and consist of sheep or goat (38%), pig (33%) and cattle (20%).[31] This familiar triad of Mediterranean domesticates, recurrent in Italy from the Neolithic onwards, seems relatively constant at Tarquinia until the second century BC. The remainder are represented by occasional dog, deer, equines, fox and hare. Cultivated grains include spelt, oats and possibly pea. Stimulated by new fashions, trade and technical knowledge, vine and olive cultivation probably expanded during the seventh century; the adjacent territory would have provided grain, orchards, vines, olives and woodland.

Urbanisation was evidently accompanied by changes in the countryside, including the foundation of new settlements, possibly new forms of land ownership, as well as trade links and population growth. Settlement is better documented in the surrounding region in the seventh century than before (Fig. 24). Sporadic finds attest occupation around Gravisca, and sites along the river Marta imply a growing network of contacts inland. Many of the finds on the valleys and hillocks within a 12 km radius of Tarquinia seem to reflect burials; the majority probably belong to small hamlets or just homesteads, but a few cases to a slightly larger settlement or village.[32] The presence of large tumulus tombs in relatively outlying locations, but surrounding the settlement, might suggest that some high-ranking individuals actually resided on adjacent tracts of land, perhaps as owner-occupiers of private estates.

Surveys around Tuscania, a secondary centre probably affiliated or subservient to Tarquinia, have also identified a growing density of sites within a 10 km radius of that town.[33] There must have been an increasingly complex hierarchy of rural settlement gravitating around various urban units of different size. Noteworthy too is the evidence for occupation around the coastal zone south of the Mignone and on the northern side of the metal-rich Tolfa massif, to which Tarquinia presumably had access. This good land south of the Mignone, which includes a number of minor centres (Monte Rovello, Cencelle, Luni) was probably also within the political orbit of Tarquinia (Fig. 17: a), while Caere perhaps maintained closer links with the southern Tolfa hills. By contrast, towards Vulci, there is little evidence for occupation along the Arrone (although systematic surveys need to be undertaken), a frontier zone perhaps less likely to be contested, lacking the particular advantage of metal resources.

3. The Rise of the City State

Legend, literature and literacy

There is no surviving Etruscan history written by the Etruscans themselves, while relevant information is limited in the work of Greek and
Roman writers who were often hostile towards other peoples and ham-
pered by restricted knowledge, a situation aggravated in the Etruscan
case by the language barrier, a long tradition of mutual rivalry and
sporadic military conflict. In fact, very little recorded or textual information was available for Italy prior to the fifth century BC. Ancient writers
could therefore either ignore the foggier past or speculate, embroider and
entertain their readers with good, but usually propagandistic, stories.
Early Italic and Roman 'history' is thus largely a concoction of moralistic
parables, folk migrations and myths of origin, enlivened by villains and
heroes with fabulous ancestries conjured up in order to provide venerable
origins or eponyms for important peoples and places. This does not absolve
modern scholarship from attempting to elucidate the surviving accounts;
aside from their intrinsic merit and interest, they can shed light on oral
traditions and bear some relevance, indirectly or even inadvertently, to
the period which they purport to represent. From a historiographic standpoint, at least they show how people in later times wished to think of
themselves or to be seen by others.

In the case of Tarquinia, the foundation stories reflect a sense of her
high status, long history and primacy in religious affairs, notably as the
place where soothsaying originated. First and foremost is the story of
Tages, a mysterious child seer, and Tarchon, the venerable city founder.
The various accounts, compressed and combined, essentially relate how
Tarchon was ploughing a field near Tarquinia when the infant Tages
appeared in a furrow, metamorphosed from a clod of earth. Struck by his
divine qualities, Tarchon took the inspired prodigy to a holy place, where
the child miraculously dictated the sacred rituals of haruspicy (divination). Ageing rapidly, Tages then disappeared or died, perhaps within a
day.

Cicero's version (*De Divinatione* 2.50-1; second century BC), in which
Tarchon is replaced by a mere *bubulcus* (ploughman or rustic) is generally
given precedence, although certain details reported by Ovid (*Metamor-
phoses* 15.552-9), the Byzantine, Ioannes Lydus (*De Ostentis* 2-3; sixth
century AD) and others may be taken as complementary to it. Cicero is in
myth-debunking mood and subjects the story to a somewhat pedantic line
of questioning:

> If a god, why did he ... hide himself in the ground ... if a man ... how could
> he have lived covered with earth? (*De Divinatione* 2.51).

However, it has been argued that Lydus' convoluted text is of equal or greater value, since it lacks Cicero's scepticism, and may possibly derive from a venerable Etruscan source, the *liber tageticus*, one of the canonical works on the art of divination, which the Romans called the *etrusca disciplina*:

> Tarchon – for that was his name – a man, [was] a haruspex, as he himself reveals ... Tarchon says in the book – which some suspect was by Tages because in it, as in a sort of treatise in dialogue form, Tarchon, indeed, puts the questions, but Tages answers each time as if he was continuing [with the exposition of] the sacred lore – that once upon a time, when he was plough-ing, a marvellous thing happened to him ... for up from the furrow emerged a child, born at that very moment apparently, although not without teeth nor the other signs of maturity. Now the child was Tages ... dealing with more sacred matters, his teaching is not presented in an open way that the impious would understand, but now in myths and now in parables ....[34]

The archaistic elements of the fable cast faint shadows from times when even heroes like Tarchon are supposed to have ploughed the fields. Furrow and clod might hark back to a chthonic or agricultural religion of Villano-van tradition, but the story sounds more relevant to the emergence of a patrician class increasingly identified with control of religious affairs, perhaps in the seventh/sixth centuries. According to Lydus, Tarchon alone was privileged with Tages' revelations.[35] Of noble ancestry, he was divinely chosen for this role, while the complexity of the rituals was no doubt another reason, or excuse, for the exclusivity of the choice. The use of writing for religious matters, generally the preserve of an elite, is of course a hallmark of Etruscan civilisation, as is the art of haruspicy, with its powerful claim to special knowledge. The myth, therefore, not only en-dorses social relations, making them seem natural or divinely sanctioned, while enhancing the status of the city, but also contributes to a sense of ethnogenesis, a recurrent feature in the growth cycle of early states, concerned with self-identity, history and legitimacy.

It was once thought that a third-century BC bronze mirror from Tus-cania depicted the youthful Tages examining a liver, watched by the bearded Tarchon (Fig. 33). Both have a kind of wizard's hat, denoting a haruspex, and are flanked by divinities (Rathlth and Veltune). Sub-sequent studies, however, have concluded that the elder man, labelled Aule Tarchunus, is more likely a descendant of the famous Tarchon, while the youthful figure, inscribed in much smaller letters as Pavatarchies, is a novice haruspex.[36] *Pava* may mean a boy (like Latin *puer*), while *tarchies* refers to Tarquinia, or possibly the Tarchon family *gentilicium*. The scene could therefore show a mature haruspex observing a pupil, possibly his son, or another member of the same gens, which liked to trace its ancestry

33. Tuscania mirror, later fourth century BC (after Pallottino 1930).

back to Tarchon, the first haruspex. It can also be argued that the boy personifies the aristocratic youth of Tarquinia and that the scene is allusive in a more general way to the long tradition of teaching the sacred art by demonstration.

Tarchon's name may derive from Tarquinia, or Tarch(u)na, which in turn could be associated with a local gens, of which he was perhaps the reputed founder. Aside from his privileged association with Tages, he is

77

referred to in his own right, at least from the time of the Greek poet Lycophron (*Alexandra* 1248; third century BC), as a mythical founder figure in traditional mould (Strabo 5.2.2); heroic exploits and a divine pedigree are ascribed to him through Herakles, Telephus or Hera, providing a link with the Lydian king Tyrrhenus (as his kinsman or delegate) and hence to Herodotus' controversial account of Etruscan origins in terms of a migration from Lydia.[37] Lydus calls him a haruspex, and his priestly role is emphasised by the Tages story. It is in this guise that he evidently appears, head veiled, as the representative of the *Tarquinienses* on an early imperial relief carving from Caere (Fig. 71). He is sometimes also credited with the foundation of other towns or the entire Etruscan dodecapolis, perhaps as a result of a later adjunctive tradition which attempted to claim reflected glory or to exalt his fame and thus the primacy of Tarquinia at a time when Tarquinia was enjoying special prominence in the Etruscan League (from 420-350 BC; see Chapter 5). The presence on the Tuscania mirror of Voltumna (Veltune), national deity and sponsor of the League, seems politically significant in this regard. In any case, Tarchon's story is intimately connected with the founding traditions of the Etruscan people as a whole.

Another venerable resident of Tarquinia, according to ancient sources from at least Polybius (6.11a.7) onwards, was a Greek, Demaratus, a member of the powerful Bacchiad oligarchy and political exile from his native Corinth. Livy (1.34.1-3) and Dionysius of Halicarnassus state that he had grown rich on the profits of mercantile activity with Etruria, and had many friends '... particularly at Tarquinii, which was a large and flourishing city at that time' (D.H., *Antiquitates Romanae* 3.46.5).[38] For Roman historians, clutching at straws in their attempts to create an early history of Rome, the main interest in Demaratus was as the founding father of the Tarquin dynasty, which ruled Rome, at least periodically, during the sixth century. Strabo (5.2.2) notes that he brought others with him from Corinth (below), which is not stretching credulity. Settling at Tarquinia, presumably some time after 657 BC when the tyrant Cypselus took power in Corinth, he married an Etruscan woman, Tanaquil, who produced two sons, Arruns and Lucumon, the latter better known as Lucius Tarquinius Priscus, the first Etruscan king of Rome.

Livy would have us believe that Lucumon's political ambitions were frustrated at Tarquinia on account of his mixed parentage: 'he was by blood an alien being the son of Demaratus' (Livy 1.34.5).[39] This prompted his departure for Rome, and implies that the position of Demaratus was effectively no more than that of a rich merchant refugee at Tarquinia, accepted by the local community, but debarred from certain political offices. Strabo makes no reference to this, but may have been following another version of events deriving from a pro-Etruscan literary tradition, perhaps developed at Tarquinia itself.[40] The prominence of Tanaquil in the literary tradition, and her not altogether sympathetic portrayal, hints at the status and power of some Etruscan women. Described as 'noble but poor' by the learned emperor Claudius (on the Lyons inscription), Livy notes her skill in steering her husband's career and effectively choosing his successor, her son-in-law, Servius Tullius, disregarding constitutional niceties in the process.

The historical authenticity of Demaratus is not actually vindicated archaeologically, but his story is at least consistent with the evidence for closer links with Greece in the seventh century, attested by imported pottery and inscriptions (below) at Etruscan sites; whether or not he is an historical figure, he personifies contact. Moreover, the Orientalising phenomenon, attested not only in Etruria but in other areas of Italy, notably Latium, by rich graves and by the avid consumption and exchange of exotic luxuries, reflects links between the upper classes, which could have facilitated mobility, through rites of hospitality, guest-friendship, gift-exchange and personal alliance. From Demaratus' standpoint, emigration must have been aided by the presence of powerful families and friends at Tarquinia with whom he had cemented bonds. Vertical, or upward, mobility was probably not so easy. In fact, although the Bacchiads were traditionally endogamous, Greek aristocrats of the Archaic period, unlike ordinary folk, frequently married strategically outside their own communities. The same may be true of their Etruscan counterparts; there is certainly evidence for it in later times (see p. 161).

Tacitus (*Annals* 11.14) states that Demaratus introduced writing to the Etruscans, while Pliny (*Natural History* 35.43.152) adds that three Greek *fictores* (craftsmen) came to Tarquinia at about this time, whose names, rather than specific individuals, suggest paradigmatic personifications of archaic arts and crafts: Eucheir (the dexterous), Diopus (the keen-eyed) and Eugrammus (the fine draughtsman). These authors were probably projecting additional elements onto the Demaratus tradition, further developing it into a pseudo-historical parable. Here again, however, the sources present no real surprises; it was commonplace in antiquity to ascribe all kinds of inventions to ancestral figures, mythical or real. Yet it is quite possible, as noted above, that some Greek craftsmen found employment at Etruscan sites.

Of more concrete value is the epigraphic evidence from Tarquinia, initially in the form of short inscriptions on pottery.[41] The earliest are in Greek and on Greek imports of the end of the eighth century, suggesting contacts with the Bay of Naples colonies, where a similar alphabet of Chalcidian origin was in use. Inscriptions on bucchero and coarse ware imply that writing was adopted locally between 700 and 650 BC, slightly earlier than at most other Etruscan sites, with the exception of Caere.

Frequently, the pronoun *mi* (= 'I') appears as part of a talking inscription in which the object itself addresses the viewer in a declaration of ownership, along the lines of 'I belong to so-and-so'. Etruscan names, such as Anth or Larth, generally follow in the genitive. Names of divinities also occur: notably the late seventh-century *miuni* (I + Uni), which may associate this divinity with cult functions on Civita (above; Fig. 34: d).[42] Apart from its novelty value, elitist associations and utility, not least in specifying ownership, writing might also have had magical or ritual connotations, as suggested by votives and such unusual vessels as a Corinthian aryballos in the form of male genitals, a bird-shaped bucchero rattle (inscribed respectively with *mi lartha sarsinaia* and *mi mulu kaviiesi*), and a jar with incised animals and a band of untranslatable letters on the collar.

Certain personal names also stand out: *numesie* on a Protocorinthian kotyle of about 700 BC suggests an Italic *praenomen* (like the Latin *Numerius*), within a longer phrase roughly translatable in part as 'I the vase of Velelthu [made, offered?] to [for?] Numesie' (Fig. 34: b).[43] Painted around the base of a Corinthian-style jug from the Doganaccia tumulus appear the words *Achapri rutile hipukrates*, combining a probably local name (like Latin *Rutilus*, meaning red) and a Greek gens (Hippocrates), transcribed into Etruscan; the meaning of *achapri* is unclear (Fig. 34: c). This might represent an individual of Greek origin, possibly the eminent

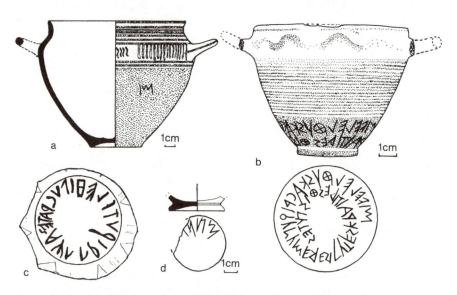

34. Seventh-century BC pottery inscriptions: (a) Protocorinthian skyphos ('*mi*'); (b) Protocorinthian skyphos ('*mivelelthuskacriqunumesiesiputeskraitilesthisputes*'); (c) jug base ('*achaprirutilehipukrates*'); (d) ('*miuni*') (after *ET*, figs 205, 157; Jucker 1969; Hencken 1968a, fig. 371g).

occupant of the tomb, or the donor of the vase.[44] While the quality and context of inscribed vases evince mainly aristocratic associations, the names reinforce the impression of a place that was receptive to exogenous materials and ideas as well as people.

Urban transformations

It has often been assumed that the Etruscan city state emerged as a result of contacts with Greek colonies, which introduced a new form of urban life and sophistication to a relatively undeveloped Villanovan society. However, this is a rather reductive and over-simplified view of Etruscan cultural evolution. As noted in the last chapter, Villanovan Tarquinia exhibits a higher level of organisational complexity by comparison with earlier times: metal-working and long-distance trade flourished, burials betray greater social articulation, while large sites dominating ample territories denote new settlement hierarchies. It is noteworthy too that Villanovan Etruria was not settled by Greeks or Phoenicians, unlike some other parts of Italy, which might imply a resistance to direct colonisation.

Nevertheless, a somewhat circumscribed assessment of Villanovan society (prior to about 750 BC) is still dictated by the absence of any great elaboration in urban layouts, which are, in any case, rather different in nature from those of sixth-century Etruscan cities. Social differences and labour division, notably craft specialisation, certainly existed, but were not particularly marked, nor is there evidence of the higher-level organisational or administrative capabilities and internal complexity of the kind often associated with early states.[45] While Villanovan Tarquinia could be described as 'protourban' insofar as it laid some of the foundations for the emergence of a more articulated social order in the Orientalising period and the subsequent Archaic city state, this does not necessarily mean that this future stage would have been attained without the additional elements, changed conditions and new stimuli of this time. Many facets of south Etruscan cities, or Etruscan civilisation more generally, can not be accounted for without reference to comparable developments elsewhere in Italy and in the wider Mediterranean world, including that of Greek and Phoenician colonies.

Moreover, several significant transformations become visible only in the later Villanovan and Orientalising periods (about 750-600 BC), notably: the more emphatic evidence of vertical division by rank; the use of exotic luxuries to express social difference; the more obvious concern with lineage; the broadening range of craft activities with implied divisions of labour; the consolidation of a nucleated civic centre; changes in architecture, building techniques and settlement layout, including the construction of a fortification wall which, on present evidence, does not

Years BC	Urban design	Regional settlement	Subsistence
1000	–	Non-hierarchical	–
900	Dispersed clusters, traditional timber buildings, thatched	Nucleated-hierarchical	Mixed farming
750	Centralising – stone masonry, cult buildings	Nucleated-hierarchical	Mixed farming & beginning of specialised olive & vine production
600	Public buildings, streets, fortifications, harbour, temples, roof tiles	Hierarchical	Mixed farming & specialist production: olives & vines
400	As above	As above?	As above?

Key features and developments, 1000-300 BC

date until the sixth century at Tarquinia; the appearance of writing, and more elaborate personal nomenclature. This suggests that significant advances occurred in the seventh century, which were crucial to the process of state formation. Rather than a gradual and inexorable development, already anticipated in the Early Iron Age, one might instead think in terms of step-like progressions in which certain significant thresholds were only crossed at particular times.

However, this does not mean that late Villanovan communities were just passive recipients of outside stimuli and that the Etruscan city state was merely imitative. The concept of a city, with its complex interlocking functions, is unlikely to be borrowed or passed from one culture to another, like a Greek pot, or implanted, except in certain colonial situations. Whatever happens in adjacent regions, state formation can only occur if it is consistent with local conditions. Furthermore, the western Mediterra-

Production	Burials	Status symbols (burials)	Years BC
–	–	–	1000
Limited craft specialisation	Limited wealth variation/display; gender/role variants	Stone chests, hut urns, metal, weaponry, personal adornment	900
Increasing craft specialisation	Marked wealth variation, & conspicuous display	Chamber tombs, luxuries, weaponry, gold, silver, exotica, trade/craft items	750
Marked craft specialisation	Marked variation, but conformity within groupings	As above & 'lifestyle' statements: banquets, 'leisure' activities	600
As above	As above	As above & sarcophagi, 'career' inscriptions, badges of public office	400

nean world of the eighth century did not yet possess a well-developed city model.

Rather than simply derivative, therefore, urbanisation and state formation in the late Villanovan and Orientalising period are better regarded as interactive processes, within an increasingly 'cosmopolitan' world, between several politically autonomous and often rival polities, which to some extent followed their own agendas but were nevertheless increasingly interlinked by the exchange of goods and by similar ideologies and aspirations.[46] Plainly, one can see points of convergence in details of appearance, due to common interests and fashions (especially those pertaining to the elite), which reflect various processes ranging from direct copying and selective borrowing or adoption with modifications en route, to independent development. In this world of increasingly good communications and information flow, people, goods and ideas moved with comparative ease. Where cultural borrowing did occur, however, it often involved an appropriation of items or forms of behaviour that were consistent with an indigenous, pre-existing ideology.

One may surmise that the key distinguishing features of Etruscan city states stemmed from local (Iron Age) traditions and the need to participate more effectively in increasingly complex relationships with their peers. In fact, despite changes in social organisation, there is a good deal of evidence for continuity between the ninth and sixth centuries, as seen for example in certain long-lived craft traditions, such as metal-working (for which the Etruscans were later internationally renowned), many aspects of burial customs, including the use of both inhumation and cremation, the prominence of certain graves and the differential use of grave goods according to local ideas about gender, role and status. Many other customs and features of later Etruscan society may also be rooted, at least in part, in earlier traditions: aristocratic pursuits, such as horsemanship, hunting, wheeled transport and parade weaponry, the family/gens system, the status of women, and perhaps some religious beliefs, public institutions, ceremonies and juridical concepts, as well as agricultural practices and diet.

In thinking about explanatory models for Etruscan state formation, the use of prestige goods and symbols in the Orientalising period is also compelling, and seems emblematic of a new spirit of experimentation and competitive acquisition. Exotic luxuries and valuables were more essential than ever to the expression and maintenance of status and were coupled with attempts at institutionalising power through the medium of monumental funerary architecture. The relevance of rival communities, especially western Phoenicians and Greeks, to the process seems essentially threefold: they created a bigger market and a new and more immediate source of goods and services; they increased the pressures and incentives to compete for the acquisition of strategic resources, not just metals and exotica, but also territory; and they inspired new artistic and technical achievements. One might say that the colonising movements of the eighth century helped to stimulate a local process of state formation. From a social, political and economic standpoint, it might also have been advantageous for all the major players (late Villanovan groups like Tarquinia as well as individual communities of western Phoenicians and Greeks) to conduct relations with each other from within at least mutually recognisable, if not identical, 'urban' structures. At the same time, Tarquinia in the seventh century seems to have been one of several fledgling western Mediterranean city states defining themselves in part by emulation, but also in opposition to each other through statements of individuality or the assertion and elaboration of local tradition.

To what extent and for whom the process may have been beneficial is difficult to gauge. One might think that greater mobility and trade would have required new guarantees of hospitality and security, that centralisation also promoted group security and solidarity, and that even competition between elites encouraged competitive displays of generosity. We would be better placed to judge if we could see more clearly to what extent material wealth or other social benefits percolated down through Tarquinian society. In conclusion, however, we may regard a period of indigenous development in the Iron Age as having established precepts for more rapid growth in the seventh century which was followed by further expansion and consolidation in the sixth century, often described as the 'golden age' of Etruria.

4. Urbs Florentissima

City of the dead

The sixth century BC can be seen as a new act rather than just a scene change in the life of the city. Several monuments and civic amenities established in this period were destined to last. The temple, city wall and harbour, for instance, were long-term investments, expressions of confidence, ambition and a commitment to the process of urbanisation which was now widespread in the Mediterranean and affecting adjacent areas. Agriculture, trade, art and crafts thrived in a climate of economic growth, cross-cultural interaction and relative stability. Nonetheless, Tarquinia seems to have developed as a self-willed centre of individual power, creativity and taste, retaining her autonomy and cultural traditions, like many contemporary cities. Her burials, for example, follow local trends, while forms typical of other Etruscan cities – the cremation urns of Chiusi, carved chambers of Caere, box or niche graves of Vulci and Veii – are absent or rare here.

Tombs were added to the old cemeteries on the eastern *poggi*, sporadic examples occur on the edge of Civita and on Cavaluccio, but the principal burial ground was now Monterozzi (Figs 35, 42). By the fifth century BC this was a vast necropolis, a testimony to urban growth, continuity and prosperity. Geophysical surveys by the Lerici foundation (p. 25) have located about 6,100 tombs (mainly sixth/third century) over the whole promontory and about 1,300 in the Calvario area alone (34,000 m^2), of which just under 10% have been excavated.[1] The records, however, are lamentably patchy; few tombs have been properly excavated and most were looted long ago. Painted tombs are the best documented, but even their spatial relationships are rarely clear.

The top of the plateau was doubtless prime burying ground, thanks to its prominence across the valley from Civita – tombs were meant to be seen. Places where the rock was harder were avoided, and old tombs were generally respected as the cemetery grew organically, despite the crush. But many questions remain. How were plots allocated? Were kin placed near each other, as one might well imagine? Some groups of similar tombs were fairly evenly spaced, facing southwards and sharing an open area around their entrances, like a forecourt, an arrangement only disturbed when later tombs filled the gaps (Fig. 36).

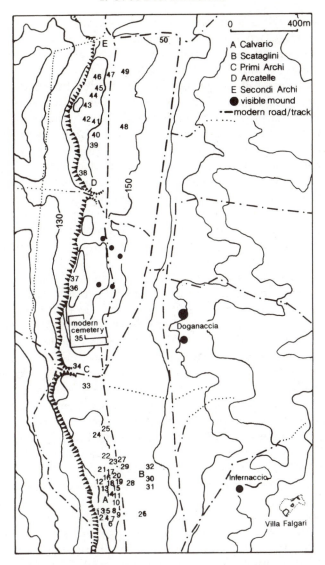

35. Monterozzi plan, with numbered painted tombs: 1 Pulcella, 2 3713, 3 Lotus
Flower, 4 Hunter, 5 Lionesses, 6 Loculi, 7 Warrior, 8 Hunting and Fishing,
9 Jugglers, 10 Charontes, 11 5636, 12 5591, 13 Cardarelli, 14 Gorgoneion,
15 Whipping, 16 Deer Hunt, 17 Double, 18 5513, 19 Little Flowers, 20 Blue
Demons, 21 Bartoccini, 22 Bacchantes, 23 Leopards, 24 Deceased, 25 Typhon,
26 Garlands, 27 Querciola I, 28 Maggi, 29 Sculptures, 30 Four Figurines,
31 Anina, 32 Mercareccia, 33 Shields, 34 Cardinal, 35 Orco, 36 Painted Vases,
37 Old Man, 38 Mouse, 39 Panthers, 40 Giustiniani, 41 Giglioli, 42 Baron,
43 Frontoncino, 44 Bulls, 45 Red Lions, 46 Pygmies, 47 Cock, 48 Bertazzoni,
49 Augurs, 50 Pulcinella (after Cataldi 1993, fig. 27).

There is no evidence in the sixth/fifth centuries for the changes in cemetery architecture and design seen at Caere and Orvieto, where orderly rows of uniform box-like rooms fronted straight streets, presumably reflecting a move towards grid-like geometry in urban planning. A comparable trend at Tarquinia, however, seems to be that tumuli diminished in size (mostly 5-10 m in diameter now), while their chambers became more standardised, and probably never held such lavish riches as the earlier princely graves. Since there is no sign of an economic downturn – rather the opposite – we may be dealing with a changing social and ideological configuration: not a move towards generalised egalitarianism, but an expression of solidarity and conformity within an expanding oligarchy, and the birth of bureaucracy. There are possible parallels here with Rome and Greece, where new legislation and codes of civic behaviour regulating funerals accompanied urban development, thereby helping to divert capital to other, arguably more useful, forms of public investment, such as sanctuaries and large building projects.[2]

Rock-cut trackways and subsidiary paths steered traffic through the labyrinthine necropolis. One route, coinciding partly with the modern *stradella comunale*, bisected the promontory and continued south-east towards Allumiere (Fig. 12: no. 4).[3] Others (Fig. 12: nos 2, 3, 7) linked up with Civita, entering Monterozzi through breaks in the scarp at Primi Archi, Arcatelle and Secondi Archi, leading on to the Doganaccia tumuli and beyond; one (no. 3) followed a natural hollow south from Arcatelle past a cluster of Villanovan shafts and chamber tombs. As always in Etruria, these were not quiet cemetery roads, contrary to current appearances, but obligatory access routes flanked by grand mausolea, reminding one and all of the venerable ancestry and prestige of the city and its ruling class. They would add pomp and circumstance to any funerary processions that plied the way from Civita to this imposing place of rest.

Unfortunately, centuries of ploughing, planting and plundering have substantially felled what was once a forest of tumuli, reduced now, with a few exceptions, to crop marks in aerial photographs, in which around 800 are visible. About 50 appeared in exploratory trenches on Calvario, superimposed on Villanovan houses (p. 42), and another palimpsest of funerary structures can be glimpsed near the Panthers tomb (Fig. 37). Between the mounds were trench and shaft graves (below) and possibly other quadrangular constructions. A shallow foundation trench held the outer ring of the drum, often faced with quadrangular or polygonal slabs and ornamented by torus and trochilus (convex/concave) mouldings, decorative projections or plinths (Fig. 8).[4] Cut-out steps, reminiscent of the ramps and stairways found at Caere and Vulci, indicate that the summit of the mound was intended to be accessible, perhaps as part of the funerary ritual.

Each mound of earth and rubble typically covered a single chamber,

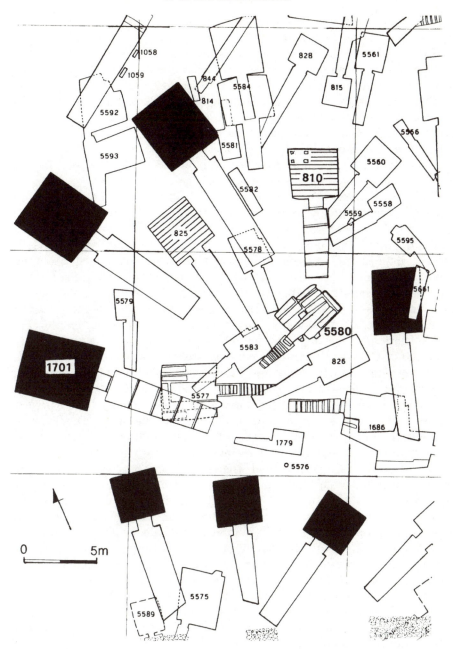

36. Monterozzi tombs near the Whipping tomb (1701). Those in black are probably late sixth/early fifth century BC; those hatched (825, 810) probably later fifth century; the rest mainly fourth/third century (after *CE*, fig. 319).

89

entered by a stepped passage (*dromos*) leading down to a narrow doorway, closed by slabs. The quadrangular rock-cut room was usually of modest size (3-6 m long). An early example is the 'hut tomb' (575-550 BC), with a pitched roof, a narrow rooftree (*columen*) carved in relief, and a few painted bands. Double or triple chambers are rarer and later in date (Bulls, Bartoccini, Hunting and Fishing tombs, 530-510 BC; Fig. 42). Some tombs had solid rock benches on two or three sides, and a wall niche, probably for a cremation urn. Less elaborate than those of Caere, the chambers evoke simplified scaled-down dwellings.

To some extent, Monterozzi must have resembled Caere's famous Banditaccia cemetery, also dotted with tumuli along the promontory flanking the town. Canina's attractive reconstruction, however, shows overly uniform and large circular mounds with too many entrances (p. 19; Fig. 9). Decorative details must also have differed. By the early sixth century, stone carvings adorned some tombs: a sculpted lion from Gallinaro, like examples from Vulci, perhaps originally guarded a tomb entrance.[5] One of the earliest depictions of men armed like Greek hoplites occurs on a limestone slab, although its original location is unknown.

One of the specialities of Tarquinia is a series of elaborately carved blocks of *nenfro*, occasionally limestone, probably painted originally (Fig. 38). There are over 70 pieces, roughly dated from the late seventh to the middle or later sixth century, possibly stone versions of wooden types, echoing richly decorated metalwork of eastern Mediterranean derivation and perhaps tapestries or textiles.[6] The figurative work occupies friezes or individual squares (metopes), framed by guilloche ribbons beside projecting slanted steps. Prancing animals and mythical beasts are the favourite motifs: panther, lion, deer, ibex, bull, eagle, sphinx, gorgon, centaur, griffin and marine creatures; horsemen and humans occur too.

A fleeing female (the rape of Thetis by Peleus?), a suicide (probably Ajax, a popular subject in Etruria), a man with a prisoner, and a sex scene, doubtless come from myth. A longer frieze may well represent Herakles and a centaur, and Achilles stalking Troilus, like the adjacent lion pursuing a deer, anticipating a kill. A squatting female, arms raised and legs apart, flanked by wild creatures, is a striking emblem, presumably of fertility and nature, reminiscent of a Near Eastern goddess. Subject choice and arrangement have precedents in the Orientalising repertoire and probably, in part, a funerary significance. For instance, the winged figures have been likened to personifications of stormy winds and harpies that carried off dead souls in Homeric myth; but the manner of rendition differs from any Greek counterpart.

Various blocks can be reconstructed, in theory at least, to form a single monumental façade, 3 m high and 2 m across (Fig. 38), but most of the pieces have only survived as broken chunks, re-used as masonry or grave

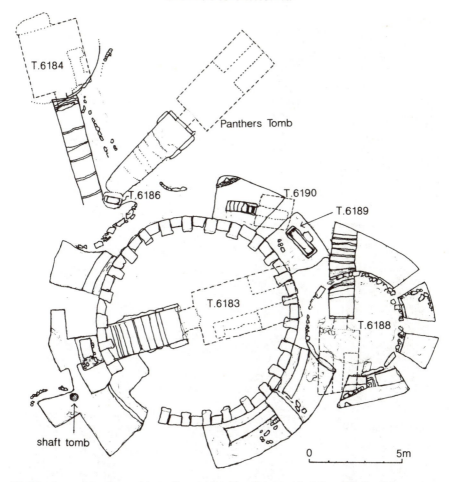

T.6184

Panthers Tomb

T.6186

T.6190

T.6189

T.6183

T.6188

shaft tomb

0   5m

37. Monterozzi tombs and tumuli near the Panthers tomb (after *PE*, fig. 71).

covers; their original function and location have therefore eluded research. Once thought to have been tomb doors, they are more likely to have been placed in front of the latter, or set above them, possibly in the entrance corridor; the real tomb doors below could have been interred. If this is correct (although it is only a hypothesis and doubts remain), the tomb entrances were spectacularly embellished.

The smaller tomb chambers were most likely for couples, probably inhumed in wooden sarcophagi, or possibly on biers or couches, but only their floor sockets or occasional bronze appliqués remain. There may have been cremation urns too; the old records mention human remains in black- and red-figure vessels. An urn-like terracotta box (about 500 BC), painted with horsemen in the style of the tomb frescos, reputedly came from a

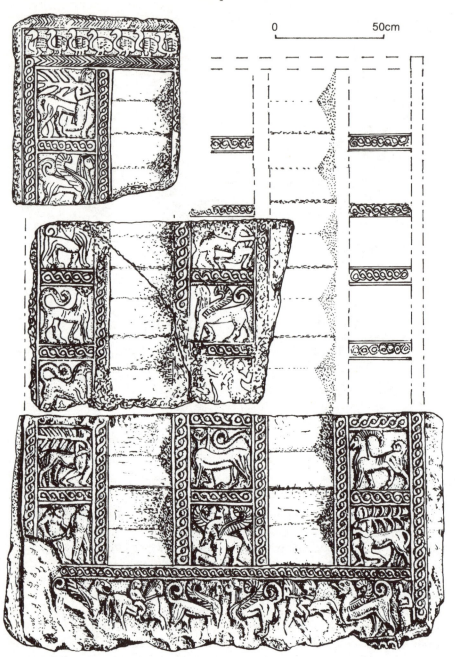

0   50cm

38. Stone slabs with step and relief carving (after photographs and Maggiani 1996, fig. 1).

chamber tomb.[7] The original number and arrangement of grave goods in the chambers is nowhere clear, but they were probably clustered on the floor, around the walls and benches. Certain tombs (Lionesses, Ship and Blue Demons, for instance) had nails in the wall, like the Avvolta tomb, perhaps for suspending garlands, often shown in frescos, or else artefacts, as represented in the later Reliefs tomb at Caere.

Although looted, the Blue Demons tomb sheds new light on funerary rites and illustrates the limits of our knowledge. The floor had sockets and a pit with burnt soil, carbonised wood and bone. Scattered iron chariot fittings, a spear and early fifth-century Panathenaic amphorae probably came from this pit; yet the wall paintings suggest a late fifth-century date. Were the amphorae heirlooms therefore? Alternatively, like the chariot, could they be from an earlier deposition? If so, the tomb must have been re-used in the late fifth century, when it was also painted, perhaps by descendants of the first occupants. They might even have been responsible for cremating the earlier remains and depositing them in the pit.[8]

Other tomb types are probably under recorded, but trench graves were still used and several dozen stone-lined cists, often packed with something resembling a lime plaster and sealed by a slab, held cremations. Bucchero urns were prevalent at Turchina, but on Monterozzi they were usually black-figure amphorae, occasionally red-figure vessels, such as a krater covered by a kylix, and either local products or Attic imports, dating from about 580-480 BC (Fig. 39B-D; below).[9] Two, found recently, held respectively the bones of an adult and an adolescent. Most lacked grave goods or had very few: a scarab, mirror, fibulae, gold ornaments, spearhead, spindle whorls and bronze lumps (*aes rude*) suggest both males and females.

The significance of these tombs is uncertain, but they are not exactly new. The cremation shafts and even the neck amphora and cover vase recall Iron Age practice and the old biconical urn. Moreover, as evidence accumulates, it seems that cremation had not disappeared, as once assumed; we may therefore infer some continuity of tradition, even if the social significance of the rite had changed. Some cremation amphorae are of good quality, but the simplicity of the shaft graves in their inconspicuous plots suggests persons of lesser rank, perhaps retainers of those in the nearby chambers. If not here, one may ask, then where are the burials of the lower classes and children? At least two hypotheses present themselves: that their tombs, dotted around the cemetery in the form of these modest trenches and shafts, were closer to the original ground surface and therefore most easily destroyed (or ignored in old excavations); or that there were other, possibly peripheral, burial zones, still unexplored, where they concentrated.

Sadly, many finds of this period lack a provenance. Row upon row of Greek or Etruscan painted vases stand like orphans in the cases of the

Tarquinia museum. We know only that they came from tombs and that they were obviously an ideal medium for conveying information and imagery, a significant contributor to that expansion of commercial, cultural and cognitive horizons which is a hallmark of the Archaic world. Eye-catching, story-telling vessels, with their skilful, sometimes masterly, depiction of human forms and stories, they seem hardly to require a functional explanation. But they had practical uses, especially for banqueting and wine-drinking. Many must have had complex histories: traded from afar, serving their owners in life, and then in death, as urns.

The range of imports betrays the extent of trade. Non-Attic products are represented, for example, by Corinthian, Chalcidian, Laconian and East Greek wares.[10] The latter include numerous Ionic cups, a Fikellura amphora of about 540 BC, amphoriskoi and lydiai (unguent vases), lekythoi, neck amphorae, a hydria, Rhodian perfume flasks masquerading as animals (580-560 BC), and a black-figure askos (Knipovitch class), possibly made by a north Ionic (Phocian?) potter in Etruria around 540-520 BC. Transport amphorae too sometimes ended up in tombs, probably holding food or drink offerings.

The flow of Attic imports, dating from around 580 BC, peaked between 530 and 475 BC, and is typified by black-figure kraters, hydriai and amphorae, including high quality products attributed to a variety of styles (Fig. 39: B), painters or workshops, such as those of Exekias, Antimenes and Lysippides.[11] A fine head jug is signed by Charinos, a potter of about 525-500 BC (Fig. 39: A). The classic cups (kyathoi, kotylai, skyphoi) and jugs (olpai, oinochoai) of banquets were endlessly popular. Graphic imagery was obviously part of their appeal, especially Dionysiac and Homeric scenes (Hector and Andromache, Achilles, Troilus), depictions of Herakles, or warriors variously in combat, departing or returning. The kyathos, which is not a traditional Greek form, was evidently destined specifically for the Etruscan market, like the so-called Tyrrhenian amphorae made in Athens from about 575-550 BC (though rare at Tarquinia).

Nonetheless, many questions remain about the use of Greek vases in Etruria and the way in which Greek production catered for Etruscan clients.[12] Products of certain workshops (or 'painters') show specific distribution patterns. For instance, the concentration of Attic Haimon and Beaume vases at Tarquinia and Vulci is perhaps due to specific commissioning by local consumers. There were probably subtle contrasts in taste and in the use of vases in this non-Greek context, recognised by manufacturers. Yet it is noteworthy that the Attic lekythos, a specialised Greek funerary vase, is unusually common at Tarquinia (22 are published), which has also produced an example, rare in Etruria, of a white-ground lekythos from a tomb.[13] Here is an indication of closer links with Greek practice, if not the actual presence of Greeks.

39. Painted vases: (A) Attic head jug by the potter Charinos (H 21 cm; *c.* 500 BC); (B) Attic black-figure amphora with Dionysus head, used as a cremation urn in a shaft tomb (H 39.5 cm; *c.* 520 BC); (C-D) Etruscan black-figure amphorae (from photographs).

Attic red-figure vases began to arrive in the late sixth century. Many are kylikes. A huge one (510-500 BC) signed by Euxitheos (the potter) and Ioltos (the painter) bears an Etruscan inscription on the base (p. 135). Amphorae, kraters, hydriai, oinochoai, lekythoi, skyphoi, stamnoi and kantharoi were still popular with local clients into the fifth century BC. Several are signed or attributable to famous names: Nikosthenes, Phintias, Hieron, Macron, Briseis, Triptolemos, Pamphaios, Kleophrades, Epiktetos, Euphronios, Brygos and the 'Berlin painter'.[14] We should remember, however, that in Etruria as elsewhere in the Mediterranean, it was metal vessels, of gold and silver above all, that were most valuable, if not necessarily the best loved. We can see both metal and fine painted vases proudly displayed on the sideboard (or *kylikeion*) in several tomb paintings (Figs 7, 45, 47).

Local production, meanwhile, diversified and intensified, anticipating the mass production of the Hellenistic period. Etrusco-Corinthian seems mainly geared to local consumption from about 590-550 BC, or aimed at smaller sites inland, perhaps to meet the needs of those for whom imports were expensive. Several forms (aryballoi, alabastra, amphorae) were for oils of various kinds. One or two amphorae (630-600 BC) may be from Caere, while three local, if rather undistinguished, 'ateliers' of 590-570 BC have been postulated at Tarquinia. The products of one (the 'Pittore senza Graffito') are perhaps recognisable in Sardinia, southern France and Carthage.[15]

Bucchero, produced throughout the sixth century, became less common during the fifth century, which saw a preference for the heavy variety with simpler decoration. Chalices, jugs (oinochoai) and other drinking forms were common funerary offerings (Fig. 40); a leg-shaped perfume flask is more unusual.[16] Stylistic analysis suggests that some were imported or made at Tarquinia under the influence of Caere, while others, also found in neighbouring centres, were Tarquinian products. Several handsome, rather 'metallic' oinochoai of 550-500 BC with relief decoration, including banquet scenes like those of contemporary tomb paintings, were probably made locally (Fig. 40: b). Related to bucchero is a glossy red ware, better known at Caere in the Orientalising period, but also current at Tarquinia, as represented by a tripod vase with stamped decoration of about 575 BC.[17]

Etruscan black-figure vases (mainly dated 540-475 BC, though some may be later) have a rather matt glaze and paler clay than their Greek counterparts (Fig. 39: C-D). One or two belong to the 'Pontic' class of amphorae, which adopt East Greek motifs, and others are associated with specific styles, or such scholarly inventions as the 'Paris painter' (about 550-520 BC) or the 'Micali painter', albeit potentially real individuals, or at least workshops, possibly based in Vulci.[18] Some amphorae, stamnoi, kraters and askoi, which vary in quality and may be inspired by Attic or

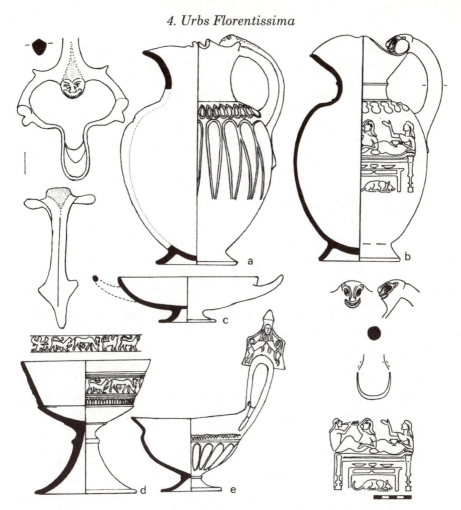

40. Bucchero vases with incised and relief decoration, sixth/early fifth century BC: (a, b) oinochoai; (c) kylix; (d) chalice; (e) kyathos (after *ET*, fig. 301;

Ionic styles of decoration, yet express local tastes and traditions, could come from Tarquinia.

Metalwork and jewellery also attest the vitality of local crafts. Despite incalculable depredations, inadequate records and the problems of separating imports from local products, one can safely assert that craft production at Tarquinia scaled new heights at this time. A speciality of Tarquinia and the surrounding region are circular bronze plaques with heads of lions, rams or the bearded horned head generally identified as the human-faced bull, Achelous, the river god (Fig. 41).[19] Roughly dated to the late sixth/early fifth century and reminiscent of later shield portraits, they were possibly applied to wooden furniture or tomb walls for apotropaic reasons. Four griffin heads from a bronze cauldron of about 600-575 BC in the Orientalising tradition, possibly East Greek products, have a parallel at Gravisca.[20]

One can trace a gradual evolution of many bronzes from Archaic into Hellenistic times, especially those associated with banqueting: various jugs (oinochoai, olpai, schnabelkannen), bucket shapes (situlae and stamnoi) with finely wrought handles, ladles and strainers.[21] Several forms are expensive versions of ceramic counterparts. One early fifth-century oinochoe may be from south Italy, while others were probably made locally. Strainers and ladles (the Latin *colum* and *simpulum*) filtered wine between krater and amphora or from jug to cup, and are depicted in tomb paintings (Fig. 46). Flat dishes were doubtless for food. Little oil and unguent flasks (sixth century) were perhaps used by athletes, as were strigils (from the fifth century), whereas cylindrical *cistae* (from the late sixth century) held cosmetics. Mirrors date from the late sixth century, some showing couples, perhaps in acts of court-ship or betrothal (Fig. 41). The emphasis is on 'domestic' bronzes in Archaic tombs, although weaponry could still be entombed, at least in the form of iron spearheads.[22]

Skilled techniques of granulation, filigree, repoussé, engraving and lost wax casting, already known in the previous century, were further per-fected.[23] Jewellery exhibits a wide range of figurative and probably amuletic motifs, such as gorgons, deities, Achelous and animal heads. Earrings and gold finger rings with decorated bezels, such as cartouche rings of Phoenicio-Egyptian inspiration, were in use from the mid-sixth century, as well as silver or bronze armlets and small ornamental fibulae in precious metal. Gold appliqués or plaques, *bullae* and elaborate ear-rings are characteristic of the later sixth and fifth century. Scarabs set in swivel-rings occur from around 530 BC until the Hellenistic period. Many were probably imported, but local gem-cutting is conceivable, using mainly red carnelians, chalcedonies, veined sardonyx and jasper, depict-ing human, mythical and animal figures, which eventually replaced the Orientalising preference for amber and faience.

To the late sixth century belong carved plaquettes from little wooden caskets, probably for cosmetics or valuables. Four bone examples in the Louvre show a chariot (*biga*) drawn by winged horses, a stag hunt and a sea creature, as well as a banquet scene whose authenticity has been disputed. Once coloured, all paint has now vanished. The East Greek or Cypro-Phoenician style also presents analogies with contemporary tomb frescos.[24] Another pair has a reclining male and a couple kissing, evidently a banquet scene, probably of the early fifth century BC.

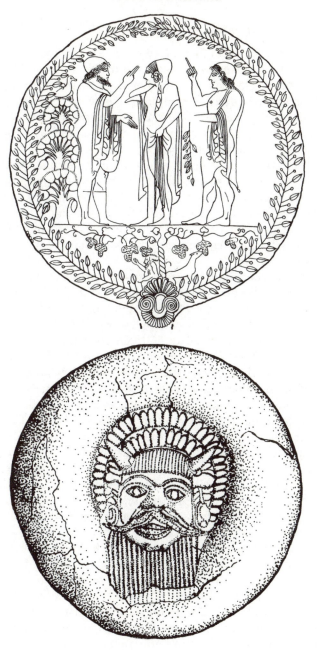

41. Above: bronze mirror (D 11.5 cm) with incised decoration, possibly a marriage scene, *c.* 510-490 BC. Below: bronze disk with moulded Achelous head inset (*c.* 470 BC) (after *CSE*, no. 16; *ET*, 295).

Tomb painting: (a) date and technique

Large paintings from antiquity rarely survive in fragments, let alone as complete murals. In terms of scale and number, those of Tarquinia are unsurpassed in the classical world other than by the frescos at Pompeii, preserved fortuitously by the eruption of Vesuvius in AD 79.[25] About 180 painted tombs are known, but the original number must have been higher: others were probably found centuries ago, and destroyed or never recorded; as many as one in four chambers known only from Lerici's photographic probes were full of earth and remain undocumented; and some preserved only a few lines or stains. The two main groupings on Monterozzi are at Arcatelle, about 1.5 km from the slightly larger one at Calvario, which is open to visitors (Fig. 35).[26] The known painted tombs (sixth/third century) are a small minority: only 3.3% of about 6,000 tombs in total, although more frequent around Arcatelle (nearly 6%) and Calvario (around 27%).

It is often said that tomb painting was the preserve of the wealthiest. However, one wonders how the cost compared with that of some fine grave goods or of construction; after all, craftsmen and painters were plentiful and mostly of lowly status in the classical world. Unfortunately, we cannot compare the contents of painted and unpainted chambers, but it is notable that not all painted tombs are large and imposing (the Deceased tomb is a mere 2.5 m^2) and that some quite large chambers were not painted, especially in the Archaic period (Figs 6, 36, 42). The latter might have had even more expensive embellishments, such as drapery or fine textiles, like those shown hanging from the wall in the frescos of the Tapestry tomb (third century BC). Wealth aside, there must have been an element of choice in tomb painting, perhaps a desire to express individuality or a personal touch, at a time of growing standardisation in funerary architecture. It may also have appealed to the followers of certain cults, such as those of Dionysus and perhaps Aphrodite.

Tomb painting began in the late Orientalising period (late seventh/early sixth century BC), flourished in the late Archaic (about 540-490 BC) and continued well into the Hellenistic period (late fourth/third century BC; see Chapter 5). Tarquinia boasts by far the longest and richest tradition of any site, with about 80% of all Etruscan painted tombs, although the custom was initially widespread, attested by one or two seventh-century tombs at Caere and Veii and by later examples at Chiusi, Blera and Orvieto. Concentrations of non-Etruscan tomb or sarcophagus paintings by neighbouring Italic peoples also exist in Campania and Lucania, dating from the fifth century. Although tomb painting has no obvious precedent in Etruria, large mural paintings in an essentially geometric idiom may have existed in the Early Iron Age. Villanovan hut urns (p. 53) are often decorated with

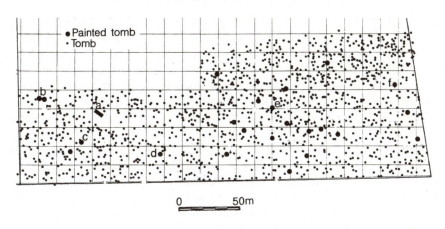

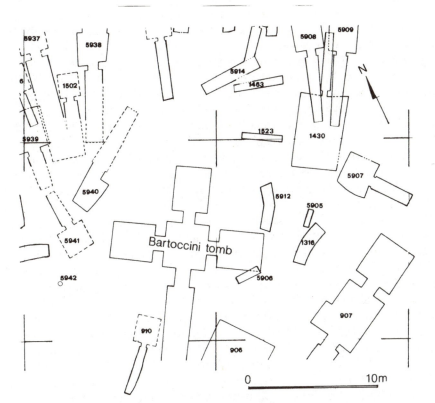

42. Above: Monterozzi, Calvario tombs identified by geophysical prospection (Lerici). Painted tombs: (a) Hunting and Fishing; (b) Warrior; (c) Jugglers; (d) Charuns; (e) Cardarelli; (f) Bartoccini. Below: Bartoccini tomb, probably originally covered by a mound, with nearby 'corridor' tombs (after Cavagnaro Vanoni 1997, fig. 3).

incised and painted motifs which might represent full-scale counterparts. It is therefore possible that there was already a tradition of painting or decorating the plastered walls of real Iron Age houses and that, therefore, the practice would not have seemed alien to indigenous society.

The Tarquinia frescos are generally dated by style, which entails comparisons with Greek art or painted vases. Some tombs are hard to date closely, especially in later periods (p. 164), but a general development can be charted with reasonable confidence.[27] Bright colour and movement typify Archaic frescos. An early formative stage, which seems freer in the choice of subject matter, includes one obvious example of mythological narrative (Bulls tomb), although some of its precepts and favourite subjects persisted well into the fifth century or later. A 'classical' style emerged only gradually and unevenly as Archaic traditions were superceded between about 475 and 450 BC, partly due to Attic influences, though some loss of thematic range resulted as scenes of banquets and sports began to dominate. The fifth-century tombs are also dated mainly by reference to painted pottery, notably red-figure vases, which flooded into Etruria and were doubtless an important source of inspiration.

For instance, the well-executed athletic scenes in the Biga tomb (490 BC) recall work by Attic potters at the transition from black- to red-figure painting. An exuberant dancer in the Triclinium tomb, combining late Archaic and Severe Styles, has been compared with figures by the Attic 'Penthesilea painter', implying a date of around 470-460 BC, while the wine vessels in tomb 5513 are recognisable types of about 450-425 BC. These and three other tombs (Funeral Bed, 4021, 810) are sometimes regarded as the work of a good 'atelier' of about 470-440 BC.[28] While several tombs of 500-450 BC are highly rated (e.g. Black Sow and Triclinium tombs) and display a sophisticated treatment of space and depth (Funeral Bed tomb), the second half of the fifth century has seemed comparatively uninspired to some scholars, an impression perhaps overstated and too influenced by the notion of a generalised economic recession at this time. However, the Blue Demons tomb heralds a change in mood and style, which seems far from stagnant.

East Greek traits appear in the figurative work of about 530-500 BC. For example, the male profiles and female dancer in the Augurs and Jugglers tombs have been likened to the style of Ionian vase painters, who inspired an Etruscan version of black-figure production at Caere, typified by elegant three-handled jars (hydriai). Other tombs (Baron, Mouse, Deceased, Bacchantes, Cardarelli) present more generic stylistic affinities with north Ionian vase or sarcophagus painting, at Phocis and Clazomenae for example, which is also encountered on Etruscan jars (dinoi) of the Campana group. Likewise, aspects of the Bulls and Bartoccini tombs have been compared with 'Pontic' vases (above), while the naturalistic motifs of the Hunting and Fishing tomb (510 BC) recall the 'little master' vase painters

43. Panthers tomb, *c.* 580 BC, rear wall (from photograph).

from Samos (Fig. 44; Plate V). It is noteworthy too that late sixth-century painted wall plaster has been found in a house at Gordion in Phrygia (west-central Turkey) and in some Lycian tombs (south-west Turkey), executed in the same fresco technique.[29] Etruscan tomb painting, there-fore, was not an isolated phenomenon with a purely autonomous development. Some of the first Tarquinia painters might even have been East Greek craftsmen who had abandoned their homeland due to growing tension and conflict with Persia from the mid-sixth century, or simply been lured to the west by wealthy patrons.[30]

However, this is rather speculative; and to say that all the best work was done by immigrants and the inferior by local apprentices would be prejudiced. One possible alternative explanation for distortions or signs of 'inexperience' is that the artist was a vase painter unused to working on a big scale. For example, the small figures are better proportioned than the large ones in the Bulls tomb, witness the shortened torso of Troilus and the corrected horse's head, placed in a rather crowded scene. The variable quality and style of work, even within certain tombs (e.g. Bulls, Bartoccini and Triclinium), might reflect a mixed crew of painters and less experi-enced assistants; the status of the commission and the client might also be relevant.

Stylistic studies are hindered by the limited number of tombs of any precise period, the force of convention and, arguably, by the absence of discernibly individual artistic personalities.[31] Attempts to assign frescos to 'workshops' have some heuristic value as an aid to analysis, but are destined to remain unverifiable. If tomb painting alone was not sufficiently commonplace to warrant full-time specialists, large-scale painting (the *megalografia* of ancient Greece) was probably known in other forms. Temples and even private houses may have had painted wall panels, as suggested by terracotta plaques (*pinakes*) from Caere and Veii. It may be that the best work – and work dealing with different subjects according to context, such as mythological works for temples – was not in tombs but in important buildings, to which the living also had access.

Initially mainly black, brown, red and yellow, by the later sixth century the range of colours included white, blue, green, and intermediate shades achieved by mixing.[32] Reds and yellows derive from iron oxides, white from lime or kaolin, dark brown and black from organic material, blue from a mix of copper, lime and silica (not lapis-lazuli) and green from copper carbonate (malachite). All of these occur naturally in Etruria, although pigments were possibly traded, as suggested by finds at Gravisca (below). In the Orientalising period and occasionally later, the paint was mixed with water and applied directly to the bare walls, which had been given a smooth finish. The Monterozzi limestone holds the colours well, by contrast with the tufa of Caere, where much has probably been lost. In the Archaic period, the walls (not usually the ceilings) were generally prepared with a thin application of clay mixed with the local powdered rock, covered by a lime-plaster skim-coat, which provides the typical creamy background. Floors were sometimes plastered, and defects in the walls made good with clay and stone chippings. On contact with the damp plaster the colours acquired a healthy glow typical of fresco painting.

As our main source of contemporary figurative imagery, painted vases are a useful point of reference, but tomb painters need not have imitated them slavishly. Vases and tombs presented different challenges of media and scale – vase painting being as much concerned with reduction as tomb painting with enlargement. The wall painter worked within an architectural format that evoked the inside of a house, highlighting the rooftree (*columen*), its support (often dividing the pediment), cornices, dados and door surrounds, with slabs of colour or finer motifs: ceiling rosettes, circles, chequerboards, dots, bands or rows of floral motifs, waves and dolphins. String and compass marks occasionally betray the use of simple devices to achieve regular bands and circles.

Fabrics could have inspired some designs; perhaps hanging drapery was used in buildings. In a few cases a tent-like structure could be intended, possibly for a lying-in-state before burial (*prothesis*), a practice

44. Tympanum banquet scenes of the late sixth century BC. From top: Tarantola; 5039; Mouse; 4780; Hunting and Fishing; Bartoccini (after Weber-Lehmann 1985, pl. 27).

attested in Greek and Italic funerary rites, and shown in two tombs (Deceased and Dying, 500-510 BC; Fig. 6). The large catafalque beneath a draped canopy in the Funeral Bed tomb might be so understood, while the Hunter tomb (510-500 BC) has the feel of a temporary pavilion, with thin supporting struts, pitched roof, hanging ducks, garlands and open or translucent sides through which a solitary deer is glimpsed (Plate IV). There is an unusual stillness here, as though a hunting party had left for the day. In the Lionesses tomb (520 BC) by contrast, one is looking through a colonnade.

When the tomb's architecture had been delineated, the pediments and wall panels were free for figurative imagery, transcending the constraints of the chamber and any domestic associations. No doubt preparatory sketches and plans were made with reference to pre-existing models. Profiles were sometimes outlined with a pointed implement or a thin black or red line. The pediments were usually viewed as discrete units, embla-zoned with counterposed animals in the Orientalising tradition, or with reclining figures. By contrast, the main walls in many Archaic tombs (e.g. Bacchantes, Baron, Funeral Bed, Hunter, Hunting and Fishing, Inscriptions tombs) were treated as a continuous frieze, like a single canvas. In some cases, painted doors provide subdivisions, or evenly spaced trees help to separate and frame the images (Figs 45, 48). Some tombs (Bartoccini, Biga, Bulls) have an additional narrow register, a two-speed narrative, with different subjects and figures at a reduced scale above the main murals: for example, sporting events flow past banqueting scenes in the Biga tomb (Fig. 45).

Alternatively, the side and end walls could be distinguished by differ-ent, albeit related, scenes. For instance, banqueters may occupy the end wall, flanked by processions, games and dancing on the sides. In the Augurs tomb (520 BC), the sombre figures, probably in mourning, beside a large door contrast with the sports and cavorting on adjacent walls (Fig. 49; Plates I-II). More obviously self-contained is the panel with Achilles and Troilus in the Bulls tomb, hanging like a picture between two door-ways (Fig. 49). In the Funeral Bed tomb, the great canopy on the end wall is the obvious focal point, but the adjacent banquet spills onto the side walls and then graduates into an area with attendants and a more open and animated field of action with sportsmen and horses.[33]

Tomb painting: (b) subject and structure

Several sixth-century tombs had just a few decorative bands, but figura-tive imagery begins at Tarquinia with the Panthers tomb (late sev-enth/early sixth century), in which two highly decorative, stylised felines are heraldically posed above an admonitory head or mask (Fig. 43).[34] The motif seems apotropaic (guarding 'the exits and entrances of the passion of life' as D.H. Lawrence believed; *EP*, 49.14) and has venerable antecedents in the eastern Mediterranean, although more easily linked in this instance with the popularity of Orientalising animal art, widely disseminated by Corinthian vases. Tympanum figures were henceforth part of the canon, ranging from big cats felling herbivores to counterposed bulls, sphinxes, marine and other scenes.

Allusions to food and drink abound in Iron Age funerary ritual. It is not without precedent, therefore, that a popular theme in tomb painting from the late sixth century is that of so-called banquets, in which individuals or couples recline, attended by servants. Evidently these were privileged venues and occasions for entertainments, relaxation and sensory pleasures, and doubtless also useful bonding sessions for an elite which relied on clientage, the reassertion of position, obligations and alliances. The setting usually proclaims good living, made manifest by fine clothing, elegant table ware, furniture, music and wine.

One of the first depictions of the reclining banquet in Etruria occurs on a terracotta plaque of about 575 BC from a palatial building at Murlo, near Siena, which shows couched couples, anticipating the tomb images.[35] The practice, evidently of Near Eastern origin, was adopted in Greece in the seventh century and probably in Etruria soon after. By contrast, Villanovan dignitaries, like their Homeric counterparts, seem to have sat upright. Good parallels for the Etruscan plaques occur in Asia Minor (for example at Larisa in the mid-sixth century). One of the oldest banquet scenes at Tarquinia, in the Bartoccini tomb (520 BC), reminiscent of this Ionic practice, shows men reclining, while the ladies perch on adjacent chairs, like spectators (Fig. 44). In the Hunting and Fishing tomb the mood is different: it is a private affair involving what looks like husband and wife, attended by a flute player, nude boys serving wine, as customary in Greek symposia, and two girls making garlands, possibly their children (Fig. 44; Plate V). The adults are elegantly dressed, the lady with her chunky jewellery and Ionic hat (*tutulus*), the man with his showy necklace and precious cup.

While the etiquette of dining and drinking could differ between mainland and East Greece, and according to the occasion, the seigneurial atmosphere of much Etruscan banqueting also stands comparison with Near Eastern ideology. One contrast between many Etruscan banquets depicted and conventional Greek symposia is that the latter were often male events, with the exception of female entertainers or courtesans (*hetairai*). Yet such occasions may also have been known in Etruria: on the side walls of the Lionesses tomb, four men recline separately on the ground in what resembles a symposium with Dionysiac connotations of East Greek type (cf. Tarantola, Frontoncino tombs, 520-500 BC; Fig. 44).[36] From

45. Top: Leopards tomb, end wall, *c.* 480 BC, based on a watercolour by G. Mariani (Blanck and Weber-Lehmann 1985, pl. 27). Below: Biga tomb, end and side walls, *c.* 480 BC, based on nineteenth-century tracings by C. Ruspi.

the early fifth century, however, coupled men, or man and woman, are shown reclining together on richly draped or upholstered couches, often in groups of three, anticipating the layout of a Roman *triclinium*. An early example is the Leopards tomb (480 BC) in which well-dressed young men and women relax together, while musicians, dancers and a procession of players and bearers of gifts grace the side walls (Fig. 45; Plate III). Couples adopt similar poses in the Triclinium tomb (and tomb 5513, 450 BC), while a cat prowls under the table (Plate VIII). These paintings support the view that Etruscan women were more prominent in certain social situations than their Greek counterparts, a theme much discussed in recent years.[37]

Various elements in these scenes (wine, food, finery, dance, games, music, talking, flirting) extol what the Romans called *otium*, or leisure, the opposite of *negotium*. A huge garlanded krater sits centre-stage in the Lionesses tomb (Fig. 46), while high-quality symposium wares are displayed at every opportunity, sometimes on a special sideboard (*kylikeion*), for example in the Painted Vases tomb (around 500 BC; Fig. 7) and in the Ship tomb (mid/late fifth century; Fig. 47), anticipating Hellenistic practice. Dancing is pervasive, and cuts across social boundaries. Elegant ladies, scantily clad young women, naked youths, male *komasts* with cup in hand, musicians, even armed warriors (probably engaged in a Greek-style pyrrhic in the Biga and Pyrrhicist tombs) all dance, individually, as couples, or groups. The repertoire was evidently wide, from the boisterous knees-up of lively adolescents to the gentler gliding steps of robed matrons (Fig. 46). Something resembling flamenco, with castanets, clapping and flutes, animates the Cock tomb (400 BC, Fig. 47), while prancing figures in the Triclinium tomb perform an exotic mime-like dance with elaborate footwork, arm and head gestures (Plate IX).

Cicero, citing Cato, tells us that according to old Roman tradition:

> ... at banquets it was the custom of our ancestors for the guests at table to sing one after the other to the accompaniment of the flute in praise of the merits of illustrious men' (*Tusculan Disputations* 4.3).[38]

This perhaps recalls an old Italic version of the rituals and recitations of Greek symposia. In the tomb frescos, several lyre players, generally male, could be singing (Plate VII); yet the one sitting on the edge of a couch in the Black Sow tomb is a well-dressed female, possibly aristocratic. In games resembling the Greek *kottabos* (Cardarelli tomb, 510 BC), wine was tossed from cup to target. A more complicated performance, probably by skilled entertainers, required balancing a candelabrum on a woman's head, perhaps in a dance, while disks or rings were thrown on to it (Jugglers tomb, 510 BC; Fig. 46).[39] Garlands, often hanging from the walls

46. Top: Lionesses tomb, rear wall, *c.* 520 BC. Middle: Olympics tomb, side wall, *c.* 510 BC. Below: Jugglers tomb, rear wall, *c.* 510 BC (from photographs).

or from the arms of dancers, underline the festive or symposiac nature of the occasion, and seem to be exchanged like presents (Deceased, Inscriptions, Baron tombs).

In addition to these party games were sporting contests of a kind widespread in classical antiquity, with athletes, sometimes naked, adjudicators, prizes and spectators, both male and female (Augurs, Biga tombs): wrestling, boxing, probably the pancration (boxing and wrestling combined, in the Biga tomb), long-jump, running, discus, chariot, javelin (in the fourth-century Warrior tomb) and perhaps other equestrian events (Inscriptions tomb; Fig. 48).[40] Boxing and chariotry seem to have been especially popular. Boxers (e.g. Olympics, Funeral Bed tombs) fought with bound knuckles and infibulated penis, to the accompaniment of the flute; their bleeding wounds were shown with a certain naturalism, or relish. Some of these competitors were perhaps professionals and of rather lowly social caste. The *triga* (three-horse chariot) and the tying of reins behind the backs of charioteers may be local specialities, and disastrous accidents were evidently part of the thrill; the Olympics tomb depicts the mayhem of a chariot crash, with a touch of comic-strip humour (Fig. 46).

A more sadistic game, unique so far to Etruria, involved a helmeted man, perhaps a masked actor, labelled *Phersu* in the Augurs tomb, inciting an angry dog to savage an opponent (a criminal perhaps?) with a bag over his head and armed with a club (Fig. 49).[41] The Latin word *persona*, in the sense of a character in a play, probably derives from this Etruscan word, and may reflect a Roman debt to Etruscan theatrical spectacles. Buffoonery and bloodshed characterised this violent show, which hints at some of the gladiatorial entertainments of Roman times, although there is no clear implication of mortal combat, let alone the systematic slaughter of a Roman arena.

Action and drama, spectacle, dance and finery, exerted considerable appeal, but not all fifth-century frescos show sports or banquets. In the Ship tomb, a double-masted trading vessel is shown manned with sails unfurled (Fig. 47). Is the adjacent figure watching (and waving?) from the shore its owner, the tomb's occupant, perhaps a wealthy merchant who commissioned the scene as a testament to his maritime interests?[42] If so, it lends a personal touch, foreshadowing the more conventional statements of family names and career achievements on Hellenistic frescos or sarcophagi.

The individual clients must also have influenced the subject matter of tomb painting, which reflects their choices, though based – rather like Christmas cards today – on a recurrent but limited range of images. In general, we must be dealing with a high-ranking group whose numbers had grown by comparison with the 'super-elite' of the great Orientalising tumuli: perhaps an established timocracy in part, but also individuals

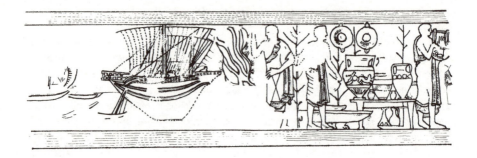

47. Above: Ship tomb, side wall, *c.* 440/400 BC. Below: Cock tomb, side wall, *c.* 400 BC (from photographs).

whose power and wealth derived from involvement in the expanded commercial networks of the sixth century. To some extent they were Hellenophiles in their aesthetic tastes and in their adherence to fashions and customs associated with an elite lifestyle, and yet many of these were already recognised and adopted widely, even by peoples on the fringes of Mediterranean urban society, in their different ways.

For over a century, critics and champions of Etruscan art have debated its origins and derivations, merits and defects. The term 'Etruscan art' has been challenged or replaced by 'art of the Etruscans', 'art of Etruria' or the potentially less problematic 'art in Etruria'.[43] In recent years, scholars have become more diffident about aesthetic judgements, while accepting that Etruscan tomb painting adopts certain techniques and conventions of Greek, and perhaps Near Eastern, art. However, the criteria of selection, adoption or participation in the broader cultural or aesthetic movements of the time are not easy to gauge. Surviving evidence is patchy for much contemporary art (pottery and, to a lesser extent, engraved mirrors excepted) and almost non-existent for Greek painting.

An extreme, negative assessment would be that the Etruscans merely borrowed techniques of representation, elite symbols and decorative motifs in a more or less haphazard, even uncomprehending manner. This view, however, is plainly too dismissive and contradicted by numerous particulars, from details of local dress to overt statements about social life, including bloody sports (the Phersu game) and the – by Greek standards – unorthodox prominence of women in certain social situations. Familiarity with foreign models goes only some way towards explaining the character, content and genesis of Etruscan art. An active process of selection, transformation and invention must have occurred. After all, it had to serve the purposes of a specific cultural environment, different from that of its Greek, Phoenician and even Italic neighbours. We should also remember that monumental graves, lavish grave goods, and tomb painting itself have little in common with mainstream Greek funerary traditions.

Tomb painting: (c) image and symbol

Further complications stem from the specifically funerary context. As a general premise, all burial rites may be said to confront the crisis of death by means of ceremony and symbolism. More specifically, one is bound to ask whether, or to what extent, this funerary art encapsulates social realities, magical or religious beliefs, philosophical messages and metaphors about rites of passage. In fact, the imagery could function on different levels and be viewed from different standpoints; one interpretation need not always exclude another. For example, 'social' readings became popular in the 1970s and 80s, but spiritual, religious and psychological dimensions cannot be ignored.[44] The former tend to emphasise the status of the deceased, the evocation and celebration of certain elite events and, thus, our transportation into a socially exclusive domain of familiarly aristocratic archetypes: wine-drinking, banquets with entertainments, sporting contests, horsemanship, hunting and allusions to the natural world. Scenes of rural life, crafts, industry, warfare or other activities of a political or civic nature are absent (at least in the Archaic period), with only rare exceptions.

But how faithful to real life is this imagery? Compared with later tomb frescos, populated by supernatural beings, there is little in the Archaic repertoire that the artist could not have actually witnessed, with the exception of mythical or netherworld scenes. This is not to say that what is depicted was necessarily painted from life or intended as a kind of documentary record, but only that convention, idealisation and foreign influences do not mask a sense of reality, locally based. (This is worth reiterating in the wake of scholarly preoccupations with comparable imagery on Greek vases, which can over-emphasise the potential for mere copying.)

For example, the deceased are shown on the funerary bed in the Deceased tomb and Dying tomb (Fig. 6), and elsewhere probably depicted alive and well, though not necessarily in this world: as an aristocratic couple reclining together (Hunting and Fishing tomb), a pose which recurs on sarcophagus and urn lids; as a white-bearded man watching games in the Jugglers tomb (or in the Old Man tomb, 500 BC); and as the man or woman in the Baron tomb, to mention only some of the more likely examples (Plate VI). In the Augurs tomb, the deceased seems to be evoked in spirit by mourners beside the door (Plate I), and in the Funeral Bed tomb by the strange crowns and hats placed on the empty bed, probably symbols of the Dioscuri and an heroic apotheosis.[45] Individual names are given in the Inscriptions tomb (Fig. 48; p. 135), some of whom must be the occupants, a practice more common in the Hellenistic period, but anticipated in the tomb of the Bulls, where the name Spurina, an eminent *gens* of the later city (p. 133), is prominently displayed.[46]

A concern with funerary rites is tangible, therefore, and sometimes responsible for what may strike modern eyes as a strange mix of frivolity and solemnity, the unworldly and the mundane. Literary sources tell us that sporting contests and other events in honour of the deceased were an ancient tradition in Greek and Roman society. So too undoubtedly in Etruria, where they also featured at gatherings of the League (Livy 5.1.4-5). Descriptions by Polybius (6.53) of elaborate performances at aristocratic Roman funerals (including masked actors imitating the deceased) also encourage the view that burial ceremonies are a major component in the Tarquinian frescos. Banquets certainly had a special

114

48. Inscriptions tomb, *c.* 520 BC (after drawings by Stackelberg, *c.* 1830; *CR*, 319).

place and a long tradition in Etruscan funerary art. Judging by the
Pulcella and Cardarelli tombs, music also had a role, as flute and cithara
were played beside the doors. Some ambiguity persists, however, because
not all banquets are certainly wakes and even the music, games and

banquets honouring the dead are also for the pleasure of the living. Hunting or nature scenes are even less obviously funerary concerns.

Religious or philosophical implications are hard to grasp. Does the somewhat hedonistic subject matter allude to an idyllic existence after death, an optimistic vision of an aristocratic Arcadia? There may well be some truth in this, a natural aspiration after all. Yet distinctions must be drawn. It seems unlikely that all the imagery shows a specific place in the afterlife. An underlying belief that some aristocratic activities, notably banquets, recur in the next world is clear, at least in later tomb painting (p. 167); and both Archaic and Hellenistic beliefs maintain the conceit that social status will still count in this other place. However, sports, games and perhaps the *komos* (revelling dance) shown on the side walls, if part of the funeral rite, must be terrestrial events, whereas certain (if not all) banquets depicted separately, and perhaps significantly, on the end walls or, even more suggestively, elevated to the tympanum, could refer to a state of post-mortem bliss.[47] The door motif in some tombs also emphasises separation between living and dead; it might represent a tomb door, but also allude metaphorically to another plane of existence beyond the tomb chamber. It presents an imposing façade, firmly shut, as one might imagine the door of a temple's inner sanctum.[48]

What then was the point of tomb painting? It was partly an expression of faith, albeit personal and private rather than public. Descending into the tombs – despite the artificial aids of flat electric lighting, new staircases and handrails – one is conscious of the intrusion, of breaking the rules by entering uninvited, a sensation heightened by so much essentially private or intimate imagery (especially in the case of Archaic tombs). Originally seen by flickering lamps or torches, perhaps by few intimates during the closing rites, the fixing of images in a time capsule is in itself an attempt to eternalise their reality. Not just the finished product but its creation may be important – the decoration of the chamber, awkward in these subterranean conditions, being imbued with magical significance as part of a religious ceremony.

All tombs are liminal places, restricted in access or out of bounds, but points of contact nonetheless. Like the microcosm of a chapel, they may also be the abode of spirits. In fact, there are several possible references to shrines in the paintings: animals in the tympanum flanking an architectural device resembling an altar could allude to sacrifices; trees and bushes may well signify sacred groves, for example in the Bulls tomb (below), where they surround the sanctuary.[49] Unfortunately, we know little about local metaphysical conceptions at this date, but Etruscan religion was obviously complex and became more so through interaction with Greek and probably Phoenician beliefs. Haruspicy and augury made play of microcosms and dualisms, as seen on the bronze model of a sheep's

I. Augurs tomb, mourner

II. Augurs tomb, wrestlers

III. Leopards tomb, musicians

IV. Hunter tomb

V. Hunting and Fishing tomb, inner room

VI. Baron tomb

VII. Triclinium tomb lyre-player, tracing by C. Ruspi

VIII. Triclinium tomb banqueters, tracing by C. Ruspi

IX. Triclinium tomb dancer, tracing by C. Ruspi

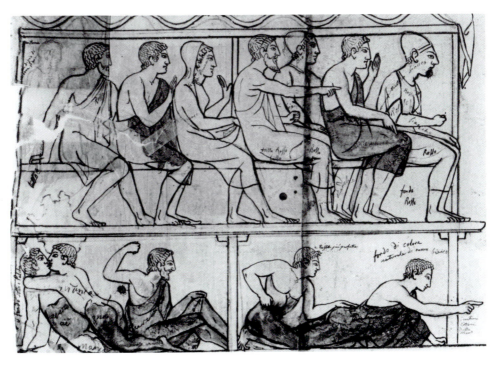

X. Biga tomb, spectators' stand, tracing by C. Ruspi

XI. Scataglini, tombs along quarried 'street'

XII. Giglioli tomb

XIII. Anina tomb, Charun and Vanth

XIV. Anina tomb interior

XV. Orco-2 tomb, underworld figures and gilded vases

XVI. Shields tomb, Velia Seitithi and Larth Velcha

XVII. Civita, north gate and city wall

XVIII. Ara della Regina temple, from south-east corner

XIX. Monterozzi, Iron Age stone burial containers, and modern entrance to a painted tomb

XX. The 'Priest' sarcophagus, mid-fourth century BC

XXI. Civita across San Savino from Monterozzi

XXII. The 'Amazon' sarcophagus, mid/late fourth century BC, marble (H 71 cm)

XXIII. Sarcophagus lid figure with young deer and *Iliad* scenes on the side, *c.* 300 BC

XXIV. Sarcophagus of Laris Pulena, the 'magistrate', 250-200 BC

XXV. Sarcophagus of Ramtha Apatrui, late third century BC

liver from Piacenza, with its many divinities and references to night and day, cosmic and terrestrial, water and fire, magically linking the animal's organ with the celestial dome. Perhaps this made it easier to accept the idea of parallel spheres of existence and to reconcile the potentially banal reality of a tomb with the idea of death as a journey to another place (below).

A religion preserved and revealed in sacred texts, a focal point of doctrine for the Etruscans, and preoccupied with the explanation of natural phenomena, might well have little need for anthropomorphic representation.[50] Supernatural and cult images feature occasionally in the early paintings, but they suggest Greek inspiration: in the tomb of Dionysus and the Sileni (520 BC, now lost), which had an image of the god himself; in the Inscriptions tomb with its possible cult statue and dedicant; and in the Baron tomb (Plate VI), with its subdued tone and symmetrical composition of figures and horsemen, probably the Dioscuri (Castor and Pollux), escorts for the departed to the underworld.[51]

Indigenous Etruscan religion must have been subjected to a wide range of influences and forces. Despite the materialism of the age – perhaps because of it – new doctrines were proliferating. Urban growth must also have provided new audiences and opportunities for street-corner mystics, sorcerers and philosophers as well as for official cults. Trade, interaction and intermarriage demand flexibility and the ability to accommodate diverse systems of belief. As trade routes opened, so too did new avenues for the transmission of cults, especially from Greece and southern Italy. By 530 BC, Pythagoras had left Samos for Croton, where he was expounding on metempsychosis and cyclical reincarnation. Dionysiac rites popular in Asia Minor, associated with vegetation, death, the underworld, as well as wine, sex and the promise of an afterlife, were spreading in Italy during the sixth/fifth century and became even more widespread in Hellenistic and Roman times (helping to prepare the spiritual ground for Christianity). Familiarity with the entourage and symbols of Dionysus, which evidently encountered equivalences in the Etruscan *fufluns*, is evinced at Tarquinia by the Dionysus and Sileni tomb, by the dancing satyrs (tomb 1999, 510 BC), perhaps too by the pervasive nudity and winged phallus of the Mouse tomb (520-510 BC), by the frenetic dancing of *komasts* in several others, by various allusions in the Lionesses tomb, and by inscriptions (on the Ioltos cup, for example, p. 135).[52] In these cases, the clients could have been initiates.

Dionysus also figured in Orphism and probably in obscure kindred cults involving initiations, purifications and even the prospect of future-world banquets and redemption. Orphic or Dionysiac connotations could be intended by the enlarged mammaries of the lionesses or the display of eggs (patent fertility symbols) in the hands of banqueters in the Lionesses and

49. Above: Augurs tomb, side wall, combat scene with 'Phersu', *c.* 520 BC.
Below: Bulls tomb, Achilles and Troilus, *c.* 540 BC (from photographs).

118

Leopards tombs (Fig. 45): 'the egg of resurrection, within which the germ sleeps as the soul sleeps within the tomb' as D.H. Lawrence put it (*EP*, 53.23), albeit unaware that eggs are recurrent in Orphic cosmogony, which was catching on in south Italy in the sixth century BC. A funerary art that was merely decorative or fixated with earthly pleasures and social status, devoid of religious or philosophical concerns, seems improbable, even pointless, especially since it was hidden from public view.[53]

Questions of motivation and association can be endlessly tantalising. For example, in the Bulls tomb, why are people copulating next to bulls just above the famous panel in which Achilles hides behind a fountain waiting to ambush Troilus, Priam's unsuspecting son, who approaches on horseback? Erotica (if such it is) may seem antithetical to the bloody drama unfolding below, where the tension is raised by the unusual murder weapon: a kind of sacrificial sabre (*machaira*) rather than a commonplace dagger. The fountain also resembles an altar. Perhaps there is no connection. Yet sex and war are hardly strangers.

In fact a fourth-century commentary on the *Aeneid* relates that Achilles lusted after the Trojan prince (Servius, *Ad Aeneid* 1.474). The potential for a homoerotic gloss existed, and for a thicker plot, as the murderer must kill not only his official enemy but the object of his desire. Ingenious explanations also identify the human-faced bull with Troy's Scamander river ('roaring like a bull': *Iliad* 21.237), which flowed red with the blood of Achilles' victims, and rebuked his cruelty. One bull (Achelous) may be rebuking the homosexual coupling, although the sodomising figure here resembles Troilus not Achilles, while the other bull seems unconcerned by an orgiastic trio. Is there a moralistic message or metaphor to be grasped? The murder scene recurs on Greek vases, although the allusion to sacrifice within a sanctuary to a vindictive Apollo may have had a special appeal in Etruria.[54]

Overall, however, sex scenes and phallic symbols are not very common. At one level they could be understood as life-affirming statements in the face of death. The same could be said of most images denoting corporeal efficiency, from athletics and hunting to the individual defecating in the Jugglers tomb.[55] Psychologically, this is all perhaps inherently or wishfully apotropaic, with the defiance of humour (itself protective) in the last case. As in Egyptian tomb painting, most people look healthy and happy. Yet in reality, of course, illness and premature death were endemic in ancient societies, where there was limited protection against pain and disease. A sense of life forces and life cycles may also underlie recurrent juxtapositions of male and female, hunter and hunted, old and young. But there is a risk of over-intellectualising and reading too much into some scenes, and of confusing casual sex with philosophies and cults. The erotica in the Whipping tomb (about 490 BC) are undoubtedly part of a Dionysiac *komos*, but the fairly inconspicuous sexual play under the spectators' stand in the Biga tomb seems incidentally matter-of-fact (Plate X). It could pass as social comment, satire or earthy humour: well-dressed polite people, including women, sit upstairs, while the cavorting riff-raff – perhaps just ordinary youths or athletes relaxing – fornicate below.

References to travel and transport, in some cases, foreshadow a leitmotif of Hellenistic painting. Horses and chariots in expectant attendance (in the Baron, Funeral Bed and Giustiniani tombs) possibly imply an underworld journey, more obviously shown by a tympanum figure riding a hippocamp bound for the isles of the blessed (Bulls tomb). Underworld journey scenes occur on the Bologna funerary stelae and were becoming widespread at about this time.[56] The sea voyage, anticipated in the Ship tomb (p. 111), might allude, wistfully, to the idea of death as a journey across water; but since this is shown quite explicitly in the Blue Demons tomb (also late fifth century), doubtless influenced by similar scenes on fifth-century Attic vases, such a heavily codified allusion seems unlikely.

An interest in symbolic linkages and metaphors, recently invigorated, has a long history of discussion. D.H. Lawrence was one of the first to consider these connections in an attempt to understand the Etruscan 'mystery of the journey out of life' and concept of a universe at once 'alive and in quivering *rapport*' (*EP*, 60.5, 62.17). The search for homologies (symbolic correspondences) involves subjecting images, which at first may seem straightforward and unrelated, to a form of scholarly psychoanalysis, in an attempt to reveal associations, allusions, metaphors and hidden meanings. It is essentially a game of associations, potentially stimulating, although easier to play with some tombs than others and vulnerable to accusations of wishful thinking and inordinate subjectivism.

The famous Hunting and Fishing tomb can be taken, at face value, as a charming emblem of Etruscan *joie de vivre*, love of nature and liberated social customs.[57] Yet the imagery is quite provocative. The double chamber has brightly painted scenes (Plate V): a return from the hunt on the first pediment, above inebriated revellers (*komasts*) dancing in a myrtle grove, probably sacred to Aphrodite, and a conjugal banquet in the second room pediment, with boys fishing, diving and hunting birds on the main walls below. A literal reading with an attempt at narration could simply go as follows: young lads return from a successful hunt, others swim, fish and catch birds, perhaps destined for the banquet of the aristocratic couple who recline surrounded by children and servants, while *komasts* frolic outdoors. Or else one might regard these as just loosely connected vignettes on the favourite themes of pleasurable pastimes, dear to the Etruscan leisured class, with some stylistic inspiration of East Greek or Near Eastern origin.

Contemporary theory, however, is also concerned with a potentially interconnected web of metaphors and symbols.[58] According to one reading, the first chamber introduces the Dionysiac theme (*komasts*), followed by a reference to the deceased's warrior virtues (the hunt), an allegorical journey (the marine scenes) to the shores of the blessed, culminating in the attainment of blissful apotheosis in the tympanum banquet. The first room seems to evoke a terrestrial ambience, whereas the second room in which the deceased actually lay (floor sockets denote a sarcophagus) is the other place. Linkages can also be found in erotic allusions under the patronage, or in praise, of Aphrodite. In the hunt, the quarry is a hare, a metaphor of the sexual chase, perhaps also suggested by the two horsemen, one of whom, dressed with leggings and a whip, could be the pursuing lover, the other his young naked prey (like the hare). The boys fishing have similar connotations, while the affectionate touches of the reclining couple gently invoke Eros.

The side murals can also be linked if one accepts that the dancing revellers are homologous with the 'dancing' dolphins, creatures with Dionysiac and netherworld associations. Likewise, the diver could be analogical if taken to signify penetration of the mysterious sea, sometimes associated with Hades or, more likely in this case, with the fertile waters which begot Aphrodite. Going one stage further, the connection between these themes – love, inebriation and the sea – would reside in the way that they all deal with transformations into altered states: a departure from everyday reality and consciousness. In this sense, the iconography of the tomb could be taken as a metaphor for death itself – the ultimate metamorphosis.

City of the living

On Civita, the seventh-century cult site was modified in the early sixth century (Figs 50-1).[59] The open precinct (alpha) and adjacent areas were resurfaced, while building beta was enlarged with a new pilaster wall (53), creating a room (11 x 8.5 m) with a ramp (614) and a bigger platform (11; 4 x 3.2 m), interpreted as another altar. The old drainage channel was enlarged (30) but still led into the pit (263), while a well was located in the open area to the south (56). New floors were laid here and in the open precinct to the north (332). Directly above the earlier deposit (349) against the wall was a little pit (351) containing the headless skeleton of a new-born infant along with charcoal remains, coarse pottery and bucchero, potentially a 'foundation offering' for the building. The excavators maintain that the area was still a cult precinct for sacrifices, votive offerings and child burials. Human sacrifices cannot be ruled out.[60]

Around the mid-sixth century, area alpha was extended and re-floored.

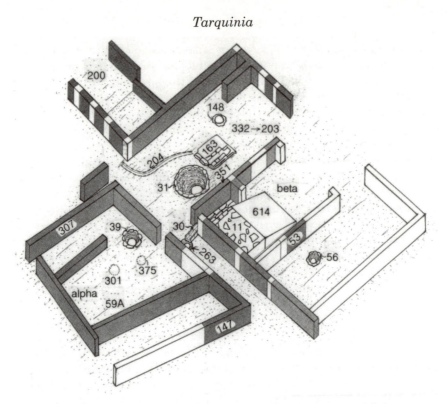

50. Civita excavations, reconstruction hypothesis (sixth century BC) (after *Tarquinia 1*, pl. 145).

Under the floor were remains of another infant burial (59A), while a nearby pit (301) contained bucchero cups of about 550 BC with pig, caprine and cattle bones, probably another votive offering from sacrifice or feast remains. By the late sixth century, a well and cistern (39) had been installed, another floor laid and 200 tile fragments buried in a small pit (375). To the south-west (area gamma) were more votive depositions of pottery and organic material including fig, poppy, grape, cereals, legumes, fruits and herbs. North of building beta the precinct was provided with a deep well, a platform, drain, stone-lined pit and new floor (148, 163, 204, 31, 203). Here again the excavators suggest cult installations: a pit or *bothros* for offerings or lustral waters, rather than a more prosaic interpretation (an ordinary cistern), and an altar or altar base, rather than some kind of work surface or *impluvium* for collecting rainwater.

Yet a work area also seems possible, since the adjacent building to the north has a jar sunk into the floor and a kiln (200) of about 550 BC, perhaps for metal-working; this area retained an industrial function into the late sixth century BC when a larger kiln was installed, associated with bellows, clay moulds and crucible fragments. That ceramic production took place in the vicinity is suggested by sporadic finds of misfired vessels. This need not seem incongruous. Close links between cults and manufacturing activity are well attested at this time; for example, at nearby Gravisca (below).

Stone slabs or broken terracotta tiles were laid for floors, and clay mortar used in stone walls. The upper part of building beta was probably of plastered mud-brick with a tiled roof. During the sixth century, adjacent buildings were given the same orientation (e.g. 147) with passageways in between, implying a rectilinear plan. Overall, therefore, while there was some continuity in layout from the seventh century, the area looked more impressive in the sixth century. There was better water provision (wells and cisterns) and manufacturing activity (kilns), but less conspicuous evidence of ritual (two infant burials and one or two votive pits).

More radical transformations occurred early in the fifth century BC when area alpha was re-floored (32) and bisected by a long drain (28), while building beta went out of use (Fig. 51). A new floor was laid (76) and the old well (56) provided with supply channels (54, 62), beside a small pit holding charcoal and pig bones (72). Several rooms erected nearby probably had a tiled roof (132-105-178). Beside wall 178 a votive deposit consisted of a bowl, cereal grains and bronze ingot or *aes rude* fragments. Kiln remains are reported nearby, possibly related to metal-working. The northern area was delimited by a wall (14) and re-floored (86), sealing off the earlier well (148), although the cistern, platform and drain (31, 163, 204) stayed in use. Between buildings alpha and beta the rectilinear trackway (8) was resurfaced, obliterating the pit (263) and thus creating a serviceable thoroughfare. It extended northward to the edge of the plateau and southward beyond the excavated area, joining an east-west roadway, paved in Roman times. This strengthens the idea that the Hellenistic-Roman street plan was based on a rectilinear street system dating back to the sixth century.[61]

The street was also provided with lateral conduits (44-45) and a subterranean drain (*cunicolo*, 474), cut into the rock, 1.7 m high and 0.6 m wide, traced for about 16 m, and reached by shafts or man-holes, spaced apart and covered with slabs (Figs 51, 52: A). There was another section further north, covered with lean-to slabs. The function of these remarkable subterranean channels has still to be elucidated; six have been recorded so far, though not fully explored (p. 172). Some might have been sewers or drains, while others seem to have been part of a water collection and supply system.[62] They lend weight to the tradition of Etruscan expertise in hydraulics. Since the water table was not easily reachable on the plateau, rain water had to be conserved in wells and cisterns, which have been found inside or near most buildings excavated to date; 36 have already been recorded on Civita. Many must have been for private use, but the larger cisterns could have been communal. Most are undated, but some

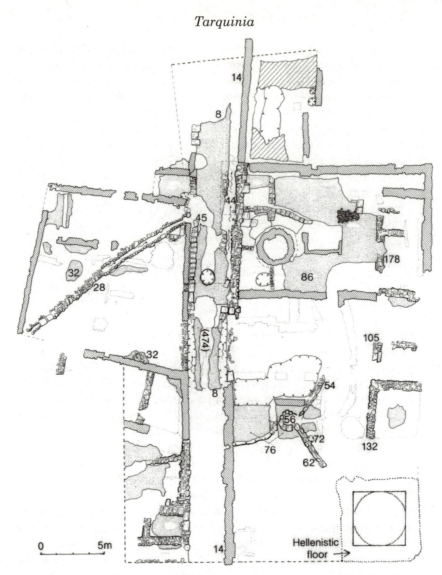

51. Civita excavations, fifth-century BC features (Hellenistic floor in SE corner) (after *Tarquinia 1*).

wells, usually from 5-10 m deep, were in use from at least the sixth century BC.

Old excavations near the Romanelli (or north) gate and city wall revealed several buildings with Hellenistic phases of occupation (p. 171), but also earlier Archaic deposits. At least one building on Romanelli's plan (Fig. 68: d), probably a shrine, may antedate the Hellenistic period. Archaic shrines are also known from architectural terracottas or soundings elsewhere: from the semicircular building, and the Ara della Regina temple (see Chapter 5).

Obscured by stone robbing and numerous modifications, the complex architectural history of the temple (Fig. 70; Plate XVIII) has been rewritten several times.[63] According to the latest investigations, the first phase dates to the early sixth century BC; it is represented by a long wall (gamma), possibly an enclosure, on the southern edge of a sanctuary complex, which already included the temple, oriented east-west, consisting of a long cella and *pronaos* (27 x 12 m) set on top of a basement (31.5 x 55 m), providing an artificial platform on the naturally sloping terrain. The design is comparable with Greek temples in south Italy, for example at Locri. Originally the building looked onto an open terrace with a small box-like structure of limestone slabs, presumably for cult purposes, which was later enclosed and covered by a Hellenistic altar or platform as part of major modifications in the fourth century (p. 172). Fragments of Archaic terracotta revetment plaques suggest a decoration of warriors and chariots in procession and banquet scenes. Later in the sixth century, this already impressive monument was probably enhanced by the addition of a four-columned vestibule (*pronaos*) and lateral wings (or *alae*).

More speculative is the idea that the temple was the hub of a federal sanctuary prior to the emergence of the pan-Etruscan shrine and gatherings at the Fanum Voltumnae. The patron god or gods are also uncertain. Zeus, Apollo or Artemis come to mind; Artemis (Etruscan Artumes) is a possible candidate given the find of a bronze rod fragment bearing a dedication, while Apollo has been suggested on the basis of a votive terracotta, but the question is unresolved. Several scholars have also been tempted to postulate an association with the origins of Tarquinia through the legendary Tages or Tarchon – some going so far as to suggest that the limestone box (or the structures erected over it; p. 173) marked the spot where Tages sprang from the furrow; needless to say, tangible supporting evidence is lacking.

It is noteworthy that magnetometer surveys indicate a large open area just to the north of the temple, a likely public gathering place, and perhaps the site of the later forum. By contrast, the idea of a wall crossing the narrow point south from the Romanelli gate, dividing Civita from the Pian della Regina, is unfounded.[64]

The fortification walls are also being reassessed (Fig. 68; Plate XVII). While much of the superstructure and the Romanelli gate probably date to the fourth century BC (p. 169), recent soundings have back-dated the first phase of construction in *opus quadratum* to the sixth century.[65] The earthen rampart, a feature with local or Italic antecedents, might also conceivably date to an early time. Roselle, Vetulonia, Veii and some other Etruscan cities had defensive walls in the sixth/fifth century; their exist-

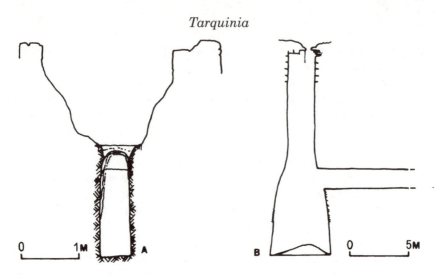

52. Civita water management: (A) underground conduit 474, section; (B)
well-cistern and lateral conduit, section (after *Tarquinia 1*, plan 14; Padovan
1999, 113).

ence at Tarquinia, therefore, should not be surprising. If one allows for
missing sections, kinks and turns, the entire circuit would have been about
8 km long, commensurate with the walls of Veii and Caere (around 7 km)
and not far behind the 'Servian' walls of Rome (around 10 km). The
enclosed area of about 121 hectares is smaller than those at Caere (148
ha), Veii (194 ha) and Rome (427 ha), although the nearby promontories
at Tarquinia are large and were inhabited at certain times; roof tiles and
pottery attest late sixth/fifth-century BC occupation on the adjacent hillock
of Cretoncini (an additional roughly 40 ha).[66]

Population size is hard to estimate for ancient cities, largely unexca-
vated, since much depends on the density of housing. If one adopted the
rather high figure of 120-210 inhabitants per hectare suggested for Etruscan Acquarossa, a population of 14,500-25,500 would result for Tarquinia
(Civita), which matches an older estimate for Caere (25,000) based on a
cemetery projection. This would also be broadly compatible with local
population density in the Middle Ages insofar as Corneto in the fifteenth
century, which covered an area equivalent to just under a quarter of the
ancient city, had a population of about 7,000. However, medieval housing
was probably denser than that of antiquity. A projection for Saturnia in
the third century AD suggests 51-94 persons per hectare, and it is argued
that 8,000-15,000 is a more likely figure for the Etruscan city at Doganella
(140 ha), comparable in area with Tarquinia.[67] Some doubts are bound to
persist, but at least these figures are more consistent than the wildly
divergent estimates of earlier research; the population of Caere used to be
placed at anything between 5,000 and 80,000. In view of the abundance

and spread of finds, and presumed regional growth since the Iron Age, one may suggest that the population of many Etruscan cities peaked in the late Archaic period; this expansion and subsequent levelling is also suggested by survey work.[68]

The range of pottery from Civita implies intensified production and consumption, adding to the impression of burgeoning prosperity and trade in the sixth/early fifth century.[69] There is plenty of good quality bucchero, with many forms matched in the tombs, rather few Corinthian imports, local Etrusco-Corinthian and some Attic and Etruscan black- and red-figure; Attic black glaze imports occur throughout the fifth century, increasing after about 460 BC. One fragment, possibly made in Vulci, suggests that Etruscan red-figure production dates back to the early fifth century. More common is plain ware (*ceramica depurata*) made locally, although some simple band decoration and forms suggest East Greek influence; it dates from the late seventh century but was still produced, with minor changes, in the third century. Terracotta roof tiles also occur, and a few antefixes of the early sixth/fifth century have parallels at smaller sites in southern Etruria and Latium, perhaps influenced by Tarquinian production.[70]

Wide-ranging trade connections are attested by transport amphorae: Etruscan (Py 1/2) types of the seventh/mid-sixth century, influenced by Phoenician shapes, and later sixth/fifth-century forms (Py 3/4); sixth-century Corinthian A-A' forms, probably oil containers; sixth-century Attic oil amphorae; 'Corinthian' B types (which are not necessarily Corinthian), but probably used for wine, from fifth/fourth-century layers; one Massaliote and several so-called Ionic-Massaliote types of the late sixth century; sixth/fifth-century Chios amphorae; Phoenicio-Punic forms of the sixth/fifth century; and Archaic East Greek types, characteristic of Clazomenae, Samos and Lesbos (Fig. 54).

Excavations have thus revealed components of a developing urban fabric: sanctuaries, an impressive temple, streets, conduits, wells, industrial installations, fortifications and vast cemeteries. With the evidence of trade and Gravisca (below), this refutes or at least undermines the idea of a Tarquinia now lagging Vulci and Caere. Admittedly, we still know little about ordinary life, residential quarters or any local equivalents of those famous places – agora, bakery, bath-house, brothel, palaestra and stoa – that play a vital role in Greek and Roman cities. Nor can we judge the extent of open or green spaces within the walls. Yet the Etruscans plainly did not lack a sense of stagecraft in urban planning. The great Archaic cemeteries, like the sculpted facades of later cliff tombs, were *coups de théâtre*, scenically placed in order to maximise their visual impact; so too no doubt were the buildings in the craggy skylines of hilltop cities (Volterra, Cortona, Perugia, Orvieto), gloating over beautiful, fertile lands, like their famous medieval successors. Urbanisation in Etruria must also have been driven by aesthetic considerations, not just for their own sake, but for the psychological and practical advantages that accrue from prestige enhancement in a world of burgeoning rivals.

Gravisca

The emporium at Gravisca (its Latin name, the Etruscan is unknown) was central to the commercial and cultural development of Tarquinia; this was the main door through which foreign influences and individuals filtered into local society, and a nodal point in a web of maritime contacts. Its establishment probably served partly to replace earlier docking places (p. 35) with better facilities, although no quayside installations have yet been found.[71] Excavations so far have revealed mainly cult buildings dating from about 600 BC, which helped to mediate between peoples of diverse origin and provide the necessary ideological sponsorship and protection required by the flourishing international trade of the period (Fig. 53).

One might think, by analogy with the Greek emporium at Naucratis in Egypt, that Gravisca at this time was a predominantly Greek colony, almost a dockland ghetto for foreigners. However, Tarquinia was highly receptive to Greek cultural traditions and there is little evidence for a policy of non-absorption or marginalisation of outsiders. For many arrivals, the main need would have been for temporary accommodation and supplies. Nevertheless, while doubtless economically and politically dependent on the metropolis, Gravisca presumably had a social and economic life peculiar to its own role and community of mariners, traders, artisans, sanctuary staff and fishermen. Like its counterparts of Regisvilla and Pyrgi, it must have been a crucible of colourful interaction, buzzing through the summer months with the excitement of comings and goings, loading, unloading, bargaining, victualling and repairs; a place of conversations in several languages, where news from the land was exchanged for news from the sea.

An agglomeration of Archaic shrines, flanking a wide street, traverses the site; perhaps, as at Naucratis, these were sponsored by particular groups of merchants. By 580 BC there was a shrine to Aphrodite, represented as a warrior in small bronze figurines found locally (Fig. 53: C). A foundry for bronze and iron-working lay nearby, of which she was perhaps the patron. Numerous votive offerings are attested and a range of fine imported pottery: Corinthian, Ionic, Laconian, Attic, bucchero and Etrusco-Corinthian, as well as small items of faience, ivory and bronze, and even pigments of the kind used in tomb painting.

The majority of inscriptions denote Greek dedicants from several differ-

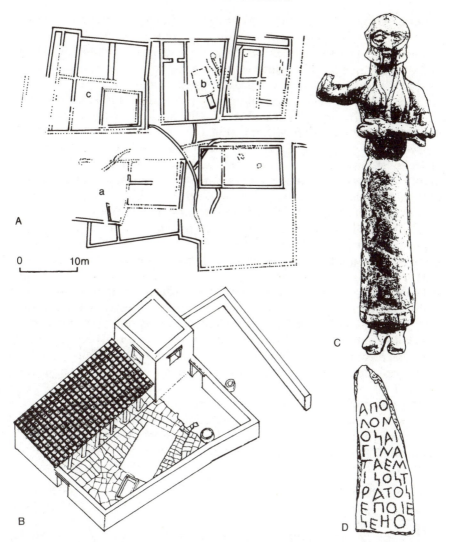

53. Gravisca: (A) sanctuary plan (shrines to: a Hera, b Adonis, c Aphrodite); (B) reconstruction of building b (Adonion) (after Torelli 1997b, figs 1,4); (C) bronze armed goddess figurine (H 19 cm), 575-550 BC; (D) stone anchor stock (H 115 cm) with dedication to Apollo by Sostratos, late sixth century (from photographs).

ent localities (Aegina, Achaea, Corinth and the Dorian Hexapolis), and especially Ionians, probably from places such as Ephesus, Samos and Miletus; the deity is also addressed once in an Etruscan form, as Turan. The most famous offering is a stone anchor dedicated to Apollo of Aegina by one Sostratos (Fig. 53: D), possibly the same famously wealthy merchant of Aegina of the late sixth century BC known to Herodotus (4.152: with whose profits 'none can compare'). By contrast, a certain Ombrikos sounds like someone from central Italy. Some dedicants' names even recur at Naucratis, a sign of the interconnected nature of maritime trade networks. The transport amphorae also reflect wide-ranging trade in the sixth century, represented by numerous Etruscan and East Greek (especially Samian) types, followed by Corinthian A, Phoenician, Attic, Massaliote and Laconian varieties (Fig. 54).[72]

By the mid-sixth century, the sanctuary zone also accommodated a cult of Hera, often associated with coastal emporia, perhaps because of her ability to integrate and mediate between groups of diverse origin. A shrine of Demeter, more commonly linked with rural fertility cults, is attested by over three thousand votive lamps and two iron ploughshares.

If these cult foundations were initially no more than a necessary or expedient political concession, intended to protect and encourage trade, their long-term effect on Tarquinia may have been more profound than anticipated. An official sanctioning of exogenous cults on local soil could only encourage their dissemination and absorption locally. Moreover, cultural interchange by this time was no longer so restricted to the elite. The pressures from Persian expansionism in the mid-sixth century on Greek settlements in Asia Minor, the eastern Aegean islands and Egypt may well have encouraged migrations westward, notably of artisans. This is one explanation for the strong 'Ionian' influence in local arts and crafts (see p. 103).

The situation in the fifth century is less clear, but the character of the place was changing. About 30 Etruscan amphorae were recently found in a building which may have had a commercial function. The sanctuary was subdivided and laid out afresh with larger buildings around 470 BC,

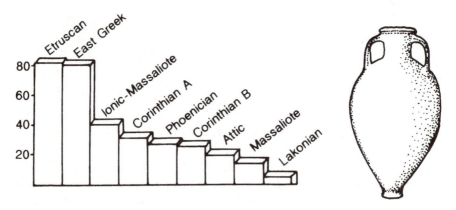

54. Gravisca, transport amphorae ratios and East Greek amphora (data from Slaska 1985).

although the cults seem more parochial than before. Judging by anatomical ex-votos, Aphrodite was mainly being invoked for health reasons, a large courtyard and porticoed annexe was used for a cult of Adonis (Fig. 53: B), while Hera's cult was in decline. By contrast, Demeter (akin to the Etruscan deity Vea) was in the ascendant, provided with a rectangular shrine and two altars; inscriptions are now mainly in Etruscan, not Greek. Another deposit, with offerings spanning the mid-sixth to the third century BC, implies a female deity with chthonic features. The older votives include weaponry, bronze and terracotta figurines, and late sixth/early fifth-century pottery, attesting links with Sicily. It remains to be seen whether traces of destruction can be tied to the Syracusan incursion of 384 BC (p. 138).

The emphasis on local cults is also consistent with deteriorating conditions for pan-Mediterranean trade in the fifth century, beset by political or military conflicts in the Greek world. Links with the Greek homeland may have been more difficult, as reflected by fewer imports (although Attic vases were still arriving). However, western Mediterranean trade need not have been so seriously affected; Etruria was still a key player in long-distance trade with Celtic Europe.

Essentially, the foundation of Gravisca shows Tarquinia coming of age as a city state, capable of taking strategic decisions and engaging formally, through civic institutions (sanctuaries), in the wider sphere of international relations. The accumulated experience of long-distance trade must also have been useful when it came to forging military alliances or organising long-range warfare. The sixth century in literary sources is also a time of piracy, strategic partnerships, treaties and rivalries, the familiar corollaries of burgeoning trade and interaction. The battle of Aleria in the Sardinian sea around 540 BC, which saw Phoenicians and Etruscans (notably Caere) allied against Phocian Greeks, was essentially a dispute over the control of Corsica and related interests. Aleria was then colonised by Etruscans, probably from Caere, although Tarquinians and others might have participated.[73] This too underscores the expanding horizons of Etruscan cities and the sometimes narrow dividing line between commercial and territorial ambitions.

Text, epigraphy and society

The literary sources for this period consist of schematic accounts or anecdotes woven into the early history of Rome by later writers, evidently based on a richly embroidered tapestry of popular traditions and sagas. A key figure in the Roman monarchy is the charismatic Servius Tullius, who supposedly succeeded the son of Demaratus, Tarquinius Priscus (traditionally in 578 BC). Cicero (*De Re Publica* 2.37.3) states that 'he was born of a servile mother from Tarquinia, his father being a client of the king'.[74] This reinforces the idea that Demaratus brought attendants with him from Tarquinia. One of the few surviving testimonies to the historical research of the emperor Claudius, inscribed on the Lyons Table, informs us that Servius was known to the Etruscans as Mastarna, a faithful companion of Caelius Vibenna. Both characters come to life in the François tomb frescos at Vulci, painted around the mid-fourth century BC, but probably referring to events of the sixth century, showing Mastarna, the Vibenna brothers (evidently lords of Vulci) and their comrades killing several opponents, including one Gnaeus Tarquinius of Rome (Cneve Tarchunies Rumach), who could be Tarquinius Priscus or another Roman Tarquin unknown to us. Literature and art therefore hint at rival cities and feuding factions, perhaps led by aristocratic warlords with their own militias, although the date and nature of the conflicts and Tarquinia's role are obscure.[75]

No special relationship linked Rome and Tarquinia, according to Dionysius of Halicarnassus (4.26.6-27). Servius is even said to have made territorial gains after conflict with Tarquinia, Caere and Veii, although there may be some confusion here with later events. However, Strabo implies that Tarquinia and Rome were on good terms under Tarquinius Priscus, during whose reign Rome adopted several Tarquinian customs:

> ... the triumphal and consular adornment and, in a word, that of all the rulers, was transferred to Rome from Tarquinii, as also fasces, axes, trumpets, sacrificial rites, divination, and all music publicly used by the Romans (Strabo 5.2.2).[76]

However, Livy (2.6) noted souring relations after the expulsion of the last king, the tyrannical and unpopular Tarquinius Superbus (the Proud), traditionally precipitated by the rape of Lucretia by his son (Sextus Tarquinius), which led to the founding of the Republic in 509 BC. Humiliated and rejected by his former subjects, Superbus turned to Veii and Tarquinia, hoping that they might support his reinstatement. And they were sympathetic to his appeal, according to Livy (2.6.4): '... all felt it was a fine thing that a man of their blood should reign in Rome.'[77] This reputedly led to the battle of Selva Arsia, where Tarquinia and Veii were allied against Rome, and in which L. Junius Brutus, the founding father of the Republic, was killed, although both sides claimed victory.[78] The role of Tarquinia was then briefly eclipsed by Chiusi under Lars Porsenna (who 'swore by the nine gods' in the poem by Macaulay), but his campaign against Rome was eventually frustrated, leaving Superbus to die in exile.[79]

One theme already emergent in the annalistic tradition is the absence of any unified or consistent Etruscan policy towards Rome, heralding a leitmotif of later Etrusco-Roman conflict (see Chapter 5). Evidently this was a world of independently minded cities, dynastic struggles, shifting allegiances and warring factions; Tarquinia and Veii were allied at Selva Arsia, but Tarquinia did not participate in the desultory fifth-century wars between Veii and Rome (or at least the Roman Fabii clan). Relations with the western Greeks were probably of greater concern. Etruscan naval success off Corsica (around 540 BC, above) and occupation of Lipari (485-475 BC) were followed by defeat at the hands of the Syracusan fleet near Cumae in 474 BC, which may have damaged Etruscan economic interests and political influence in Latium and Campania. Coastal cities like Tarquinia, which relied partly on maritime trade and had historic links with Campania, must also have suffered a loss of prestige. Added to evidence of political changes in Italy (especially in Rome) and an increase in armed conflict elsewhere in the Mediterranean (between Persians, Greeks and Carthaginians notably), this is generally given as a reason for economic and cultural stagnation in fifth-century Italy, or at least a relative downturn by comparison with the effervescence of the previous century.[80]

Cumae was possibly remembered with sufficient bitterness two generations later to persuade various Etruscan cities (we are not told which) to send a small force of three penteconters in support of the Athenian expedition against Syracuse in 414 BC (Thucydides 6.103.2), which ended in disaster for the allied invaders. One of the finely engraved first-century AD marble slabs from Tarquinia, known as the *elogia Tarquiniensia*, might refer to this conflict. These Latin inscriptions ornamented the base of a monument near the Ara della Regina (p. 175), commemorating illustrious ancestors of the Spurinna family (Fig. 56). They mention an armed expedition to Sicily led by a magistrate (*praetor*), Velthur Spurinna, son of Lars, although interpretation is dogged by missing sections and problems of dating; the association with the Sicilian campaign of 414-413 BC is not universally accepted. In fact, one wonders whether the Romanised Spurinnae of the early Empire would have wanted to commemorate a defeat, when other interventions in Sicily had had a more successful outcome: the occupation of Lipari, for example, or the campaign in 307 BC to help Agathocles against the Carthaginians, Rome's traditional enemy (see p. 139).[81]

Apart from their Romanocentric and patchy attempt at historical reconstruction, literary sources say little about Tarquinian society in the seventh/sixth centuries BC, while epigraphic evidence is meagre. Etruscan cities in this period (and some in the fifth century) were reputedly headed by kings, such as Lars Porsenna at Chiusi, Thefarie Velianas, Orgolnius and Mezentius at Caere, and Lars Tolumnius at Veii, but the nature of kingship is elusive. Velianas, for example, known from the Pyrgi inscriptions, is referred to in Phoenician as king and in Etruscan as *zilath*, a magistrate (p. 161).[82] Livy (1.8.1-3; 5.1.5) also mentions that kings or high officials were elected by the members of the League. In Rome, kingship was not necessarily strictly hereditary nor limited to Roman patricians, and may have involved a complex form of election, even though, as it turned out, kings of Rome often were relatives and sometimes usurpers. Their eviction marks the triumph of a small oligarchy, not the birth of democracy.

We do not know the name of a single king of Tarquinia. The story of Tarchon (p. 75) could support the notion of an original ruler invested with religious and political power, but it is curious that when Tarquinius Superbus came seeking support for reinstatement, Livy makes no mention of a king at Tarquinia, while Dionysius (5.3.2) speaks only of magistrates and a popular assembly (*ekklesia*). This may be merely anachronistic, as conventionally maintained, or a simple omission, but it makes us question the existence of a monarchy and the assumption that all Etruscan cities were alike, or that kingship precluded the existence of other political bodies (such as the *comitia* and *curia* in Rome). It also transpires from the *elogia* of Aulus Spurinna (see p. 139) that Tarquinia already had republican institutions when Caere was still monarchical, although the date is uncertain. Livy (4.17; 5.1.3) implies that the mere appointment of a king at Veii in the late fifth century BC was enough to antagonise other members of the League (see p. 138). If Dionysius is discounted, we can only assume that Tarquinia made the transition to republican oligarchy at some point in the fifth century, perhaps soon after Rome.

One would like to know more about possible analogies in socio-political organisation between Rome and Etruria. Did the political and military (centuriate) reforms of Servius Tullius have counterparts here? Class conflict in Rome during the fifth century seems to have had parallels in Etruscan Italy, perhaps inflamed by economic difficulties, tensions over land ownership and urban growth. The literary sources, somewhat simplistically, suggest that Etruscan society was divided between masters (*dynatotai*) and slaves (*oiketai*), with some people of semi-servile status (*penestai*) enjoying limited rights of property ownership.[83] Perhaps these were tenant farmers who worked the land in exchange for a share of the produce. In the fourth century BC, evidence for ex-slaves (freedmen) grows and we hear of political crises in Arezzo and Volsinii stemming from an evolving dialectic between plebeians and patricians (see Chapter 5).

The trend towards increasing numbers of uniform chamber tombs in the sixth/fifth centuries fits the idea of an expanding, multi-layered ruling class, benefiting from enhanced possibilities for wealth accumulation. Perhaps this also encouraged rivalries and the division of certain powers, leading to the proliferation of aristocratic honours and offices of the fourth century. If Orientalising lords indulged in extravagant displays of ances-

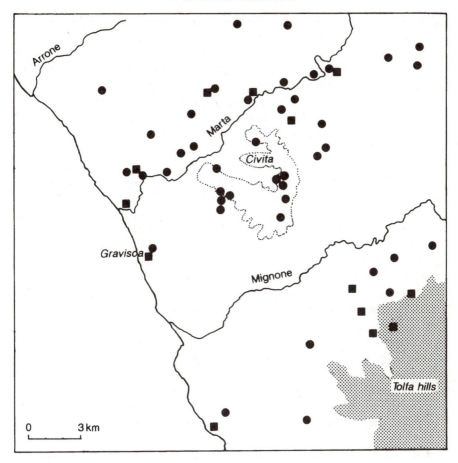

55. Archaic (sixth century BC) sites and findspots (circle = burial, square = settlement) (after *TE*, fig. 13).

tral and individual power, their successors were more circumspect, within an increasingly complex framework of urban social life. Nevertheless, the tomb frescos indicate that traditional aristocratic ideals were well entrenched.

Inscriptions become more common in the sixth/fifth century BC, although they largely attest private rather than public or overtly political uses.[84] Names or short statements recording ownership or dedications on prestigious artefacts are still typical. The fine Oltos kylix (see p. 96) declares: 'itun turuce venel atelinas tinas cliniiaras' ('Venel Atelina dedicated this to the sons [= the Dioscuri] of Tinia [= Zeus]'). Individuals are sometimes labelled in tomb paintings, as heroes or divinities are named on Attic vases. In the Inscriptions tomb, figures may be designated by a single *praenomen*, such as Velthur (though possibly a slave) or, in one case with the patronymic, Laris Larthia (= Laris son of Larth), but more usually by the *praenomen* + *gentilicium*: Avile Recieniies, Arath Vinacna, Laris Fanurus and Larth Matves (who possibly owned the tomb); even the dog ('*aefla*') is named. This was still a society that communicated orally and through visual imagery, although the written word was gaining ground.

Rural life is only gradually being illuminated by regional surveys and excavations at small sites.[85] The Tuscania and Albegna valley surveys attest increasingly dense and complex interlocking settlement systems and hierarchies. Clusters of farms and hamlets probably also existed around Tarquinia; there are several potential candidates along the Marta, though apparently not along the Mignone (p. 74; Fig. 55). It is quite possible that city dwellers also farmed surrounding lands, commuting back and forth at dawn and dusk. For the rural population, the metropolis was doubtless a market to which agricultural surplus was brought and exchanged, and where long-distance trade (through Gravisca) and local or regional production and consumption intersected.

The subsistence requirements of a growing population centre would make corresponding demands on the agricultural hinterland. As olive and vine assumed greater importance, there must also have been a need for formal and stable land titles. One might expect the surrounding territory to have been more closely controlled and affiliated to the urban centre than before, and to have been at least as large. The zone of political influence, moreover, quite likely extended inland as far as Lake Bolsena, referred to by Pliny (*Natural History* 95-6, 209) as the *Lacus Tarquiniensis*. Recent research suggests that the Marta river was linked by a man-made channel to the lake at about this time, a project possibly undertaken by Tarquinia as a precaution against lake flooding and, one might add, in order to increase the capacity of the river and its potential for irrigating her own territory.[86]

5. Tarquinia and Rome

Dream fluently, still brothers, who when young
Took with your mothers' milk the mother tongue,

In which pure matrix, joining world and mind,
You strove to leave some line of verse behind

Like a fresh track across a field of snow,
Not reckoning that all could melt and go.

Richard Wilbur, 'To the Etruscan Poets'

History according to Livy

We begin with a brief digest of literary and epigraphic sources. Livy's early history of Rome is of limited (and debated) use as a source of information for Etruria, although it represents the fullest surviving narrative from antiquity for the last phase in the development of the Etruscan city states. From the fourth century BC, they were increasingly entangled in a fateful relationship with Rome, described by Livy in an engaging though very partial and partisan manner. He was also writing long after the event, with minimal documentary support, for an audience little interested in Etruscan history per se and not particularly concerned with historical details or accuracy. As a result, the Etruscans are a frustratingly faceless entity in his one-sided account. While the Romans dominate the stage with valorous speeches, debates, ingenious stratagems, heroic leaders and exploits, not even the names of their Etruscan counterparts seem to have been known, and characterisation is hardly attempted. As a history of events, much also remains unverifiable. And yet, for all the bias, omission and anecdotal colour, the underlying pattern of growing rivalry, periodic confrontation and eventual submission of the Etruscans is not really in doubt. However hard to ignore, nonetheless, Livy should not be allowed to prejudice an assessment of the archaeological evidence; the latter, in fact, tends to illuminate different aspects of the period.

The fourth century opens with a dramatic account of the destruction of Veii in 396 BC after a protracted struggle.[1] In retrospect, Rome's first conquest of a major Etruscan city, her long-standing rival on the right bank of the Tiber, seems ominous. The other Etruscan cities, aware of Veii's predicament, failed conspicuously to rally in support. One reason or excuse was their dislike of the king at Veii 'for personal reasons no less than for political' (Livy 5.1); another was their preoccupation with troublesome Gallic settlers elsewhere in Etruria. Tarquinia did eventually send a light force into Roman territory, perhaps encouraged by a sense of duty towards a former ally, concern at the growing prospect of Roman victory, or the chance to engage in some profitable raiding while Rome was under pressure, as Livy (5.16.2) rather cynically states. Whatever the reason, the incursion had little impact on the course of events. A skirmish near Caere supposedly ended badly for the Tarquinian side, with the loss of booty. Subsequently – the date is controversial – the Romans replied by raiding *in agrum Tarquiniensem* (Livy 6.4, 7, 11) and destroying two small towns, Cortuosa and Contenebra, whose whereabouts are uncertain.[2]

Caere seems to have been quietly neutral at first, or even supportive of Rome. This also seems symptomatic of a structural flaw on the Etruscan side, even if the consequences of disunity and prevarication in the face of Roman expansion could not have been predicted. Livy gives the impression that these were difficult years for everyone, typified by tensions between Etruscan, Roman, Latin and Campanian neighbours, internal political dissension and external threats. In 390 BC, shortly after the triumph over Veii, marauding Gauls inflicted a humbling defeat on Rome herself, who was assisted by Caere during the crisis. For the next three decades, nothing is known of relations with Tarquinia. Perhaps more worrying to central Italian communities was the rise of Syracuse, whose charismatic leader, Dionysius I, had successfully countered the Phoenicians in Sicily, enrolled Gallic mercenaries in his army and sacked Caere's port at Pyrgi in 384 BC, making off with spectacular quantities of loot. He was also undermining Etruscan interests in the Adriatic.

As Rome recovered, however, the potential for conflict was, if anything, even greater than before. Veii's demise had left Tarquinian territory bordering Roman not far from Sutri, a flashpoint too with the Faliscans of Falerii. Somewhat predictably, Livy (7.12.5) accuses Tarquinia of starting what sounds like a frontier squabble in 359 BC, which subsequently escalated into a more serious confrontation, resulting in the defeat of a Roman force in 358 BC under Gaius Fabius, who

> showed neither prudence or skill in his battle with the Tarquinienses. And yet the disaster experienced on the field was overshadowed by the fact that the Tarquinienses slew three hundred and seven captured Roman soldiers as a sacrifice – an act of savage cruelty that greatly emphasised the humiliation of the Roman people. (Livy 7.15.9-10).[3]

5. Tarquinia and Rome

The crisis evidently deepened in 357 BC as allied Faliscans refused to repatriate Roman deserters. Camped near Sutri, a Latin colony, the Romans were then routed by a joint Tarquinian and Faliscan force, panicking during the first encounter at the spectacle of Etruscan 'priests bearing serpents and blazing torches before them, advancing like Furies' (Livy 7.17.3).[4] A counter-attack followed only to be outflanked by an enlarged Etruscan army, which advanced to the salt beds at the Tiber mouth. Caere was also recruited to the Etruscan coalition. Yet this was apparently the high tide of the Etruscan advance; Livy (7.17.8-9) then speaks, albeit vaguely, of Roman successes under Rutulus and Plautius and under Fabius and Quinctius in 353 BC, when 358 Tarquinian prisoners of noble birth were singled out for beating and beheading in the Roman forum in retribution for the earlier sacrifice of Roman prisoners at Tarquinia. A whiff of literary artifice hangs over the story, though it was also reported by Diodorus Siculus (16.45.8), who gives the number executed as 260.

Fearful of defeat and probably a hesitant ally, Caere sued for a separate peace with Rome, obtaining a 100-year truce (*indutiae*) in 353 BC.[5] Their citizens had previously enjoyed reciprocal rights of 'public hospitality', but the juridical nature of the new relationship is uncertain. Livy (7.20) may have exaggerated Caere's submissiveness – her ambassadors are described as feeble supplicants – but it would be surprising if she regained equal terms with Rome after such a volte-face. Whether she was granted citizenship without suffrage (*civitas sine suffragio*) is also debatable; this is easier to associate with a later date of 273 BC.[6] As war weariness set in, Tarquinians and Faliscans perhaps retired into the relative security of their walled cities. A truce was then agreed and evidently respected for the next 40 years.

Livy's version of these mid-fourth-century clashes emphasises the prominence of Tarquinia. However, while no significant changes resulted in territorial possessions – Sutri was still at the border and Rome's Veian annexations intact – it was evidently Rome that emerged strengthened, her initial defeats reversed, her executed prisoners avenged and northern border restored. With the defection of Caere, moreover, the threatening prospect of an expanded Etruscan alliance must have receded.

The *elogia* of the Spurinna family (p. 133), fragmented inscriptions commemorating events and people otherwise unknown to us, might well be relevant to this period (Fig. 56). They mention one Aulus Spurinna, son of Velthur, a praetor of Tarquinia, who seems to have got rid of Orgolnius, a king of Caere, suppressed a slave revolt at Arretium (Arezzo) and taken nine towns (*oppida*) from the Latins. An intervention at Caere might have been intended to weaken pro-Roman sentiment there, while that at Arretium sounds like an act of patrician solidarity on behalf of the local

139

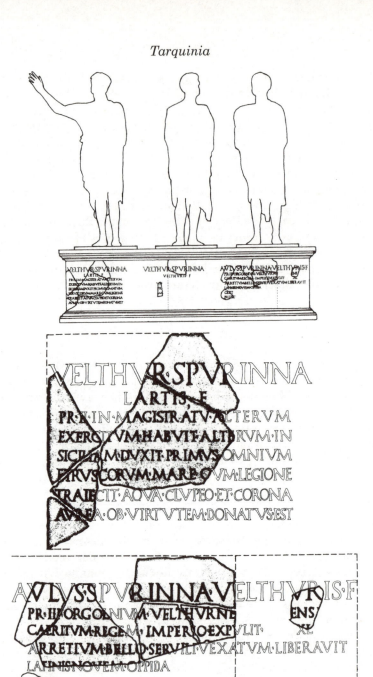

56. In praise of ancestors: the *elogia* of the Spurinna family as reconstructed by Torelli (1975). The statues are conjectural.

oligarchy, with Tarquinia in the role of policeman, perhaps as head of the League. This revolt presumably pre-dates other outbreaks of class warfare at Arretium, crushed by Roman intervention in 302 BC (p. 162), and at Volsinii (Orvieto) in 265 BC (Livy 10.3.2; Zonaras 8.7.4-8). Yet the fragmentary nature and uncertain date of the *elogia* are problematic; a fourth-century context seems likely, but a reference to unknown events of the fifth century is not inconceivable.[7]

The literary sources return to Etruscan affairs in the late fourth century, when the balance of power had shifted further in favour of Rome, battle-hardened from the Samnite Wars and with a reformed army (maniple formations were replacing the rigid phalanx) and a string of Latin and Campanian 'allies' to draw upon for manpower and money. The Faliscans, doubtless impressed and intimidated, had already requested a more friendly treaty (*foedus*) in 343 BC to replace the former truce. Livy's war of 311-308 BC is sometimes rather arbitrarily dismissed as a fabrication, but his sources seem no worse than before.[8] As usual, the narrative is suspect in some ways, perhaps duplicating events and exaggerating Roman successes, although the general trend of Roman advances into central Etruria and Umbria seems credible; the claim of collective Etruscan retaliation (Livy 9.32.1) is perhaps less so.

Tarquinia is hardly mentioned, possibly due simply to the mixed nature of Etruscan forces, but more likely to her minor role, or even abstention; her territory was perhaps little affected. This is also hinted at by the uneasy truces of 308 BC in which she alone was granted *indutiae* for 40 years, a renewal of the previous truce (if not a confusion in the annals), whereas the other parties settled for just one year (Livy 9.41.5; Diodorus Siculus 20.44.9). If Roman successes are to be believed, these sound like good terms for Tarquinia, raising suspicions that territorial concessions must have been made.[9] Livy, however, mentions only that the Roman army under Decius obtained some grain from her; perhaps that was a kind of indemnity. The special deal with Tarquinia may also suggest that Rome's policy aimed at prising her away from other Etruscan towns, as it had done before with Caere.

Etruscans were involved in another engagement in 311 BC when 1,200 mercenaries fought in Sicily for Hamilcar, the Carthaginian general, against Agathocles of Syracuse (Diodorus Siculus 19.106.2).[10] This is unremarkable, except that in 307 BC the policy towards the old enemy seems to have been reversed, as 18 Etruscan ships were sent (we know not exactly by whom) to help Agathocles against the Carthaginians (Diodorus 20.61.6-7). The change is puzzling; was it an attempt to win new friends in Sicily in order to counteract Rome's growing power and influence?[11]

Central Etruria and Umbria were again the focus of conflict in the next reported round of fighting between 302 and 293 BC. Tarquinia is not mentioned specifically. The question recurs: did she play a part, or simply stick to the treaty of 308 BC? We hear of Etruscans first harassed by Gauls, subsequently making common cause against Rome, and then of allied Gauls and Samnites dramatically defeated in 295 BC at Sentinum in Umbria. A memory of huge battlefield losses (25,000 in Livy 10.32.1), if little else, reverberates in Roman tradition. Rusellae was captured and *indutiae* granted, following payment of fines, to Volsinii, Perusia and Arretium in 294 BC. After 293 BC, we are navigating without Livy, whose second decade is lost, but there are echoes of protracted fighting, notably at Lake Vadimon in 283 BC, campaigns against Etruscans and the Gallic Boii, a triumph for the consul of 281 BC, possibly over Tarquinia, defeats of Volsinii and Vulci in 280 BC, and the confiscation of Caeretan territory in 273 BC.

One by one the old cities fell, although we are not told of the specific circumstances – whether following dramatic battles, heroic resistance or peaceful capitulation. By 281 BC, or perhaps 268 BC (the date is unrecorded), a *foedus* was probably contracted with Tarquinia, whose citizens – *Tarquinienses foederati* as stated in a third-century AD inscription – became unequal 'allies' with diminished autonomy, committed to contributing manpower and supplies to Rome when required.[12] The terms of the new order, however, are unclear. Citizenship rights were probably not granted and territory was doubtless ceded as *ager publicus*. Yet the Roman citizen-colony at Gravisca was not founded until 181 BC 'in Etruscan territory, formerly taken from the people of Tarquinii' (Livy 40.29.1). This is considerably later than the imposition of Roman Cosa in 273 BC in the territory of Vulci, and of Pyrgi and other Roman sites in the territory of Caere, in the mid-third century BC. It might suggest relatively lenient treatment initially.

Disaffection perhaps existed among the new Etruscan allies, but we know nothing of rebellions or such embers of discontent as Hannibal's propaganda was later keen to fan. In this connection, a tomb epitaph of about 175-150 BC from Monterozzi (Villa Tarantola) has sometimes been taken as evidence of Carthaginian recruitment. It commemorates one Laris Felsna, a name with Perugian parallels, the son of a slave or freedman, who supposedly died aged 106. However, the text is ambiguous: all it seems to say is that Felsna was at Capua during the Hannibalian campaign in 216 BC.[13] Indeed, he could well have fought on the Roman side in the heroic defence of Casilinum, for example, along with 460 other Perugians (Livy 23.17.8-11). Likewise, too much should perhaps not be made of the curious fact that the Roman commander, Cn. Fulvius Flaccus, charged with treason after defeat by Hannibal in Apulia, opted for exile in Tarquinia in 211 BC; his sounds like a case of military incompetence or cowardice.[14] In effect, therefore, nothing overtly seditious is documented.

Grudgingly or not, Tarquinia was soon contributing sailcloth for Scipio's Carthaginian campaign of 205 BC (Livy 28.45.14).

Livy's essentially militaristic history should not induce us to ignore other consequences of the changing fortunes of the time. Rather than military defeat alone (in fact, we cannot be sure that Tarquinia actually was defeated militarily *sensu stricto*) the socio-political repercussions of protracted conflict were probably equally or more serious for Etruscan society. One might anticipate disruption to the wider regional economy and trade, growing insecurity, the undermining of the social system through a weakening of bonds between aristocratic families and cities, a certain loss of cohesion, credibility and prestige by the traditional governing class, and an erosion of ideological and cultural values.

With the foundation of the colony at Gravisca in 181 BC, probably designed partly to consolidate Roman naval power in the Tyrrhenian, and of market towns such as Forum Cassii (Vetralla) in the second century BC, accompanying the development of new road systems (Via Clodia and Aurelia), the pace of Romanisation must have increased. The establishment of another Roman colony at Tarquinia in the time of the Gracchi is disputed, or its significance generally played down, but possibly this too brought a small influx of settlers.[15] Changes in land ownership must have ensued. One may imagine tensions between incomers and old families, whose power and influence was waning. Plainly, the Social War and subsequent enfranchisement of Etruria by 89 BC marks a watershed in the history of the region, and the start of a new chapter in Tarquinia's history, as a Roman municipium (below).

Monterozzi and Scataglini

Tombs of the fourth/second century BC are scattered over several hills around the town, but the greatest concentration is on Monterozzi and the adjacent Scataglini estate.[16] By this time, limited space remained on the upper plateau for more chamber tombs, which had to be fitted into the gaps, often encroaching on older graves, or into areas where the bedrock was less suitable. Old tombs were perhaps re-used or even forgotten (but evidently not destroyed) when families died out or moved away and there were no relatives left to tend and maintain the grave. Saturation point was reached in the second century BC, although depositions were still being added subsequently.

Certain families known from inscriptions had larger, architecturally more elaborate or painted tombs (below): for example, the Shields tomb (Velcha *gens*) is distinguished by side rooms and windows; the Orco (Velcha, Murina *gens*) by extensions; the Ceisinie and Cardinal (Vestrcni) by size (up to 17 m wide), pillars or ceiling coffers (Fig. 3); the Charuns

143

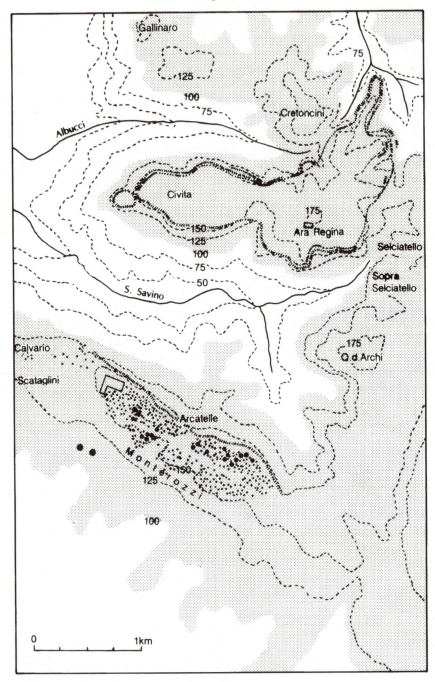

57. Site contour map (dots = tombs and tumuli).

tomb by different levels. The Mercareccia tomb (around 300 BC) has an upper chamber with carved roof beams pitched upwards to a central aperture (Fig. 2), which forms the base of a rock-cut shaft leading to the surface, imitating the atrium ceiling of early Roman houses. An internal staircase led to a lower chamber with benches and carved roof beams. Nonetheless, Hellenistic tombs generally make few obvious or detailed allusions to domestic architecture and their flat ceilings are often featureless.

About 60 corridors apparently intended for tombs were never completed. In certain cases, this may have been because the rock became harder, or because another tomb was encountered unexpectedly, but the reason is often unclear.[17] Perhaps those commissioning the tomb ran out of funds, changed their minds, or died elsewhere. Sometimes these corridors were used like trench graves for simple burials.

The few chambers found intact have the grave goods and deceased on benches, or additional burials on the floor. Iron nails in tomb 5430 suggest that certain items or drapery could still be hung from the wall, as shown by the Giglioli or Tapestry tomb frescos (and some Archaic tombs, p. 93). Quadrangular chambers with benches, usually accessed by a stepped corridor, could easily hold three corpses, and up to a dozen or more in some cases. Cremations, represented by pottery urns, seem less common, but they are not easily quantified (below). Skeletal data is therefore scarce, as from all Etruscan cemeteries.[18]

Judging by inscriptions and sarcophagi, aristocratic tombs often contained married couples. A few intact but otherwise unexceptional chambers seem to reflect this: in Monterozzi 6046, of about 300 BC, an adult male aged about 52 and female of about 42 lay on opposite benches, with ten pottery vessels on the rear bench (Fig. 58). However, in tomb 5698 a single man lay on each of three benches, while a female, inserted last, was on the floor. Tomb 5580, of similar date, was amplified by the creation of hollowed-out benches designed to hold seven or eight inhumations and perhaps cremation urns in two wall niches (Fig. 36). Though partially robbed, it contained about 100 pottery and metal artefacts. Modest single burials with few grave goods are recorded in niches or separate trench graves. One can only guess to what extent these different burial combinations reflect variations in family structures, but the tombs were plainly not just for couples.

Research on about 40 skeletons, mainly from chamber tombs of the fourth/third centuries, suggests that only about 25% of the adult population passed the age of 40, while only one individual was over 60.[19] This is roughly consistent with findings from other Etruscan sites. Inscriptions on half a dozen aristocratic sarcophagi of Tarquinia (below) nevertheless record age at death ranging widely from 25 to 82; the advanced age of Laris

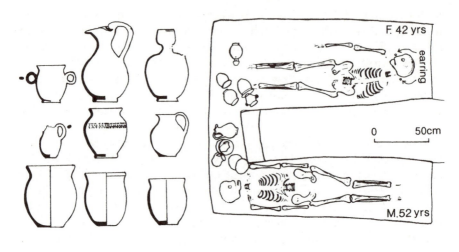

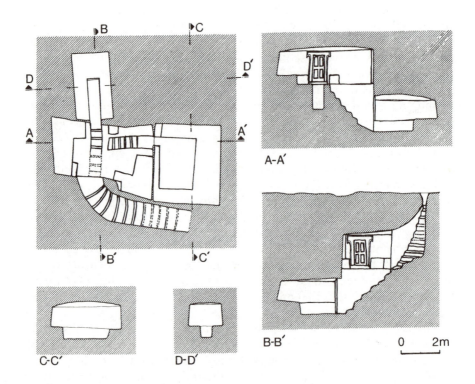

58. Above: Monterozzi tomb 6046, late fourth/early third century BC. Below: Monterozzi, Charuns tomb, third century BC (after *ET*, 314-15; Cataldi 1993, 49).

Felsnas (106 years, above), as stated by his epitaph, is obviously exceptional. Child mortality was no doubt high, but burials of young children are hardly recorded. However, many tombs were empty or not carefully excavated; teeth and a small cranium fragment of a two- to four-year-old were recently found in tomb 6270.

Cremations are probably also under-recorded, and rarely allow assessments of age or sex. One exception is tomb 6270 in which adult bones (of a 20-30-year-old), possibly originally in a casket of perishable material, were identified on a bench, associated with a fibula and an iron spearhead, reminiscent of the old Iron Age practice of cremation for 'warriors'. As before, the reason for cremation is not obvious. In some cases it may even have been a secondary treatment, or perhaps a space-saving solution.

Measurements of bone calcium, strontium and zinc suggest relatively little meat in the diet and a high dependence on carbohydrates, cereals or vegetable foods. This is roughly comparable with several ancient societies, although the suggestion of a decrease in meat consumption in Etruria after the Archaic period is not a generalised phenomenon in the Mediterranean. Judging by tomb design and grave goods the persons concerned were of fairly modest status, but since comparable data is lacking for richer tombs, one cannot tell whether eating meat was linked to class; one might suspect that it was. One roughly 50-year-old female (tomb 5698, above) boasts the earliest archaeologically recorded case of a bone metabolism and hormonal disorder (*hyperostosis frontalis interna*, or MSM syndrome), generally attested by a thickening of the frontal skull and sometimes associated with obesity in older women.[20]

A rather high incidence of dental caries and wear is attested. Enamel hypoplasia (under-development) in ten individuals was possibly caused by illness or poor nutrition in infancy. However, Etruscan dentists were surprisingly advanced and among the first to replace missing teeth (sometimes by filing down animal teeth), correct tooth alignment or hold loose teeth with orthodontic bands. Two of these from Tarquinia (sixth/fourth centuries BC) are made from alloyed silver and gold, metals that were obviously known to be the most suitable for dental work.

South-west of Monterozzi, the gently sloping terrain of Scataglini provided better opportunities for expansion (Fig. 59).[21] Before the late fourth century, the area had been used as a quarry, served by a roadway (33 x 3.2 m) leading into a central court (9 x 10 m) cut into the rock (Plate XI). Present appearances are deceptive, however, since the tombs were inserted only after the road and court, designed to facilitate the extraction of limestone, had been at least partially back-filled. This is why several doorways are unevenly spaced and why the Anina tomb, though centred on the square, had an entrance corridor built higher up (since removed).

The excavated tombs comprise 34 trench graves, 125 single and 16

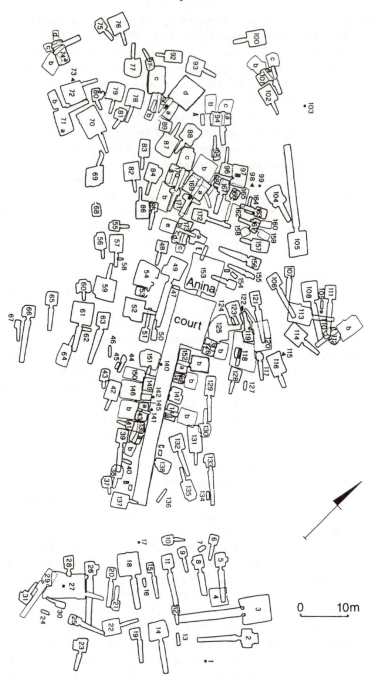

59. Scataglini cemetery plan (after *Scataglini 1*, pls I-II).

multiple chambers, mostly of about 325-275 BC, though later insertions occurred in the second/first centuries BC and sporadically in the early empire. The rock-cut trenches (*fosse*), covered with slabs, were probably meant for single inhumations, attested in the odd case, including that of a child; one held a cremation. As on Monterozzi, corridors intended for chamber tombs were sometimes unfinished, but used for single inhumations.

The chamber tombs, like those of Monterozzi, were generally entered by a descending ramp or steps leading into a quadrangular room, often provided with benches and occasionally with niches and minor architectural embellishments, such as semi-columns, a tympanum, or pillar. Size variations suggest some tombs were intended for single inhumations, others for two or three individuals, and the largest for numerous members or even different branches of a family, to be used over generations, as occasionally confirmed by inscriptions. The two-storey tomb with an upper-level chamber and one to three rooms below, reached by a staircase, was also in use by the late fourth century (Fig. 58); the upper room could hold burials and was not necessarily a vestibule or cult chamber as sometimes thought. Depositions were on the benches, stepped back in tiers in the Anina tomb (Plate XIV), in hollowed-out benches covered with a lid, in sarcophagi, and sometimes added on the floor (Fig. 60). Large slots (*loculi*) or small niches in the wall held inhumations or cremation urns, though the latter have been found on the benches too, and in small rock-cut trenches or stone chests.

The original appearance of the cemetery, nevertheless, is hard to imagine. Any superstructures have long since vanished and modern ploughing has further chiselled away at the old land surface; yet some contemporary tombs, at Tuscania for example, had monumental facades and were clearly meant to impress, like their Archaic predecessors. Sculptural embellishments were probably visible. One lucky survival from Monterozzi is a fourth-century limestone figure of a finely draped and bejewelled woman on an inscribed base; another is a *nenfro* female bust framed by an aedicule or shrine, surmounted by pillars, resembling betyls (cult stones), probably indebted to south Italian or Punic traditions, and perhaps originally set above a tomb door (Fig. 61). Columnar *cippi* with inscribed bases (for males and females) were occasionally carved with a human head, such as that of Arnth Paipnas. Large fragmented relief panels with battle scenes may come from a funerary monument in the open, if not a tomb. Other sculpture fragments include Charun figures, possibly lions guarding entrances, and altars, as well as a head carved in relief inside a Scataglini tomb.[22] One might envisage a kind of funerary theme park with prominent figurative imagery imparting lessons in family history, social status, civic pride and eschatology, while providing a focus for commemorative ceremonies and cults.

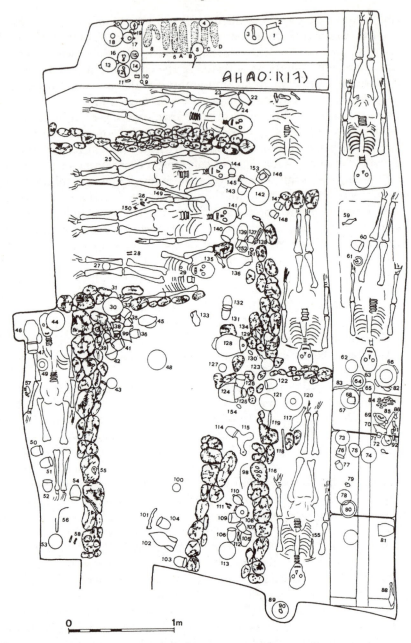

60. Scataglini tomb 112, lower chamber, with 13 inhumations and four
cremations, *c.* 250/200 BC. The painted inscription on a sarcophagus lid reads
'*Ceisi Thana*'; Ceisi is a *gentilicium* recorded elsewhere in southern Etruria
(after *Scataglini 1*, pl. LIV).

5. Tarquinia and Rome

Few tombs illustrate the original range and wealth of goods, and bias is exemplified by the comparatively large quantity of plain or simple band-painted pottery (cups, plates, jugs, unguentaria, askoi, urns and jars) ignored in centuries past by treasure hunters more interested in jewellery, metals and painted vases. Black-glaze ware (oinochoai, kylikes, cups, plates and paterae) of the fourth/second centuries BC, like bucchero before, drew some inspiration from metalwork. Much of the Civita (non-funerary) sample was probably locally made, with glaze of uneven quality, possibly in small kilns from workshops scattered around the site or its territory.[23] Red-figure wares of Faliscan, Etruscan (Caere and Vulci) and local workshops gradually replaced Attic imports; Faliscan kylikes and Genucilia plates are typical of fourth-century contexts. Certain forms are over-painted, decorated in silhouette or rather mediocre imitations of Apulian Gnathian pottery. Transport amphorae (Corinthian B and Massaliote types) are also known. Flagons (lagynoi) and unguentaria are especially

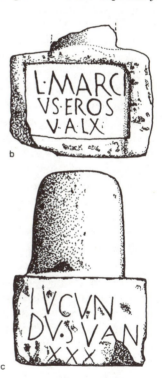

61. Funerary stone sculpture: (a) Monterozzi, probably third century BC, an aristocratic Etruscan woman; (b-c) Scataglini tomb 69, *cippi*, *c.* 100 BC, inscribed in Latin: L(ucius) Marcius Eros V(ixit) A(nnos) LX, and: Iucundus V(ixit) A(nnos) XXX; both individuals of probable slave origin (after photographs, and *Scataglini 2*, pl. CCXLV).

common in third/second-century tombs, which sometimes contain 'Graeco-Italic' transport amphorae, while Roman lamps, glass unguentaria, Megarian bowls and Arretine ware occasionally appear in re-used tombs.

Bronze items (Fig. 62) consist of oinochoai, censers (thymiateria), candelabra, unguent flasks (balsamaria), strigils (skin scrapers), mirrors, sometimes decorated with mythical figures, various appliqués and studs probably from wooden and leather objects, and metal (*aes rude*) fragments. Iron is represented by spears, nails and strigils. Despite looting, wealthier tombs contained fine gold jewellery: rings, earrings, necklaces with a variety of pendants, beads and *bullae* (personal amulets), as well as figurative appliqués (possibly from furniture and clothing) and elaborate leaf diadems flaunted by rich men and women; such items also appear in tomb frescos and sculpture.[24] Toiletry articles of carved bone include small boxes, spatulae, *specillae* (probes) and mirror handles. The list goes on: pebbles, shells, little terracotta animal figurines and fruits, glass or alabaster gaming pieces, and real food offerings, occasionally attested by animal bones. Noteworthy too are little terracotta theatre masks, comparable with those of Greek Sicily and Magna Graecia, as well as Dionysiac masks and figurines of sileni, satyrs, Pan or Dionysus himself.[25] These probably reflect a continuing Dionysiac tradition, seen also in certain frescos and sarcophagi (below).

Fine jewellery, perfume vases and toiletry items are associated with well-to-do females, and strigils, drinking cups, tools and weapons with males. Strainers, oinochoai, skyphoi, kylikes and kantharoi represent the traditional paraphernalia of wine-drinking. Despite stylistic changes with the passage of time, grave goods seem to conform to rather conservative, formulaic notions in keeping with earlier traditions. There is perhaps a certain fin-de-siècle weariness in the rather florid offerings of the period. In a sense, it was the end of an era; funerary practices of Roman and later times are comparatively austere. However, the social and gender implications have been little studied. Jewellery, mirrors and toiletry sets may have been rather intimate, personal items – gifts on important occasions, such as marriages – but at the same time generically emblematic of gender and class. Yet they were presumably only token offerings, a small percentage of the deceased's actual possessions inherited by their children.

Status is more vividly proclaimed by sarcophagi, inscriptions and by the size and elaboration of tombs. For instance, the large Monterozzi tomb 5512 is distinguished by sarcophagi, inscribed *cippi*, and wall painting as well as by an abundance of bronze, iron, lead, alabaster, glass and bone articles. Even this is surpassed by tombs with fine frescos or aristocratic sarcophagi (below). By contrast, the humble appearance of burials in simple niches (*loculi*) or trenches is compounded by their modest contents. Those close to or within the corridors of chamber tombs may have been

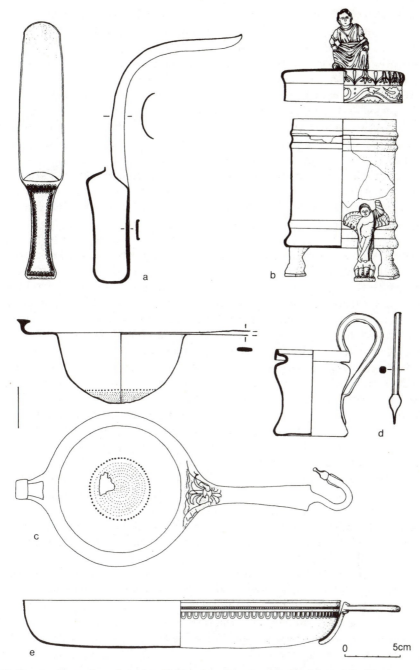

62. Bronze items from late fourth/third-century BC tombs: (a) strigil; (b) cista; (c) strainer; (d) kyathos; (e) platter (after Bini *et al.* 1995).

linked with the latter in a subservient way, as retainers or slaves, like the earlier shaft graves (p. 93). Overall, we may infer a complex social matrix with various gradations in wealth and distinction, as also suggested by inscriptions (below). Archaeology thus warns against taking too literally the notion of a society split simply between masters and slaves.

What of the wider economy? In the manufacture of fine pottery, Tarquinia does not look like a serious rival to Falerii, let alone to the booming south Italian workshops, nor perhaps to Caere or Vulci. This may seem paradoxical given the prominence of the city at this time, but perhaps the existence of other specialist centres discouraged competition. One might also link the presence of mid-fourth-century Faliscan imports at Tarquinia with the political alliances of the time. In any case, pottery was less important in ancient economies than its archaeological abundance might appear to suggest.

Metal production seems more distinguished, as before, represented by utilitarian and luxury items, although much has been lost and distinguishing local products from imports is problematic. One may suspect some greater local expertise in the production of sarcophagi, jewellery, architectural terracottas and perhaps textiles and gemstones. While undoubtedly self-sufficient in essentials, different Etruscan cities probably had certain craft traditions that were to some extent complementary – as in the case of fine pottery – which stimulated inter-city trade.

The agricultural wealth of Tarquinia must have exceeded that of smaller states like Falerii. We know little about the rural economy of the fifth/fourth centuries BC, but there is no clear evidence of recession; the apparent prosperity of provincial centres belies this notion. During the later fourth century there appear to be strong cultural, and probably economic, ties between Tarquinia and sites such as Norchia, Tuscania, Musarna, Sorrina, Castel d'Asso, and smaller sites around Viterbo. Only in the third century is there some evidence for more widespread disruption in Etruria, which can be associated with military conflict and Romanisation.[26] However, in the Tuscania region just to the north, a surprising degree of stability in rural settlement is reported, as well as evidence of cultural continuity in the form of wealthy chamber tombs spanning the fourth/second centuries BC.

Local coinage of the late fourth/early third centuries provides further clues to economic conditions and political aspirations.[27] A few dozen coins come from the tombs, based on subdivisions of the libra: the *as* (with boar's head, spear and astral symbol), *semis* (ram's head/shepherd staff), *quadrans* (anchor/dolphin), *sextans* (plough/yoke/value sign), *uncia* (crescent/A) and *semuncia* (caduceus/A) from two series, probably minted locally (Fig. 63). Circulation was evidently limited; only one Tarquinia coin has been tentatively identified at Tuscania (around 320 BC), whereas Greek coins of south Italy and Sicily first appear in Etruria in the fifth century BC and are widespread from the fourth century. One or two late fifth-century coins from Himera and Agrigento in Sicily are known. Roman coins spread during the third century, first with the ROMANO series and then in greater numbers, exemplified by the ship prow *sextans*. The Scataglini tombs contained a handful of Greek examples of the later fourth/third centuries from Campania, Apulia, Rhegium, Syracuse, possible Sikel-Punic types and about a dozen Roman. A likely explanation for the lack of local third-century issues is that production was inhibited by growing Roman dominance and perhaps treaty impositions.

More common as currency in the fourth/third centuries BC were metal bars (*aes rude*) weighing between 480 and 670 g, sometimes stamped (*aes signatum*) and occasionally placed in tombs with coins (Fig. 63: e). The 'A' sign on some of them and on an *uncia* has been variously regarded as part of a TA (Tarquinia) monogram, a levelling device (*libella*) or, most likely, the Greek letter, standing for the *as* or for a primary coin in a series.[28] It is interesting to find the same sign displayed prominently, along with a boar's head and amphora, in the late fourth-century shield frescos of the Giglioli tomb (Plate XII), which has prompted the hypothesis that the tomb's founder, Vel Pinies, a prominent city magistrate, had some special responsibility for coinage and the choice of these emblems. The military regalia depicted in the tomb might also allude to a martial dimension of Vel Pinies' magistrature, and remind us of the recurrent association between currency and war, whether in the form of soldiers' pay, booty, or reparations. It has been argued, therefore, that Tarquinia attempted to formalise coinage emissions in the second half of the fourth century BC and

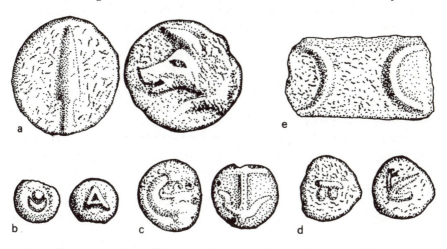

63. Tarquinia coins: (a) as; (b) semuncia; (c) quadrans; (d) sextans; (e) aes signatum (after Catalli 1988).

to create a currency zone in the surrounding area to rival that already developing on its southern border, where the first Roman issues (*aes grave*) were circulating among Latin allies and probably at Sutri as well as Caere.

Coinage, of course, is propagandistic or symbolic as well as practical. The ram's head, shepherd's crook and plough could refer, albeit indirectly, to the traditional importance locally of animal husbandry and cultivation. Tarchon, after all, was also a ploughman (p. 76). The anchor and dolphin might allude to maritime activity, although the dolphin is also generically symbolic of Tyrrhenians; the boar and spear could be a mythological reference, but not easily specified, while crescent moons and astral motifs may have calendrical or cult connotations (the Dioscuri, Juno and Jupiter have all been invoked in one way or another). Early Roman issues, however, are emblematic of the increasingly forceful assertion of Roman hegemony, which eventually ended any hopes for an independent local currency.

Names and faces: sarcophagi and inscriptions

In the fourth/third century BC, the more illustrious dead were often entombed in hollowed-out benches, sometimes painted with garlands (perhaps alluding to canopies above funeral beds), drapery, or spiral motifs, and covered by a stone lid, carved with simple architectonic motifs, such as a *columen*, *acroteria* or volutes.[29] These tombs within tombs typify collective vaults, like that of the Anina family, dating from about 300 BC, and helped to preserve individual identities (Plates XIII-XIV).

Separate free-standing stone sarcophagi commemorated high-ranking persons. They appear during the fourth century, but they are not entirely new: there were wooden, if not stone and terracotta, versions in earlier periods. Their development can be roughly charted, starting with those on which the lid figure lies flat, like a medieval effigy, as if asleep or lying in state, or else in a more life-like pose (Plates XX, XXII-XXV).[30] Those with a gabled lid reiterate the old metaphor of the tomb as a house; others allude to altars. From the late fourth century BC, lid figures are generally semi-recumbent, propped on one elbow, reminiscent of a banquet couch rather than a bier. Males often hold a libation bowl or *patera*. The more roughly carved and painted examples in *nenfro* of the later third century suggest a declining, or changing, tradition. Terracotta sarcophagi, more typical of the third/second century, also vary in quality, and are generally not equal to the best stone examples. One specimen from Scataglini tomb 90 of around 250 BC finds good parallels at Tuscania and might be from the same workshop.

Inscriptions on sarcophagi or painted on tomb walls permit several chambers on Monterozzi and Gallinaro to be ascribed to specific aristocratic *gentes*, whose family trees can sometimes be reconstructed. For instance, there were 14 sarcophagi and one stone urn in the Partunu tomb (mid-fourth/late third century), 21 in the Pulena (mainly third century), six in the Alvethna (late fourth/third century) and over 30 in one of the Camna tombs (third century). To these names of influential families of the mid-fourth/third centuries we may add the Velcha, Cuclnie, Curuna, Pumpu, Ceisinie and others.[31] However, they were not all social equals; their sarcophagi vary in raw material, style, and quality of finish. Local *nenfro* sufficed for the majority, but a few superior examples occur in limestone or marble.

The late fourth-century sarcophagus of Larth Alvethna with its finely carved lid figure, perhaps a haruspex, stood apart in the centre of his tomb, like a venerable *paterfamilias*, while much plainer examples were set around the wall. Likewise, of the 21 sarcophagi in the Pulena(s) tomb, that of the mature Laris (popularly known as the 'magistrate', around 250 BC), who seems to have been of Greek origin (hence 'Creice'), projects seniority (Plate XXIV). His son, Velthur, has only a plain gabled lid. In semi-recumbent pose, Laris holds an open scroll (like the Roman *volumen*, originally cloth) showing his *curriculum vitae* with details of descent, distinctions and offices held. These included writing religious texts (*libri haruspicini*) and some, probably priestly, responsibility for cults of ancestors and of at least two deities, Catha and Pacha (Bacchus), while he also made a libation of wine and honey in honour of Culsu, another deity.[32] Word and image extol his credentials. This is one of the longer Etruscan inscriptions to have survived (59 words in nine lines, bearing faint traces of red paint), although the last six lines are not translatable with much confidence.

The 'priest' sarcophagus of Laris Partunu (around 340 BC), made from Greek marble of Paros, is unusually fine: the bearded lid figure in a long chiton with ceremonial stole, wearing an earring in Punic fashion, is holding a *pyxis* (incense box) and solemnly gesturing, doubtless in fulfilment of some sacred task (Plate XX). This could represent a Punic priest, but perhaps not Laris himself. Did the latter obtain the sarcophagus secondhand? Similar types are known from Carthage and were perhaps made to order by Parian craftsmen.[33] The sides have well-restored painted figures of warring Greeks and Amazons, and a famous scene from the *Iliad* of Achilles sacrificing Trojan prisoners at the funeral of Patroclus, into which the artist – presumably local – has inserted Etruscan underworld figures. Although it was fairly frequently depicted in the fourth century (for example on the François tomb at Vulci), one may imagine that this particular story resonated loudly at Tarquinia around the time when the 307 Roman captives were reputedly sacrificed (p. 138); in this case, the defeated Trojans could be allusively Romans. A more ambitious attempt to invest the scene with political significance proposes that the hooded female warriors are Carthaginians fighting Sicilian Greeks, and that the Punic character of the sarcophagus reflects a mid-fourth-century axis of friendship between Tarquinia and Carthage.[34]

Velthur Partunu (the 'magnate', late fourth or perhaps early third century BC), son of Laris, had a fine-grained limestone sarcophagus, no doubt a marble substitute, but well finished and originally painted (Fig. 64). The lid figure, bare-chested and head wreathed, propped on soft cushions, holds a *patera*, while crouching lions and sphinxes stand guard. Greeks, Amazons, centaurs and Lapithae in typically animated scenes on the box panels seem antithetical to the serenity of the figure above. Here perhaps is a juxtaposition of war and peace, life and death. The epitaph

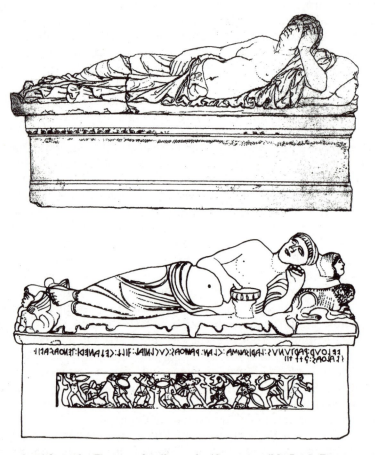

64. Sarcophagi from the Partunu family tomb. Above: possibly Laris Partunu, a son of Velthur (below), the so-called obese (probably early third century BC). Below: the so-called magnate, inscribed 'Velthur Partunu son of Laris and Ramtha Cuclni was *zilch cechaneri* and lived 82 years' (late fourth century BC) (after Herbig 1952).

records his position as *zilch cechaneri* (see below) and advanced age, although the face on the lid is quite young; it reads as follows:

velthur partunus larisalisa clan ramthas cuclnial zilch cechaneri tenthas avil svalthas LXXXII ('Velthur Partunus, the one who is of Laris, [and] the son of Ramtha Cuclni, praetor of sacred functions (he) served; years he lived 82').[35]

Another high-ranking member of the Partunu family, also called Laris (the 'obese' or the 'thinker', late fourth/early third century) is shown with prominent belly and breasts of polished veined marble (Fig. 64). Corpulence, but not obesity, is a feature of some Etruscan sarcophagus figures and was doubtless meant to imply status or *gravitas*. A fashionable image locally, it was evidently lampooned by the Romans: Catullus (39.11) and Vergil (*Georgics* 2.193) refer to an *'obesus Etruscus'* and a *'pinguis Tyrrenus'*. Like the proverbial Etruscan love of luxury (*tryphé*), or the lustful Etruscan (p. 167), this belongs in a long list of ancient stereotypes, from cheating Greeks to drunken Celts, although it seems a relatively mild jibe, and most Romans would presumably have been happy to be portrayed with the far from unmanly facial features of these Etruscan lid figures.[36] People who lived barely 80 km from Rome can hardly have looked very different from the Romans themselves.

Aristocratic females are also prominent. An inscription informs us that Larth Camna (early/mid-third century BC) set up a tomb for himself and his successors, who included Arnth and his wife, Ramtha Apatrui, shown reclining in her fine robes, an impressive matron whose epitaph names her husband and relatives (Plate XXV). Ramtha Huzcnai, the mother or grandmother of a magistrate (*zileteraias*), Larth Apaiatru, as recorded by the lid inscription, was given a particularly elegant sarcophagus (the 'Amazon') made of Greek island marble carved with Actaeon being savaged by his dogs on a gable end (Plate XXII).[37] The painting in tempera on the sides with action-packed scenes of Amazons battling Greeks, probably done locally, is in tune with Greek realism in painting of about 350-320 BC.

Plainly, Greek myths and sagas were as popular as ever, especially those involving Amazons, Homeric battle scenes and incidents of high drama, like the fratricidal duel between Eteokles and Polynikes. Equally, there is no doubting the local character of much imagery: the fighting Etruscans and Gauls (Camna tomb), and underworld figures such as Vanth and Charun, who lead dignitaries to Hades, sometimes on a chariot, accompanied by musicians and officials bearing official insignia. The sarcophagus of Arnth Paipnas, surmounted by a three-headed Cerberus, shows the deceased flanked by these funerary attendants on the side panel, while lions clutch sheep on the lid. With parallels in fresco painting (below), much of this stems from a distinctly Etruscan eschatology, although more specific religious connotations are also implied: by the deer drinking from paterae (Plate XXIII), Silenus masks and symbols including the scroll motif, suggesting the persistence of Dionysiac cults.

Etruscan sarcophagi mark an early stage in the development of ancient portraiture in Italy. The more schematic facial modelling generally lacks much individuality or any accurate illustration of age; archetypes rather than likenesses generally sufficed. Terracotta lid figures, in particular, can be highly, almost absurdly, schematised, although even a rough modelling of facial features can impart a sense of character. Some high-quality work in stone seems at least vaguely allusive to the individual concerned, within contemporary conventions. Aristocratic women, however, like the aristocratic Ramtha Apatrui, aspired to a rather standardised Hellenistic model of beauty that changed little into Roman times. The face of Seianti Hanunia of Chiusi, recently reconstructed from her skull, when compared with her rather bland sarcophagus image (in the British Museum), illustrates the point.[38] The aesthetic ideals of fifth-century classicism, to which the bearded *cippus* head of Arnth Paipnas is also indebted, were not easily renounced. Nor perhaps are the somewhat restricted ambitions and audience of this particular form of funerary art likely to have spurred much innovation. Nevertheless, some of the lid figures described above, with unusually furrowed brows, sunken eyes, flabby jowls or a bent nose, point to a more purposeful attempt at individualised commemoration, and an underlying interest in character.

Aside from funerary sculpture, hardly a fraction of what once existed survives; the finest works in bronze have gone. One bronze sculpture from Tarquinia (the 'putto Carrara'; Fig. 4), bearing a dedicatory inscription to Selvans, is roughly dated to the late fourth or early third century BC. It is a good example of a naked squatting child wearing a *bulla*, a popular type of the Hellenistic period, though unlikely to represent the legendary Tages, as once thought. Nevertheless, there may have been little statues of Tages at Tarquinia in similar style, not unlike the baby Herakles or Mars figures that were fashionable in fourth-century Etruria.[39] This particular figure was evidently originally set on a stone plinth, and it might possibly have come from the Ara della Regina temple (p. 7).

Literacy skills were now more advanced and probably more widespread than before, but still closely linked with high status and political office, especially priesthoods. The Tarquinia inscriptions, including epitaphs on tomb walls, inscribed stone *cippi*, sarcophagi and a bronze plaque, possibly a legal decree, are the most numerous and informative of any Etruscan site.[40] Some provide a *gentilicium* and *praenomen* followed by a patronymic, rarely a matronymic, and the age, distinctions or magistracies of the deceased. Thus we know the names of more than 50 local families, from

Acnatru to Zertna. However, terms such as *lautni* (freedman), *etera* (clients?), or *lautneteri*, denoting lower-class or servile origins, are lacking. Cippi written in Latin appear in the second/first century BC, signalling a language change as a result of increasing Roman influence.

Marriages between influential families (such as the Ceisinie/Matulna, Partunu/Cuclnie, Clevsina/Alsina) are amply documented and doubtless often served to secure alliances and power. Some long-range connections are implied. For instance, the Pumpu, Alsina, Pinie and Ane (of the Typhon, Alsina, Giglioli and Querciola II tombs) are variously encountered at Vulci, Chiusi, Cortona, Perugia and Volsinii, while the sarcophagus of Thanchvil Apunei, married to a Curuna at Tuscania (around 280 BC), may be a lady from Tarquinia. Certain epitaphs in the Scataglini tombs (Anina, Spitu) also point to family ties with central Etruria, notably Perugia and Chiusi. Significantly, the names from this cemetery are not those of the most prominent Monterozzi tombs, and may reflect a preponderance of middle-ranking *gentes* in Scataglini. In fact, Larth Anina is the only known *zilath*. In the Etrusco-Roman period, most of those buried here were of Etruscan descent, but some Latin names appear and one or two of potentially humble origin.

Magistracies are denoted by several titles, whose meaning, though not always certain, may be qualified by additional terms.[41] Foremost is *zilach* (the 'zilachship'; *zilath* refers to the individual), generally equated with the Latin praetor, a high-ranking position and probably normally held for a set time period. The *zilath cechaneri* seems pre-eminent, recorded three times at Tarquinia, twice with a member of the Velcha *gens* and perhaps depicted in the Meeting tomb with various symbols of *summa potestas* (see below). This may equate with the person called *sacerdos* by Livy (5.1.5), or *autokrator* by Dionysius (3.61). *Zilath mechl rasnal* (probably akin to the Latin *praetor rei publicae*) occurs twice in Tarquinia, but not in the provincial towns, and most likely means a supreme magistrature, possibly with powers extending over the surrounding territory. Other forms of *zilath* also occur in provincial towns suggesting specific roles. *Zilath eterau* possibly had some responsibility for aristocratic young men, like the Latin *praetor iuventutis*. An eponymous time-recording formula, as in *zilci velusi hulchniesi* ('during the zilathship of Vel Hulchnies'), resembles Roman equivalents ('during the consulship of ...'), while numerical suffixes imply that the office was sometimes renewable, but otherwise presumably annual.

A more junior position may be *marunuch*, with various civic or religious remits, perhaps sometimes connected with building activities or cults of Bacchus and Catha (a female divinity) as part of a collegial institution. A parallel might be the Roman quaestor or aedile. Other official roles are documented: *cepen*, probably a priest or priesthood; *eisnevch*, alluding to the sacred or sacrifices; *purth*, perhaps a rather specialised office with civic duties; *macstrevch*, which recalls Mastarna (p. 132) and Latin *magister* (as in *magister populi*, or dictator), perhaps a military position; *eprthnevch*, which is obscure but seems high-ranking; and *camthi*, possibly a relatively junior religious charge held even by teenagers and women, perhaps as heads of associations of young aristocrats (akin to the Latin *camillus*). It seems likely that there was an assembly of magistrates or ex-magistrates, resembling a Senate, or the *ordo decurionum* of the later municipium.

The profusion of high-ranking titles, specified and specialised, reflects the greater institutional complexity of later Etruscan society. It may be that by this time Tarquinia had a particularly elaborate administrative structure, befitting its political prominence and status as a centre of learning and religious lore. Within the ruling class, there was doubtless scope and competition for political advancement, augmented by strategic marriages and by the federal nature of certain offices. The *cursus honorum* perhaps began with the *marunuch* and culminated with a zilachship (more usually the *zilach mechl rasnal*, exceptionally the *zilach cechaneri*), via several other positions. This challenges a stereotypical notion of a politically fossilised and rather arcane society. Yet despite continuity in the trappings of officialdom into the second century BC, the real power of later magistrates must have shrunk – like the territory of their state – by comparison with that of their fourth-century forebears. In a city neutralised militarily and with its autonomy curtailed, local military traditions (as vaunted by the Giglioli tomb) were presumably in abeyance, or else limited to mercenary service elsewhere. The career path for a Tarquinian aristocrat may therefore have inclined towards the civic and religious, rather than the military route of his Roman equivalent.

How did the system maintain equilibrium? Was a desire for upward mobility from the lower orders resisted or accommodated? It is in the fourth century BC that literary sources first inform us of tensions and conflicts within republican oligarchies brought about by the ambitions of an increasingly restless and politically active plebeian class. At Arezzo, the latter acceded to positions of power, albeit temporarily, only to experience a backlash, at least twice, associated in the *elogia* with the Tarquinian, Aulus Spurinna, and then with the Roman consul, M. Valerius Maximus in 302 BC (above). Tarquinia's oligarchy was perhaps more firmly entrenched and less inclined to relinquish power than those elsewhere. In the provincial towns, a coterie of influential families, some related to those of Tarquinia, monopolised public office: the Apatru and Alethna at Musarna, the Atna, Vipinana and Curuna at Tuscania. Yet the situation was probably more fluid than before. If people of humbler origins assumed the *gentilicium* of their patrons they would be largely hidden from our view. Latin incomers, such as the citizen colonists at Gravisca, must also have presented a challenge to the old order. We will return to this question later.

Painted tombs

The dating of the later tomb frescos on stylistic grounds is often surprisingly problematic and liable to fluctuate by up to a century, thanks in part to uncertainties about the duration of Hellenistic art styles in general. For example, the Typhon tomb has recently been dated from about 250-225 BC, rather than 200-150 BC, and some scholars now maintain that no painted tombs are actually later than the third century BC.[42] If that is the case, and if tomb painting is indicative of the tenor of cultural life, then the late third/second century would appear to be a time of recession and crisis. We could ascribe this to the loss of independence, the ravages of the Hannibalian war, if not to a spell of social unrest and class conflict of the kind which affected parts of central Etruria.

The Scataglini tombs of the late fourth/early third century show that paint was sometimes used to enhance architectural features as well as for inscriptions and small-scale scenes, but infrequently for large-scale figures, such as those of Charun and Vanth in the Anina tomb. Large murals occur in about a dozen chambers, spread over the Monterozzi plateau, belonging to prominent families. A few tombs also had painted relief carvings or decorative stucco work, all sadly deteriorated or lost, though sometimes recorded by antiquarian descriptions and illustrations: for instance, animal friezes in the Mercareccia tomb, and a monstrous creature (Scylla?) in tomb 4822.

The frescos are generally more sophisticated than before in the use of colour for highlights and textures, as seen in folds of clothing, elaborate hairstyles and *chiaroscuro* effects, exemplified by the shiny vases of the Orco-2 tomb (Plate XV). Ornamental and floral motifs may allude to draperies and real garlands used in funerary ceremonies. Facial expressions are more varied, with angled poses as well as profiles, while crowd scenes are more realistic, juxtaposing people at different levels and depths (Typhon tomb). These changes reflect advances in Hellenistic painting, pioneered in the Greek world, but also encountered over a wide area, for example in Macedonia and south Italy. There are precedents for certain subjects in earlier tomb painting, as seen in the fifth-century Blue Demons tomb, but changes of emphasis and mood are evident. Journeys or processions to the underworld are popular, requiring some imaginative leaps into Hades, where the deceased may encounter relatives, mythical heroes and supernatural creatures. The underworld has become a recognisable place, depicted with reference to a range of contemporary imagery and conventions, of both local and Greek inspiration.

65. Orco-2 tomb, late fourth century BC, scenes from the underworld. Above: Agamemnon and Tiresias, with *eidola* in between (from photograph). Below: Pirithous, Tuchulcha, Theseus, snake and Charun (?), side wall (after *MonInst* 9, 1869-73; Dennis 1878).

5. Tarquinia and Rome

The mood is not necessarily gloomy, as often maintained, although strange creatures abound in the underworld. Charun is prominent, generally a haggard tramp-like figure with hooked nose, lurid blueish skin, fiery wild hair, scruffy tunic and somewhat incongruous wings (Plate XIII; Figs 66-7). His most distinctive emblem is a great mallet for banging on the doors of Hades, or for banging into place the wooden crossbar that secured city gates and that would now secure the fate of the deceased. However, he has variable guises, as in the tomb of the Charuns, where one is holding a sword. Rather than a single Charun, there may have been a number of underworld officials so labelled, but they are not essentially or necessarily malign. Gatekeepers rather than ferrymen, they have little in common with the Greek Charon.[43] Vanth, a female counterpart and a torch-bearer, is also basically a servant of the dead (Plate XIII). By contrast, a winged Tuchulcha is an ass-eared, bird-beaked, snake-brandishing demon in the Orco-2 tomb (Fig. 65). In the Cardinal tomb (known mainly from misleading eighteenth-century illustrations), there is no shortage of these spirit-world figures standing by or directing proceedings.[44] Whether borne in a cart, on horseback or walking with attendants, the deceased are consigned to these escorts who guide or goad the way to an underworld archway, evidently modelled on a real city gate.

That death is ineluctable is obviously just part of the message. It may be that the journey is a potentially unpleasant rite of passage or even a kind of test, which the great and the good endure stoically, and that Orphic or Pythagorean ideas of purification come into play. In the Orco-2 tomb, the depiction of Sisyphus (now also recognised on the sarcophagus of Laris Pulena) could have moralistic overtones, while the human figures clinging like insects to the riverbank reeds recall the souls (*eidola* or *animulae*) destined for reincarnation of Greek and Roman eschatology (Fig. 65), described in Vergil's underworld: 'about this river like bees in a meadow on a fine summer day, settling on flowers of every kind … the souls of countless tribes and nations were flitting' (*Aeneid* 6.704).[45]

Simultaneously, the prospect of elite associations and encounters with gods and heroes of epic poetry is a claim to fame, with cultural snobberies and class consciousness magnified by pervasively Homeric references. Hades, Persephone, Theseus, Agamemnon and others now badly eroded await the deceased, confirming their superordinate status. In less elaborately painted tombs, like those of Scataglini or the Querciola-2 tomb (Fig. 67), the departed could at least look forward to being reunited with relatives, an encounter touchingly depicted at the gates of Hades, where the shades of those long gone come to greet new arrivals, sometimes with a welcoming handshake, under the watchful eyes of Charun.[46] Here at least was a credible aspiration and comfort for ordinary folk.

For the rich, untroubled by Christian notions of renunciation or social

66. Above: Orco-2 tomb, late fourth century BC, head of Hades; Orco-1 tomb, mid/late fourth century BC, Charun. Below: Bruschi tomb, third century BC, detail of funerary procession with musicians, attendants, inscriptions (mentioning the Apuna family) and probably Charun leading the deceased (a magistrate?) on horseback (after *DD*, fig. 33; *MonInst* 8, 1864; *CR*, 298).

levelling, it must have been reassuring to think that – in an afterlife also populated by weird and ugly creatures – social status, with its fine clothes, toiletries and family reunions, would be respected and banquets enjoyed between husband and wife with musicians in attendance and servants who still know their place. In the Shields tomb, we see two generations of the Velcha family: Velthur and his son Larth, a distinguished magistrate, reclining in traditional pose, while their richly attired wives (Ravnthu Aprthnai and Velia Seitithi) sit demurely on the banqueting couch in dutiful admiration, or in affectionate receipt of that putatively symbolic egg, which reminds us of certain Archaic frescos (p. 119; Plate XVI). Yet the mood is palpably formal now. These venerable ladies were not here to be shown dancing or lying with their men, unlike their more relaxed maternal ancestors. Velthur reappears in an adjacent panel, hieratically enthroned like Zeus, while his wife points to him as if he were some great clan leader, in a flattering *elogium* of aristocratic status; they are practically deified.

Traditions and behaviour patterns were changing. Sex scenes are absent. The straitlaced funerary iconography of the period could hardly be more out of tune with the blatantly sensationalist account of Etruscan sexual mores by the fourth-century BC writer, Theopompus (in Athenaeus, *Deipnosophistae* 12.517). The banquet was also being eclipsed by iconologies of public life, now fully accepted into the formerly rather secluded, domestic ambience of the aristocratic tomb.

The parade of military regalia and symbols of *auctoritas* or *imperium militae*, such as the curved staff (*lituus*), or military cloaks (*paludamentum*) of the Giglioli tomb (p. 155; Plate XII), are a dour reminder that armed service was the order of the day. Henceforth, serried ranks of toga-clad officials are recurrent, shown most evocatively in the Bruschi tomb (Fig. 66) and again in the Meeting tomb (Fig. 67) by numerous aides bearing double axes, lictor's rods and spears on behalf of an *éminence grise* (his hair is realistically grey), Larth son of Arnth, an unusually high-ranking magistrate (*zilach cechaneri*). Perhaps this shows a special appointment connected with formal alliances between two or more cities, such as those sanctioned by the Etruscan League for military purposes. In any case, it is a life-like scene and a suggestive precursor of the Roman taste for processional pomp and commemorative relief, epitomised by the Ara Pacis (but perhaps already current in earlier Roman triumphal art). We might further surmise herein a desire to re-assert the socio-political role of an aristocracy increasingly concerned with stability and continuity at a time of rapidly changing fortunes and a shifting balance of power. The last tomb paintings show a society looking forward as well as back.

67. Top: Anina tomb painted inscription, between Vanth and Charun, to Vel Anina, who died aged 22. Middle: Querciola-2 tomb, meeting with Charun figures, probably at the gate of the underworld (third century BC). Below: Meeting tomb, probably third century BC, toga figures (after *Scataglini 1*; *CR*, 344, 307).

5. Tarquinia and Rome

Urban topography

Several tracts of city wall are still visible, much of it good ashlar in local limestone, revealed in patchy excavations prior to 1946, and preserved best on the northern edge of the plateau (Figs 13; 68).[47] Generally, only a single or double row of stones was found, with occasional traces of a rubble rampart behind, 3 m wide. Wall towers are absent, although the trapezoidal foundations of a possible watchtower (3.7 x 3.3 m) lie near the westernmost point. While nothing survives around Civitucola, the Castellina promontory was strategically enclosed. A Doric capital and pilaster fragment could imply that there was once a temple here, yet the hillock, albeit distinctive, is rather peripheral and unlikely to have been a 'citadel', for which the Ara della Regina area (below) is a better candidate.[48] The wall crossed the promontory (Fig. 13) and seems to have followed the southern scarp back towards Civitucola, although it is mostly missing, probably due to erosion.

A perimeter road of stamped earth and stones, up to 9 m wide, hugged the outside wall at certain points. Another road, nearly 7 m wide, backed against the Romanelli (or north) gate. South of the Ara della Regina, trackways joined, one heading towards the temple, where resistivity surveys also suggest gridded roads, about 36 m apart.[49] At least five gates may have existed, although only the Romanelli gate, located at a natural entry point, has been revealed. Here the fine masonry, with occasional mason marks, survives up to eight courses and over 4 m in height (Plate XVII). Two facings enclose a rubble fill up to 3 m thick. The main feature is an inturned pincer-like entrance, probably once incorporating two sets of wooden doors under a turret, with a chamber below and a space in front where attackers could be fired on from two directions. Those approaching from the west would have had their right sides exposed, which are vulnerable since shields are normally on the left arm. At least two construction phases were noted as well as a rampart accessible by steps and stretches of pilaster walling on the interior face.

Some uncertainty persists about the date of the walls, which Romanelli placed in the fourth century BC on the basis of rather general inferences: for example, Rome's 'Servian' wall has a Livian date of 378 BC and the literary tradition attests armed conflicts in the fourth century. The pincer design of the gate also seems more in tune with the increasingly sophisticated arrangements of later fourth-century fortifications encouraged by new developments in siege warfare, seen in Sicily for example.[50] By this time, the Tarquinia walls were well developed and had perhaps been expanded and improved, even though an earlier phase of construction is now dated to the sixth century (p. 125). It is not clear whether the pilaster 'block and fill' masonry is necessarily later than the ashlar masonry in this area.[51]

169

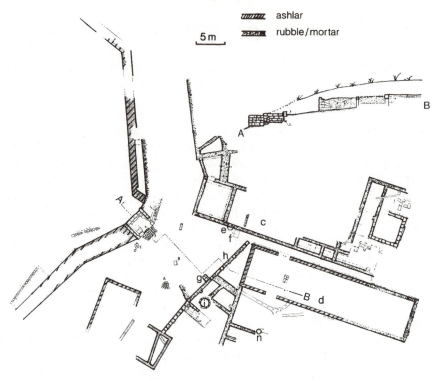

///// ashlar

▀▀▀ rubble/mortar

5 m

68. North gate area excavations (after Romanelli 1948).

To the south-west of Civita are remains of a semicircular podium, 28 m in diameter and up to 5.6 m high, of ashlar masonry in stepped courses against the slope (Fig.13: e). A shrine with a health cult is implied by the numerous fourth/second-century BC terracotta votives from the vicinity, including heads (three male, nine female and two children) and various anatomical parts, notably feet (15 examples), penises (12), uteri (10), tongues, windpipes, hands, arms, a heel, heart and breast.[52] One arm with three ulcers is unusual in showing the condition for which, presumably, a cure was being sought. Votive offerings of this kind are typical of later Etruscan 'popular' religion. Many of these shrines were perhaps used by the populace, regardless of class, although in this case two female heads with fine earrings, resembling those of Velia in the Orco or Shields tomb (above), suggest aristocratic women. Architectural terracottas also point to a Hellenistic date, although one or two fragments indicate a sixth/fifth-century BC phase.

Hundreds of terracotta votives (Fig. 69), predominantly sexual organs, as well as feet and heads, were also sealed by stones in a large pit near the Ara della Regina (but probably not associated with the temple). They

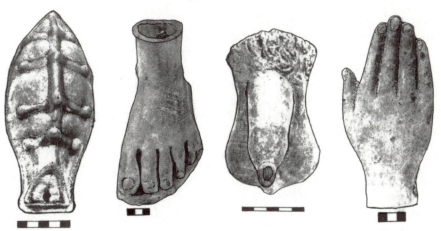

69. Terracotta votives from Civita (after Comella 1982).

imply a particular concern with health and reproduction by dedicants of rather low social status, slaves probably included, in the third/second century BC.[53] Another votive deposit, just outside the Romanelli gate, included nine two-faced heads of the second century BC, probably honouring the tutelary deity of the gate. Four male heads and one female are of an unusual double-faced type, possibly representing a youthful Janus (Etruscan *Ani* or else *Culsans*), and Demeter and Kore, resembling others from southern Italy and Sicily.

Information from the older excavations on Civita is sketchy and dogged by uncertainties about the dates and functions of buildings uncovered. In the north-west zone, a long rectangular building with a cistern contained finds of mixed date, prevalently Roman, while a long apsidal structure was flanked by a corridor, with column bases, perhaps re-used (Fig. 13: a, b).[54] Nearby rooms may have been residential. Unseparated stratigraphically, the finds include bucchero, Attic red-figure and Archaic terracotta fragments.

The main area investigated was behind the Romanelli gate (Fig. 68), where there were at least three superimposed roadways, the last two perhaps Roman and early medieval.[55] On entering the city here, one was confronted by a long building in ashlar masonry (d: 34 x 8.5 m), probably a shrine. Its foundations enclosed a pit full of animal bones, perhaps sacrifice remains and, at a slightly higher level, Hellenistic pottery and bronze items, resembling votives. Adjacent structures of rather inferior build, flanked by a long pilaster wall (h) and enclosing a pit (i), are perhaps of Hellenistic/Roman date. A stone-lined well (n), 10 m deep, contained oil lamps, glass, bronze and iron fragments, much of it Roman, and some misfired pottery, perhaps discarded from a nearby potter's yard. Another

171

long adjacent building (c) had some rooms with drains, terracotta piping and black and white mosaic flooring, but the function and date are uncertain. An earlier well (e), rich in bucchero, Italo-geometric and Proto-corinthian pottery and terracotta plaques signals occupation from Archaic times. Four terracotta bath tubs (*à sabot*) of Hellenistic type, were placed upside down nearby as if in temporary storage.

Beneath the ancient street level were more rock-cut tunnels (*cunicoli*) of the kind seen in area alpha, which was in use by the fifth century BC (p. 123); about 1.5 m high and 0.5 m wide, they were just large enough to crawl along, and accessible from vertical shafts or manholes (f, g) on the street above, spaced about 12 m apart, and covered by slabs. Three joining branches were followed for 54 m in various directions. Whether these were drains, sewers or water conduits, designed to channel rain water for use, has yet to be established.[56]

A *nenfro* block was recently discovered on the surface in this area, probably from a local shrine, inscribed with the names of two gods in capital letters, dated to the fourth/mid-third century: *Suri*, often assimilated with Apollo, who was a major deity in the Etruscan pantheon, and *Selvans*, a god of woods (like Latin *Silvanus*), but also a guarantor of boundaries.[57] There is also some evidence of a long, probably continuous street, up to 4 m wide, crossing Civita from east to west, resembling a *decumanus*, though it remains to be seen whether it can be dated earlier than the Hellenistic period.[58]

On western Civita, the sanctuary and roadway, revealed in recent excavations, changed little between the fifth and third centuries BC.[59] The old buildings may have been crumbling by now or even abandoned, although the north-south street was resurfaced and remained serviceable, equipped with a central drain, probably to channel water into the conduit below. A new building of unknown function with small rooms and geometric floor mosaics composed of red and white tesserae with marble insets, and elegant stucco on adjacent walls, was in use from at least the third/mid-second century BC (Fig. 51, lower right). Apart from a paved Roman road to the south, no other significant building is known here after this date, and the topsoil produced few Roman finds. The area seems neglected or undeveloped by comparison with the city centre, presumed to be in the vicinity of the Ara della Regina (Plate XVIII).

After an Archaic phase (p. 125), this temple was substantially modified in the early fourth century BC, as suggested by the style of architecture and the majority of terracotta decorations. It is broadly consistent with a 'Tuscan' temple as described by Vitruvius (not a peripteral temple as originally reconstructed).[60] It must have loomed large in views of the city from the south (Fig. 70). The enlarged basement (77 x 35 m) had 15 courses of tiered ashlar masonry over 7 m high on its southern side, on which the shrine consisted of the *cella*, anteroom and vestibule, set back between the corridors (*alae*). Rooms were perhaps now added to the rear.[61] The eastern façade was given a new scenographic entrance with two projecting corners enclosing a grand staircase (15.5 m wide) leading up to an intermediate level, from where two more stairways beside a central ramp led to the main floor. On the north side are stretches of street paving, about 4.5 m wide, with more paving and a small altar base near the south-east corner.

The superstructure is difficult to reconstruct. Architectural fragments include smooth column drums and bases, torus (convex) mouldings on the north basement, volute capitals and pillars with semicolumns. These were mostly of the grey *nenfro* traditionally worked locally and perhaps intended to provide colour contrast with the limestone ashlar. The pitched timber-frame roof was covered by tiles and mould-made revetments, including simas (gutters) with relief lotus and palmette decoration, geison revetments, and maenad and silenus antefixes, some of which are comparable with those of roughly contemporary Etruscan temples, notably that at Orvieto (Volsinii).[62] Particularly impressive is the famous figurative sculpture (Fig. 70; found at point z), a Hellenistic work in a classicising vein, originally placed above the pediment near the ridgepole (*columen*): it consists of a large terracotta slab (114 x 124 cm, restored) with two winged horses in high relief, yoked to a chariot (on an adjacent missing slab). A deity perhaps originally stood in the chariot or was about to mount it. Another fragment shows part of a draped female figure.[63]

On the lower terrace, protruding beyond the temple platform and thus disrupting its symmetry, two adjacent structures were erected (Fig. 70: x, y), resembling an altar and precinct, the latter perhaps surrounded by a metal or wooden transenna. They stand on top of the Archaic box-like structure (p. 125), and seem to preserve the location of an important place. It is tempting to speculate that the little precinct marks the spot where some prodigy occurred, but perhaps fanciful to associate this with Tages' appearance in the furrow (p. 75).

More obviously, the renovated temple, like the city wall and some of the large fourth-century tombs, reflects a new interest in big building projects and the public image of the city. On one level, this may be accounted for in terms of a generalised economic revival in southern Etruria and more efficient (or exploitative) relations between Tarquinia and the surrounding territory, although we do not know how labour for such projects was drafted, organised or paid for. If improvements to the fortifications can be explained most simply by concerns about security, the magnificence of the temple proclaims status and political ambitions, perhaps connected with the importance of Tarquinia (increasingly obvious after the demise of Veii) within the alliances of the time. The architectural references to Archaic precedents must also have emphasised the antiquity and pre-eminence of

70. Ara della Regina temple plan (77 x 35 m), phases (a: 600-550 BC, b: 550-500 BC, c: 400-350 BC, d: 300-250 BC) and terracotta winged horses (H 114 cm) (after *ET*, fig. 361; Bonghi Jovino 1997, 87).

the city's religious traditions – the importance of the building deriving from its appeal to myth and historical memory in the collective consciousness of the community.

Municipium and oblivion

The passing of the *lex Julia* bestowing municipial status and citizenship rights on Etruscan and Umbrian towns by 89 BC was a political watershed. Along with Cortona, Ferentium, Horta and Tuscana, Tarquinia was incorporated into the Stellatina tribe, an administrative division that formerly included Capena, Gravisca and the Latin colony at Nepi. It was probably a relatively advantageous association, with the potential to muster political influence. Tarquinia evidently escaped the confiscations associated with the Sullan settlements.[64] Henceforth the town seems to have been governed on conventional Roman lines by *quattuorviri* (*iure dicundo* and *aediles*). Limited evidence exists for other magistrates: *quinquennalis*, *curatur*, *praefectus* and *quaestor*, and a town council (*ordo*) of *decuriones*.

The late Republican period saw the persistence of essentially Etrusco-Hellenistic cultural traditions, but after the first century BC the character of the city is harder to gauge. The Roman remains, ironically, have suffered even more than the Etruscan on account of their greater exposure. Modest burials occur on Cretoncini and Gallinaro and are sometimes attested by insertions into older tombs on Monterozzi, but no specifically Roman cemetery or monumental tombs are known.[65] Funerary customs were changing. In the surrounding territory, cremations are known from *colombaria*, while fragments of tile tombs occur in topsoil. Monte Quaglieri has remains of a suburban villa with Arretine vases and mosaics, a late medieval bridge over the Marta could have Roman foundations, and surface finds of Roman pottery have suggested small-scale occupation on surrounding land; but the Roman and later periods are the least known.[66]

In the town centre, the Ara della Regina temple was maintained in the early empire, when some roof tiles were replaced and two small interconnecting rooms added on the north side. They contained some of the early imperial inscriptions (the *elogia*, discussed above), taken from commemorative monuments once standing nearby.[67] Surrounding streets were re-paved in places and a marble fountain basin (*labrum*) was set up in Augustan times, inscribed with neat letters giving the name of the *quattuorvir*, Q. Cossutius, who seems to have donated it instead of games (*ludi*) (Fig. 70).[68]

Roman brickwork, mosaics and a cistern, probably belonging to atrium and peristyle houses, are vaguely recorded north-east of the temple, and a large pilastered building, known from a drawing by Sangallo (p. 5), was possibly a water reservoir (*castellum*) linked with the baths uncovered in

1829, near the town centre, about 200 m west of the Ara della Regina. These are called the Tullian baths after second-century inscriptions naming P. Tullius Varro as the first sponsor of the construction, soon after AD 161, and his son, L. Dasumius, who continued the work in the reign of Antoninus Pius. The lengthy inscriptions on two marble slabs (erected in their honour by a *libertus*, P. Tullius Callistio) document two remarkably full and distinguished careers, packed with honours and appointments (see below).[69]

The building itself is little known. Terse notes mention a large brick and *nenfro* structure with a porticoed area, perhaps a palaestra, and an imposing polygonal hall with vaulted ceiling decorated with glass mosaics, probably a vestibule, where the inscriptions were prominently located for all to appreciate. In addition, there were rooms with hypocausts, marble pools, fine black and white mosaics of animals, nereids and sea monsters, cipollino columns, Corinthian capitals and verde antico. A good deal of terracotta and marble statuary probably came from here.[70] Nothing survives today and the documentation is inadequate, although it attests the presence of rich patrons and the desire to satisfy local aspirations with the provision of public buildings and typically Roman amenities. An inscription suggests that there was also another older set of baths, otherwise unknown, repaired by the emperor Antoninus Pius. In the same period (AD 180-183), we know of the appointment of a *curator*, L. Fabius Cilo, with special responsibility for Gravisca.

However, the condition of the old town quarters and the extent of new building are difficult to assess. Were peripheral areas decaying? There is still insufficient evidence to challenge Pallottino's first assessment of Roman Tarquinia as a place that enjoyed only moderate and temporary prosperity under the empire, notably in the second century AD. A sense of encroaching parochialism and demotion to provincial status is hard to avoid and was, arguably, inevitable. The main source of wealth now was presumably local agriculture, but confined to a much reduced territory. The subservience of neighbouring centres and the stimulus of a bustling port nearby were long past. There is, nevertheless, a risk of imposing preconceived notions. For example, it has sometimes been assumed that the countryside was everywhere in crisis. Yet the Tuscania survey suggests the presence of rural farmsteads in the early empire, some larger than their Etruscan forerunners, but with little sign of abandonment or replacement in favour of large villa estates. Further north, by contrast, the effects of conquest seem more dramatic, and large estates are known. In short, the Roman municipium merits more attention than it has hitherto received and needs to be understood on its own terms. The gloomy leitmotif of decline and melancholy nostalgia is perhaps easily overstated and potentially misleading.

If archaeology falls short, epigraphy comes to our aid. Religious titles, notably that of haruspex, imply continuity of tradition but also a rather self-conscious desire, promoted by Roman antiquarian interests and political programmes of the early Empire, to honour and preserve specific Etruscan customs. Interesting examples of the first century AD can be linked with the emperor Claudius, whose Etruscological interests are well documented, and with a law of AD 47 granting official support to priestly institutions (Tacitus, *Annals* 11.15). In fact, the Roman state was already consulting Etruscan diviners in the fourth century BC; it was a Spurinna, probably descended from the Tarquinian family, who warned Caesar to beware the Ides of March (Suetonius, *Julius Caesar* 81); and in Rome there were still Etruscan haruspices who were consulted in AD 408 when Alaric's Visigoths attacked.

The Tarquinia inscriptions present short commemorative eulogies (like *fasti* or *elogia*) to certain members of a distinguished college of 60 priests (*collegium LX haruspicum*), experts in the interpretation of religious phenomena, especially omens, and the conduct of ritual. These *haruspices peritissimi*, by contrast with the street-corner fortune-tellers and sooth-sayers lampooned in Latin literature, came from elevated ranks of the aristocracy and enjoyed the special prestige of a learned elite, charged with the guardianship of the *Etrusca disciplina*. They may well have had

71. Marble relief (reign of Claudius, H 78 cm) from Caere, with Etruscan cities (Vetulonia, Vulci, Tarquinia) personified (from photograph).

a base at Tarquinia, as also in Rome, and a *schola*, in recognition of the fabled importance of the city as the birthplace of Tages (p. 75). We may recall that Tarquinia is personified by a veiled priest on a early imperial marble relief (Fig. 71).[71]

The inscriptions refer to the interpretation or expiation of prodigies, such as lightning strikes, invocations of spells, consecrations to Jupiter and *Iustitia*, individual contributions to religious lore (*discipulina*) preserved in written form (*carmina*), and questions of jurisdiction, including the role of the Roman *decemviri sacris faciundis*, another sacerdotal elite who kept an eye on the activities of the *collegium*. The individuals thus commemorated were presumably citizens of Tarquinia, rather than of other Etruscan towns who also had members in the *collegium*. Like the *elogia* of the Spurinnae (p. 133), the inscribed marble slabs probably originally adorned a monument in the centre of the city, another example of the predilection for public commemoration. They also denote a feeling of civic pride based on local tradition and the old gentilicial obsession with genealogies and political or religious titles, which characterises the municipium's sense of identity, and perhaps a need to re-define this identity after the crises of recent centuries.

Since the character of the town had been changing gradually since the third century BC, the conversion to municipium presumably did not come as a sudden shock to the socio-political system, even if there were casualties. Certain families were doubtless better placed than others to exploit political changes and make new friends and alliances, leading to high office for some, but obscurity for many others.[72] For example, we know of a Republican senator, T. Numisius Tarquiniensis, possibly from Gravisca, who was a *legatus* in 167-169 BC; and from Cicero's case *Pro Caecina*, of M. Fulcinius, a local banker (*argentarius*) who had financial business in Rome probably in the mid-80s BC, and a distinguished wife, Caesennia; once widowed, she married Caecina, an aristocrat of Volterra and Cicero's client. Two possible descendants are C. and L. Fulcinius Trio, respectively praetor in AD 24 and consul in AD 31.

The Caesennii (Ceisinie) are certainly a local aristocratic family, associated with a painted Hellenistic tomb, for whom records exist from the late Republic to the third century AD. For example, L. Caesennius Lento was Caesar's legate in Spain in 45 BC, while L. Caesennius Paetus acceded to the consulship in AD 61, and was closely connected to the imperial family by marriage to Flavia Sabina, daughter of Flavius Sabinus, nephew of Vespasian; several of their descendants had distinguished careers. The Vestricii and Spurinnae (immortalised in the *elogia*) were old Tarquinian families, who had already entered the Senate by the reign of Claudius, if not earlier, and whose names fuse in the person of T. Vestricius Spurinna, a friend of Pliny the Younger, and governor of Germania Inferior, who erected the *elogia* monument honouring his ancestors.

The Tullii Varrones can be traced back to a civil magistrate (*decemvir*) of Nero's day, then praetor under Vespasian and proconsul in Macedonia, perhaps married to Dasumia Polla, daughter or sister of the Spaniard, L. Dasumius Hadrianus, consul in AD 93. His son, P. Tullius Varro (junior), who first sponsored the baths (above), as attested by the inscription, had a brilliant career, holding important positions in the provinces (*proconsul* in Baetica and Africa, *legatus Augusti propraetore* in Moesia), as well as the consulship in Rome in AD 127, *quinquennalis* at Tarquinia (the highest position in the municipium) and five times *praetor Etruriae*. This last title harks back to the old *zilath mechl rasnal* (p. 161) of the Etruscan League and was presumably now a slightly quaint honorific title with religious and commercial connotations, reinstated under the auspices of Augustus.

The family was also related by marriage in the second century AD to the Rufii *gens* of Volsinii, and had large landholdings (*fundi*) in the territory of Viterbo. Albeit of Latin origin – Varro is a good Roman *cognomen* – his son, L. Dasumius Tullius, consul in AD 152, is referred to as Tuscos, perhaps simply because he liked the idea of Etruscan descent. A member of various sodalities and an augur, he probably accompanied his father abroad, susbequently becoming prefect of the *aerarium Saturni*, *legatus propraetore* in Germania and Pannonia, and serving with Marcus Aurelius against the Marcomanni. Well-connected in the provinces, he was also a *patronus* of Lugdunum (Lyons). Other inscriptions naming local worthies of senatorial or equestrian class, of Latin origin, include C. Lucilius Proculus, military tribune with the *Legio V Macedonica* in Syria in the second half of the first century AD. Two other members of the family were *quattuorviri*.

It appears, therefore, that a few old Etruscan families with Latinised names retained prominence in the municipium, yet most others seem to have vanished. There is no trace, for example, of the Partunu, Velcha, Pumpu, Pulena and Camna. In fact, less than 20% of late republican and early imperial names known from Tarquinia are Etruscan, and less than 10% are certainly of Tarquinian origin. New names of solid Roman derivation are much more frequently associated with public office after the first century AD: Lucilius, Papirius, Petronius, Sevius, Valerius, for example. The change may be attributed partly to a Latin influx deriving from the foundation of Gravisca, if not from the disputed Gracchan colony, as well as expropriations and a weakening of the old families.[73]

Whatever their origin, the new ruling class evidently embraced some political and religious traditions of former times without any sense of discomfort or contradiction, especially in the Julio-Claudian period, when Etruscan ancestry even had a certain cachet. Allusions to a venerable

Etruscan past could doubtless be useful propaganda for ambitious municipial politicians. This must also have fitted a desire for renewal after the upheavals of the late republic, encouraged by the socio-political programme of Augustus, with its emphasis on reconciliation, incorporation and a return to old values – including the rediscovery of Italic traditions – as exemplified by some of the literary, artistic and antiquarian interests of the early empire. An inscribed Arretine potsherd from Gravisca suggests that the fomer cult of Adonis (p. 131) was now revived after more than a century of abandonment.[74]

Nevertheless, much had obviously changed: an altar base, possibly erected in AD 13, attests a cult of *Iustitia Augusta*; one inscription is possibly dedicated to *Divus Augustus*, another to Drusilla (probably after AD 41), Caligula's sister, deified in AD 38; a fragment from an equestrian statue or arch honouring Nero, was perhaps erected through the auspices of L. Caesennius Paetus (see above); and an inscription of AD 182 to the deified Marcus Aurelius supports the idea that a building dedicated to the cult of the imperial family lay in the vicinity of the Ara della Regina.[75] These were the new rivals to the old city gods, and their veneration is a reminder of the competition for imperial favour that characterised provincial capitals and towns in the early empire.

By the late empire, we know of few prominent families of Etruscan origin in the upper echelons of power, a sign of their final absorption by Rome. Moreover, there is little evidence of private patronage of public works in Etruria after the Antonines. Tarquinia provides some of the few exceptions of the third century AD, though this does not significantly alter the general impression of urban decline: C. Fabius Lucilianus, probably a rich senator, and father of a Numidian legate and consul under Alexander Severus, sponsored some building work near the Ara della Regina; and Q. Petronius Melior, around the time of Gordion III (AD 238-44), followed the example of the Varrones by restoring the *thermae*, although he showed little respect for their memory by having his own inscription cut on the back of the Varrones' original slabs. Perhaps there was a shortage of marble. At Gravisca, there is evidence of private house construction from a rather modest (80 m^2) third-century *domus*, abandoned by the early fourth century, and of a much more comfortable private residence of the fourth century with a courtyard, nymphaeum, private baths and *opus sectile* decoration.

The later history of Tarquinia is even more obscure. The traditional, perhaps excessively melodramatic view of decline and abandonment, aggravated by the ravages of barbarian hordes or Arab raids, could be misleading – a romanticised reaction to the end of classical antiquity. Admittedly, the passage of Alaric's Visigoths through the territory in AD 409-11 could have been traumatic; Castrum Novum seems to have been deserted and it must have been a fearful resident of Gravisca who hid a famous hoard of 174 gold *aurei* (coins from Valentinian I to Honorius, AD 364-423) under the floor of the late Roman *domus* (above) at about this time. Furthermore, Gravisca was proving to be rather insalubrious in the summer. Rutilius Namatianus, *praefectus urbi* at Rome under Honorius, noted the problem while sailing home to Gaul in 416 AD, and the fact that he chose to sail, rather than take the Aurelia, may also point to the latter's state of disrepair:

> Inde Graviscarum fastigia rara videmus
> Quas premit aestivae saepe paludis odor
> Sed nemorosa viret densis vicinia lucis
> Pineaque extremis fluctuat umbra fretis.
>
> (Then we sight Gravisca's scattered rooftops
> where often a marshy odour oppresses in summer,
> yet the wooded environs have verdant clustering groves
> and shadows of pines quiver by the water's edge.)[76]

On the other hand, there were coastal marshes even in Augustan times, and the place was at least still inhabited in the fourth/sixth centuries AD. The port may have had some continuing commercial activity, and not just as a fishermen's hamlet, judging by the presence of African oil amphorae (fourth/fifth century AD) and Byzantine pottery from coastal findspots in the region. There is mention of a bishop (*episcopus ecclesiae Graviscae*) in AD 504, possibly associated with the tradition of a local martyrdom under the emperor Decius (AD 249-51), and evidence of late Roman villas and possible granaries in the general area. Gravisca was possibly abandoned in AD 549, at the time of the siege of Centumcellae by Totila, or in the seventh century as a result of the Lombard dominion.[77]

Rather less can be said with confidence about late antique or medieval Tarquinia (Civita). In the fifth century AD, the names of three Tarquinian bishops are recorded: Lucianus, Apuleius and Proiectitius, possibly attesting North African origins, which might be connected with the exodus of Christians from that region as a result of the Vandal occupation. A rock-cut chapel ('San Savino') with traces of painted wall plaster has also been excavated on the southern edge of the Pian della Regina, associated with a cult of Santa Restituta, martyred in north Africa, and possibly dating from the late fifth/early sixth century; there are records of the church between 816 and 1198.[78] It is even conceivable that the Ara della Regina was eventually used for Christian worship; simple inhumations of a late date were inserted at various places. In the ninth century there were four churches on Civita, assigned to the bishops of Tuscania, under the control of the Abbey of San Salvatore at Monte Amiata.

Corneto, meanwhile, had evidently grown sufficiently in size and status by 1006 to be called *vico et castello et turre de Corgetu*. Nearby harbour facilities must have been functioning tolerably well from the tenth to the twelfth century, providing a temporary stopping place for Crusaders' fleets, including that of Richard Lionheart in 1190, and permitting commercial links to be maintained with Pisa, Genova and Venice. In the thirteenth century, Corneto is referred to as *horreum urbis* on account of its grain production, although by the seventeenth century the population seems to have dwindled to about 2,350.[79]

Medieval occupation on Civita, by contrast, is only dimly indicated archaeologically by traces of walls around Castellina, the last stronghold of a much depleted population, which came to a violent end in 1307, when the castle belonging to the Vaccari family was attacked by the inhabitants of Corneto. The event marked the culmination of a long period of petty resentments and rivalries between the two neighbouring but separate communities on the parallel promontories. Surviving documents suggest that Tarquinia was then abandoned and its few remaining inhabitants and some of its land absorbed by Corneto. Civita itself was acquired in the fifteenth century by the Roman Ospedale di Santo Spirito. Local variations of place names proliferated as 'Tarquinia' (Turquena, Turchina) was applied more loosely to adjacent land, confusing the memory of the original location of the Etruscan city. Ancient Etruria was long gone, but its discovery was about to begin.

Notes

See pp. 197-8 of the Bibliography for the abbreviations used in this section.

1. Discovery and Loss

1. Pallottino (1937, 13-38) for a detailed history of research, summarised in *ET*, 39-47; also Dasti (1878) on Corneto. From a large bibliography on the history of Etruscan studies, see Hus (1980, 297-349) for a synthesis, Cristofani (1983), the exhibition volumes: *BE*; *AE*; *FE*; *EE* (with references); Vickers (1985-86).

2. Pallottino (*DD*, 9) has also referred to the 'fascinating and yet painful' history of research in terms of discovery and loss.

3. Morandi (1995) for Santa Maria di Castello.

4. 'Post Cornetum, turritum et spectabile oppidum, gemino cinctum muro et ex alto colle maria longa despiciens. Huius in finibus Tarquinii fuerunt, olim civitas, nunc nichil preter nudum nomen ac ruinas, unde qui Rome regnarunt Tarquinii prodiere': Petrarch, *Itinerarium ad sepulcrum Domini* (*'Itinerarium Syriacum'*), 25; translated here by Allan Hood; for Bandini, see Weiss (1988, 55-6, 119).

5. 'Is Coritum mons est, veteris primordia Troiae, / Cornetum quo nunc urbs opulenta sedet. / Urbs muro non cincta fuit; mirabilis hic mons; / Conditor haud habuit pulvere calcis opus. / Oenotriae gens nulla prior. Monumenta supersunt, / Maxima et in multo plura reperta solo. / Sunt immensa albis exausta palatia saxis: / Multa nimis magnae mansio gentis erat. / Sive intus fontes excisa sedilia circum, / Spiramenta locis dant penetrare diem. / Celatum in quodam pulchrum est spectare lacunar: / Illa, reor, Coriti regia regis erat; / Sculpta ea perlegerunt oculi memoranda, / sed illud Priscum longa dies attenuavit opus, / Quin etiam effigies veterumque sepulcra virorum / Sunt et semideum, sunt simulacra deum. / Illic nulla tamen signata est litera testis: / Carment[um = is?] nondum venerat Italiam. / Plurima sunt oppleta, aditus si cura fuisset / Scrutari in multis multa reperta forent'. From Pallottino (1937, 20), and translated here by Allan Hood. See also Dasti (1878, 73-6); Dennis (1878, I, 392); Jannot (1982); De Grummond (1986, 25).

6. For this idea: Pallottino (1937, 20); Panofsky (1964); *CR*, 28-9, 335. However, Chastel (1959) notes that the source could easily have been a Roman standard-bearer, of which there are many on Trajan's column. For a more cautious view of Etruscan influences on Renaissance art, see also H. Blanck in *EE*, 240-5.

7. Pallottino (1937, 93, fig.13); *FE*, 40 (with references).

8. Cristofani (1983); Leighton & Castelino (1990) with references.

9. *Voyages du Père Labat en Espagne et en Italie*, vol. 5 (Amsterdam 1731, 33-42).

10. 'Raro è di goder tanto, perché le pitture appaiono belle e fresche al primo apparire delle grotte, ma dopo che l'aria c'entra liberamente, in pochi anni tutto si smarrisce e la malta, sopra cui sono, s'inumidisce e va cadendo': quoted by Cristofani (1983, 104) with references; *BE*, 45 (with eighteenth-century descriptions of the Mercareccia and Cardinal tombs).

11. *BE*, 123-7.

12. '... c'est-à-dire, au passage des âmes dans les Champs Elysées': quoted in De Caylus, *Recueil d'Antiquités Egyptiennes, Etrusques, Romaines et Gauloises*, vol. 4 (Paris 1761, 113).

13. 'An account of some subterraneous Apartments, with Etruscan Inscriptions and Paintings discovered at Civita Turchino in Italy', communicated from Joseph Wilcox by Charles Morton, *Philosophical Transactions*, Royal Society, London, vol. 53 (1763, 127-9); Haynes (2000b, 319-20).

14. 'O Pargoletto, che nel bronzo annoso / Serbi l'arte, e il valor d'etrusca mano, / Non ti lagnar se lunga etate ascoso / Nel Tarquinio giacesti altero piano: / Dono d'un Cuor gentile or vai fastoso / Di Roma augusta al REGNATOR SOVRANO, / E fra i recessi del Museo famoso / Ergi il volto ridente in Vaticano. / Forse già fu col ciglio alto indovino / Da gli Aruspici tuoi vaticinato / Il luminoso tuo nuovo destino; / E il lavoro immortal voller celato / A l'antica Terrena onda vicino / Per maturar di tua grandezza il fato'. See Springer (1987, 48-9).

15. Pallottino (1937, 22-3); Cristofani (1983, 194); *BE*, 128-32; Ridgway (1989) with further references.

16. G.B. Piranesi, *Diverse maniere d'adornare i camini ed ogni altra parte degli edifizi desunte dall'architettura Egizia, Etrusca, e Greca con un ragionamento apologetico in difesa dell'architettura Egizia e Toscana* (Rome 1769, 18-19).

17. 'Sospetto che abbiano chiamato Etrusco tutto ciò che non hanno capito': *AE*, 109, 140, n. 6.

18. Stendhal (1932, 208-9); see below, n. 28.

19. Avvolta (1829, 96, my translation): 'quasi estatico mi fermai a vedere tutto ciò che poteva vedersi in quella posizione, e particolarmente fissai lo sguardo sul guerriero giacente sopra il letto ... che mi si presentava di contro, ed in pochi minuti lo vidi quasi sparire sopra il letto; mentre più l'aria s'introduceva dentro la tomba, più l'ossidata armatura andava in minutissimi pezzi, non restando ... che il segno di quanto avevo veduto. Fatta ingrandire l'apertura ... feci calare un lavoratore per aiutarmi a discendervi; cosa che eseguii subito, facendo divieto che nessuno entrasse senza mio ordine. E però a tutto mio comodo vidi, esaminai, e notai tutto quello che posto era dentro la tomba, e che sono persuaso non recherà dispiacere di sentirlo descrivere ... e ne fui talmente sorpreso, che non posso esprimere quale effetto cagionasse nell'animo mio quanto avevo veduto; ma posso assicurare essere stato il più bel momento della mia vita'; also reported by Hamilton Gray (1841, 529); Dennis (1878, 388-9). An essay by Cardarelli ('La tomba del guerriero') in *Il cielo sulle città* (1939; see below) is inspired by the account, as well as the poems noted below.

20. 'Ce fut une évocation du passé qui n'eut pas même la durée d'un songe et disparut comme pour nous punir de notre téméraire curiosité': A. Noel des Vergers, *L'Étrurie et les Étrusques* (Paris 1862-64, vol. 2, 47).

21. Dennis (1878, 450).

22. Michaelis (1908, 56-84).

23. For an evaluation of the chaos and criminality surrounding the discovery of the Etruscans, see Ridley (2000, 323-37).

24. Hamilton Gray (1841, 272); *BE*, 188.

25. Moltesen & Weber-Lehmann (1991, 23); Banti (1967); *EE*, 417-18.

26. In the series entitled *Monumenti Inediti*: *BE*, 46. See *DD*; Colonna (1978; 1984c); Blanck & Weber-Lehmann (1987).

27. *DD*, 14.

28. 'Nous avons eu occasion, il y a trois ans, de voir M. Ruspi travailler à des nouvelles copies de ces peintures singulières .... Nous nous sommes assuré que M. Ruspi n'ajoutait rien au dessin vraiment sublime et aux brillantes couleurs des originaux. Jamais, par exemple, il n'a voulu corriger les mains qui ressemblent tout à fait à des pattes de renoncules. Mais nous apprenons que, depuis trois ans, les couleurs de ces fresques ont bien changé. Un chien lupo, placé au pied d'une des tables, dans un des tableaux représentant une cérémonie funèbre, et dont on admirait la vérité et l'esprit, a disparu entièrement': Stendhal, 'Les Tombeaux de Corneto', in H. Martineau (ed.), *Mélanges d'Art* (Le Divan, Paris, 1932 ed., 208). The first publication seems to have been in 1840; see also Hus (1976, 438, n. 3; 447).

29. Probably from G. Micali, *Monumenti per servire all'opera intitolata storia de gli antichi popoli italiani* (Milan, 1832); *BE*, 186-7.

30. Quote from Bentham (1842) by Colonna (1978, n.23); see also Hamilton Gray (1841, 4-7, 12).

31. See *DD*, 17; Sassatelli (1984); Moltesen & Weber-Lehmann (1991) with further references; Weber-Lehmann in *EE*, 414-31.

32. See above, n. 28; and A. Hus in *EE*, 446-9.

33. '... je me sens indigné contre les Romains, qui vinrent troubler, sans autre titre que le courage féroce, ces républiques d'Étrurie qui leur étaient si supérieures par les beaux-arts, par les richesses et par l'art d'être heureux ... C'est comme si vingt régiments de cosaques venaient saccager le boulevard et détruire Paris ... Les Romains ont été un grand mal pour l'humanité, une maladie funeste qui a retardé la civilisation du monde ...': Stendhal, *Rome, Naples et Florence* (1826; Gallimard, 1973 ed., 503-4, 508); also quoted and discussed by Hus (1976, 441; 1980, 329).

34. For *EP* (*Sketches of Etruscan Places*) references, see below, n. 45.

35. *BE*, 137-9.

36. Hamilton Gray (1841, 20, 229).

37. See the biography by Rhodes (1973); *BE*, 140-3; Haynes (2000b, 322) with further references.

38. Dennis (1878, I, 304).

39. Pallottino (1937, 29-30).

40. Dennis (1878, 302).

41. See, for example, 'Le Vase Étrusque' (1830) by Mérimée, or the poem by H. Ellison (1811-1890), 'On an undeciphered Etruscan urn, with an inscription'.

42. Ricks (1969, 1160-1).

43. R.C. Trench, *Poems from Eastern Sources* (London 1842, 217-18).

44. Many of Lee-Hamilton's poems have references to archaeology and antiquity. See, for example, Fletcher & Stokes (1984).

45. There have been numerous reprints. More recently, for example: 1972 (Folio Society) with a foreword by Lawrence Durrell; 1986 (Olive Press) with an introduction by Massimo Pallottino; the definitive annotated 1992 edition (Cambridge University Press, De Filippis ed.), with a popular version in Penguin (1999). All my page and line references (*EP*) are to the 1992 edition.

46. However, see the synthesis by Sagar (1985, 278-323).

47. A. Huxley, *Those Barren Leaves* (1925; ch. 9); *Point Counter Point* (1928; pt 4, ch. 5); on Forster's 'Macolnia shops' (in *Abinger Harvest*, 1936) see Haynes (2000b, 322-3).

48. Huxley, *Point Counter Point* (Chatto & Windus ed., 1949, 312).

49. '... quasi in atto di alzarsi e disposti a favellare, come se ne avessero abbastanza d'esser morti': V. Cardarelli, *Il sole a picco* (1929; Mondadori ed., 1962, 183).

50. From 'Nostalgia' (1942); for the full poem: *Opere complete* (G. Raimondi, ed., Mondadori, Milan, 1962, 416); and further commentary in Burdett (1999, 162-3), whose translation I have altered slightly.

51. In prose fiction, Tarquinia has helped to inspire detective novels, a children's story by H. Brinsmead, *Time for Tarquinia* (Hodder & Stoughton, Sydney,1981); and, albeit set in Caere, *The Augur's Daughter: A Story of Etruscan Life* (Rubicon Press, London, 1987) by the Etruscan scholar, Sybille Haynes.

52. Dasti (1878); Naccarato (2000).

53. Pallottino (1937, 33-8); *TE*, 111-2 (with references).

54. For example, D'Atri (1977); Bartoloni (1981); Delpino (1991); Toms (1998); Iaia (1999b).

55. Pallottino (1937).

56. Romanelli (1948).

57. Regular reports appeared in the journal *Prospezioni Archeologiche*, published by the Lerici Foundation. See *EC*, 49-52; Cavagnaro Vanoni (1987) for an appraisal, with bibliography.

58. See *TE*, 61-7.

59. Bradford (1957) for a summary and further references; for aerial photography at Tarquinia, see *Tarquinia 1*, 5-17.

60. Cavagnaro Vanoni (1996); *Scataglini 1-2*.

61. See bibliography: *MAT*.

62. See *TE*, 45-51 (with references); Torelli (1975).

63. Del Lungo (1999). An interesting source of information is the late thirteenth-century Corneto archive, published by Supino (1969).

64. Perticarari and Giuntani (1986); see also Cataldi (1997).

65. 'Was gut ist, ist Griechisch: was Schlecht, Etruskisch': see Chapter 4, and Arias (1989, 648) for this quote and an historical overview.

66. For examples of Etruscan themes and references in modern art and popular culture, see *FE*.

67. The Tarquinia museum has just recently exhibited the new findings from the Civita excavations.

68. See, for example, *CR*, 91-9; Bettini (1987).

69. Statistics from *DD*, 65-70; *PE*, 201-3.

70. Hamilton Gray (1841, 215).

2. Origins and Growth

1. Pallottino (1937, 96-8); Hencken (1968a, 5-17) on topography.

2. Pallottino (1937, 99-106) for old controversies about the location of the Etruscan settlement; see Chapter 1.

3. *Tarquinia 1*, 9; Pelfer (1998); Mandolesi (1999, 194).

4. *ET*, 200-2, 381-3; *Tarquinia 1*, 92-9, 103-44; *TE*, 8, 59-61.

5. Gianfrotta (1988, 13); *Tarquinia 1*, 7-8, 13-14.

6. Pallottino (1937, 41); Fantini *et al.* (1988) on malaria.

7. Hencken (1968a, 10-17); Pelagatti (1989); *Tarquinia 1*, 5-17.

8. Barich *et al.* (1968); *ET*, 55-62; Fugazzola Delpino (1988); Mandolesi (1999, 155-78). For sporadic Neolithic-Copper Age finds from Civita: Mandolesi (1999, 145-6).

9. Recent general surveys: Bartoloni (1989); Bietti Sestieri (1992).

10. Mandolesi (1999).

11. Cassano & Manfredini (1978); Mandolesi (1999, 165-6) with further bibliography.

12. Pottery chronologies are not so reliable as to permit this close dating (*Tarquinia 1*, 146). If ceramic types, particularly from settlements, are longer-lived than generally allowed, this phase could be later (i.e. Villanovan, ninth century, or even early eighth century BC). Arguments for lowering and compressing the chronology include the shallow deposits and lack of a clear typo-chronological evolution of pottery types (those in later layers differ little from those in layers below). For the second Iron Age hut: *TE*, 30-2.

13. However, the bronze pendant could date to the late eighth century BC, while material of 750-700 BC covered the burial. A later dating would also allow it to be associated with the nearby burials of the mid-eighth/early seventh centuries. Skeletal reports in *ET*, 197-9; Fornaciari & Mallegni (1987); *Tarquinia 1*, 100-2.

14. *Tarquinia 1*, 165; Bonghi Jovino (1996, 454); *TE*, 24.

15. Chiaramonte Treré (1987); *Tarquinia 1*, 219; and, for example, *The Etruscans*, 274; Haynes (2000a, 28). The pathology of individual 293 has also led to discussions about the treatment of abnormal or handicapped children in antiquity, a subject with a certain resonance at Tarquinia in view of the Tages story (p. 75).

16. Two reconstruction drawings (*Tarquinia 1*, pl. 143:1-2) seem rather fanciful, based on little more than post-holes. The Iron Age site presents obvious difficulties: poor preservation and complex stratigraphic relationships.

17. Cataldi (1994, 61); Mandolesi & Pacciarelli (1990); Mandolesi (1994; 1999, 44-5, 58-60, 112); Iaia *et al.* (1998); *TE*, 7-10, 14-18; Pacciarelli (2000, 165-70). Mandolesi (1999) assigns surface finds of Iron Age incised ware to the ninth century BC; but they could be later, perhaps even late eighth/early seventh century, since comparable material comes from the Civita layers of this period (*Tarquinia 1*, pls 114-23); it is not certain, as often assumed, that the latter should be dismissed as 'residual'. This would change certain conclusions and, for example, obviate the need to propose lacunae on Cretoncini between the mid-eighth and late seventh century.

18. Linington *et al.* (1978); Linington (1982a; 1982b); *CE* 47.

19. Pacciarelli (2000, 170) on the possiblity of more than one phase. Bruni (1995, 218-9) suggests a link with Villa Tarantola-Ripagretta tombs, rather than Arcatelle.

20. See Mandolesi (1999, 136) with references.

21. Mandolesi (1999, 169) assigns the Calvario material broadly to the Iron Age (*iniziale* and *recente*). See also Pacciarelli (2000, 170).

22. E.g. Di Gennaro (1988); Bietti Sestieri (1992, 40); although survey sites are sometimes rather speculatively dated. Rendeli (1993) and Barker & Rasmussen (2000, 60-3) for a critique.

23. Di Gennaro (1986, 137); Rendeli (1993, 227) is more sceptical.

24. Pacciarelli (2000, 171-6).

25. Bartoloni & Delpino (1975). On Villanovan Campania: Bietti Sestieri (1996, 307-8, 328-354); Cornell (1995, 153-6). South Italian vases at Tarquinia: Hencken (1968a, fig. 127g); Delpino (1984; 1989); *CE*, 62; *EM*, 59; *ET*, 76.

26. Bartoloni (1989, 165); Gras (1987, 144) with references.

27. Hencken (1968a, 541-58; 1968b, 97-112) emphasised central European connections.

28. E.g. a skyphos of about the mid-eighth century BC, and hydria, perhaps slightly older: *CE*, 60-1; *ET*, 216.

29. For the jug (Fig. 18: c), see *ET*, 78 (dated around the mid-eighth century BC); *Principi* 128, (with bibliography, here dated late ninth/early eighth century).

30. Pallottino (1937, 133-56) and Hencken (1968a), with references to original publications by Pernier and others; Bartoloni & Delpino (1970); Buranelli (1983); *CE*, 50-64; *EM*, 57-60, 74-81; Toms (1992-93); Delpino (1995); Iaia (1995); Zifferero (1995); *TE*, 81-93 (Villa Bruschi-Falgari). For tombs around Civita: Mandolesi (1999, 146-9) with references. Major studies are by Toms (1998) and Iaia (1999a). The conventional chronology is followed here, despite the possibility that the Iron Age began earlier, in the tenth century BC: see Iaia (1999a, 14-22); *TE*, 3-5. However, the conventional dating for the later tombs may be too high. For example, many of those of phase IIA2-IIB2, which Iaia (1999a) and others date from 775-750 BC, in my opinion could well be later (i.e. 750-725 BC). Nor am I convinced by the suggestion of Delpino (1989) that certain bowls on stands from Villanovan tombs necessarily date well before the mid-eighth century BC and therefore betray 'precolonial' Greek influence.

31. D'Atri (1977); Pacciarelli (2000, 242-50), for Le Rose.

32. Hencken (1968a, 24, fig.13, a-b); the second example, however, looks as though it might have been an urn or stone chest cover. Finds of *nenfro* cippi are reported from the Savino valley: Cataldi (1994, 62). For mounds in the Tolfa-Allumiere region: Domanico (1995): *EC*, 120.

33. Toms (1998); this does not include the Villa Bruschi tombs.

34. Bruni (1995, 236-7); Iaia (1999a, 115).

35. Bietti Sestieri (1992, 108).

36. Iaia (1999a, 118) notes the case of a child burial at Veii with a helmet cover.

37. Hencken (1968a, 192, 198); Toms (1992-93).

38. Tuck (1994).

39. De Angelis (2001, 297-8).

40. *CE*, 50, 53; Bartoloni *et al.* (1987); Iaia (1999a, 22-3).

41. See also Maggiani (1997) for a discussion.

42. Hencken (1968a, 115).

43. Pallottino (1937, 161-2); Hencken (1968a, 593-6) for tables and discussion.

44. Zifferero (1995, 259) suggests the pendants are prototypes of Roman bullae.

45. Hencken (1968a, 191) 'Dolium with turtle girdle'.

46. Hencken (1968a, 201-20); Kilian (1977).

3. The Rise of the City State

1. For major studies of this period at Tarquinia (with further references), see Pallottino (1937, 181-234); Hencken (1968a); *ET*, 203-46; Bruni (1995). Records of 150 chamber tombs and 80 trench graves (Pallottino 1937, 187) are obviously only a fraction of the original numbers. Mandolesi & Pacciarelli (1990, on Cretoncini); Gras (1987, 143, on Gravisca).

2. One association of a Protocorinthian *oinochoe* (700-675 BC) with a biconical urn, crested helmet and Villanovan pots is controversial (Romanelli tomb 66: *Ceramica*, 251-2 with references; Toms 1992-93, 146). However, I am not convinced that it must be rejected *a priori*. If the *oinochoe* were an early example of its type (about 700 BC), the tomb would be only 50 years or so later than the warrior tomb at Veii and about contemporary with the Tarquinia Warrior tomb (p. 56) and with the crested helmets seen on the tripod stand (Hencken 1968a, 363). Moreover, the use of Villanovan crested helmets in the early/mid-seventh century is shown by tomb 89 at Verucchio (e.g. Torelli 1997, 52-86, with references). A period of co-existence between traditional urn burials, traditional pottery production and early Greek imports seems natural. Why should the local burial rite have disappeared just because the first imports arrive? It is also possible that poorer tombs, lacking imports, have been wrongly back-dated to the earlier Villanovan period by default.

3. *ET*, 224-30; Bruni (1995, 236, n. 81).

4. Bruni (1995, 238); Ridgway (1997).

5. *TE*, 95-9.

6. Hencken (1968a, 345-52); *EM*, 74-80; *Principi*, 214-5.

7. The tombs were often called *tombe a corridoio* or *egizie* in the nineteenth century (Bruni 1995, 220). Westphal noted 600 mounds in 1830, Gell mentioned 300, and Pallottino 100 (1937, 187, 194), though many of these could have belonged to the sixth century. *EC*, 120 (Caere).

8. Pallottino (1937, 183); Hencken (1968a, 364-78); *CE*, 93-5.

9. *ET*, 221-3.

10. *ET*, 277-92.

11. Pallottino (1937, 186); Hencken (1968a, 378-80; Doganaccia); *ET*, 203-14; Cataldi (1993b, 84-8); *ET*, 206. Rendeli (1993, 236) underline their territorial significance; Naso (1996a, 74, n. 20) with further references.

12. For example, the altar and forecourt at Grotta Porcina and the vestibules in the Cuccumella necropolis at Vulci; Colonna (1993); Torelli (1997, 122).

13. Avvolta (1829, 95-100); Pallottino (1937, 67, 184); Hencken (1968a, 397-401).

14. Avvolta (1829, 97) found only burnt bones of the warrior; was the corpse cremated and then 'reconstructed' with armour and dress?

15. Naso (1996a) with a discussion and further references.

16. E.g. Torelli (1981, 71-83); Cornell (1995, 82-5).

17. E.g. *The Etruscans*, 255-71 (for a recent discussion).

18. A question much debated: e.g. d'Agostino (1990); Barker & Rasmussen (2000, 259-61) with references.

19. Canciani (1974); *ET*, 149-51, 233-4; *Ceramica*, 12-13; Ricci Portoghesi (1968); Bruni (1994), with further references.

20. *Tarquinia 2*, 43-97.

21. *ET*, 151-3, 224-37; Palmieri (2001).

22. Hencken (1968a, 402-6); *Oro*, 277; *ET*, 47-8, 221-3.

23. Hencken (1968a, 350); Haynes (2000a, 17).

24. For example, the stepped slabs (*lastroni a scala*) have been dated by some from the second half of the seventh century (see Chapter 4, n. 6).

25. *ET*, 93-111; *Tarquinia 1*, 167-81, 219-20; *TE*, 21-44.

26. *ET*, 141-2; Bonghi Jovino (1987).

27. Bonghi Jovino (1991, 171, n. 2) with references; *The Etruscans*, 274.

28. Bagnasco Gianni (1987); Torelli (1987); *Tarquinia 1*, 175-8.

29. Bonghi Jovino (1991).

30. *Tarquinia 2*, 2; Mandolesi & Pacciarelli (1990, 25).

31. *ET*, 200-2, 381-3; *Tarquinia 1*, 92-9, 103-44.

32. *TE*, 17-19, for a disucssion.

33. Rendeli (1993, 237-45); Iaia & Mandolesi (1993); Barker & Rasmussen (2000, 144-7).

34. Pallottino (1937, 234-48); *ET*, 29. See especially Wood (1980). This translation from Wood (1981, 96-7).

35. Cicero (*De Div.* 2.50), however, states that the whole of Etruria assembled to hear the sacred lore, which was then transcribed. Discussion also in Bonfante & Bonfante (2002, 10).

36. Pallottino (1930); Cristofani (1987a); Torelli (1988); Pairault Massa (1992, 143-5) for different readings.

37. Pallottino (1930; 1937, 234-48); Briquel (1984, 225-59). See also Bonfante & Bonfante (2002, 10) for references to Tarchon as the inventor of divination.

38. *The Roman Histories of Dionysius of Halicarnassus* (Heinemann, Loeb ed., 1939); see also Cicero, *De Rep.* 2.19.34.

39. Livy, *The Early History of Rome* (Penguin Books, Harmondsworth, 1960).

40. Ampolo (1976-77); Cornell (1995, 133); Rasmussen (1997); but compare Musti (1987) and Briquel (1988).

41. Pallottino (1937, 232-3); *TLE*, nos 78-157; Hencken (1968a, 420-3); *ET*, 172-8.

42. *CIE, 3,1*; Bagnasco Gianni (1987; 1996, 163-87).

43. Jucker (1969); Cristofani (1971).

44. Hencken (1968a, 381, fig. 371g).

45. Bietti Sestieri (1997), by contrast, argues that Villanovan centres were already organised as federations of states in the tenth/ninth centuries, an idea supported by some prehistorians (notably A. Guidi). See also Pacciarelli (1994). For counter-arguments, see for example Harris (1989).

46. One theoretical framework for the Etruscan case is that of peer polity interaction (Renfrew 1986), which avoids an overly polarised position of local versus external causation.

4. Urbs Florentissima

1. Linington *et al.* (1978); *CR*, 22; *ET*, 312-6; Cavagnaro Vanoni (1987; 1997).

2. See, for example, Cornell (1995, 105-8).

3. Pallottino (1937, 48, 68); Hencken (1968a, 10-17); *Tarquinia 1*, 5-17.

4. Bradford (1957, 131-9); Linington *et al.* (1978); Linington (1980); *PE*, 122. See Banti (1967) on nineteenth-century drawings, including a 'stepped' tumulus.

5. *The Etruscans*, 368 (Gallinaro lion); Hencken (1968a, 389) for the warrior relief.

6. Pallottino (1937, 197-207); Brendel (1995, 119-24); Bruni (1986) suggests an earlier dating going back to 650 BC; *ET*, 273-7; see Maggiani (1996; 2000b) for discussion and reconstruction.

7. *ET*, 297-8 (terracotta box); de la Genière (1987, 205); Ferrari (1988, 80).

8. Cataldi (1987); *PE*, 150-3.

9. Pallottino (1937, 250-8) also mentions a stone sarcophagus; de la Genière (1987); Bruni (1995, 235); Cavagnaro Vanoni (1997, 118-19); *TE*, 101-2.

10. Martelli (1981); Pierro (1984); *CE*, 206-8; *Tarquinia 2*, 261-3 (with references).

11. Pallottino (1937, 265-77); Campus (1981); Tronchetti (1983); Pierro (1984); *ET*, 51-2; Cataldi (1993b, 122-3).

12. Spivey (1991); Lewis (2003) for a discussion.

13. Bruni (1995, 236, n. 80).

14. Pallottino (1937, 284-96); Ferrari (1988); *ET*, 51-2; Cataldi (1993b, 123-5).

15. Szilagyi (1972); *CE*, 164; *Ceramica*, 23-30; *Tarquinia 2*, 177-204.

16. Camporeale (1972); *ET*, 293-5; *CE*, 145; Gran-Aymerich (1988); Bruni (1989).

17. *ET,* 296-7.

18. Pallottino (1937, 277-84); Ginge (1987); Spivey (1987); *Ceramica,* 31-42.

19. Pallottino (1937, 352); Brendel (1995, 213-14); *ET,* 296.

20. Pallottino (1937, 209); *Principi,* 129-30.

21. Bini *et al.* (1995).

22. Pallottino (1937, 353).

23. Pallottino (1937, 355-63); *ET,* 48-50; *TE,* 116-22.

24. Pallottino (1937, 349-51); Brendel (1995, 179-81); Martelli (1985); *ET,* 295-6; Briguet (1988) suggests the Louvre banquet scene is largely a nineteenth-century restoration.

25. The bibliography on tomb paintings is vast and continually growing. Much of the groundwork was laid by Pallottino (1937, 296-347; 1952). Markussen (1979) gives a useful collation. The best illustrated catalogue is by Steingräber (*CR*). Important new contributions include exhibition volumes (*DD, PE*), Cavagnaro Vanoni (1987), Arias (1989) for the history of research; Thuillier (1985), Weber-Lehmann (1985), Cerchiai (1987), Moltesen & Weber-Lehmann (1991), Naso (1996b), Torelli (1997a, 122-51); d'Agostino & Cerchiai (1999). For later Etruscan painting see also Chapter 5.

26. Pallottino (1937, 81-2) first attempted to elucidate the layout and evolution of the cemetery. For a distribution map, see *CR,* 388-9. Cavagnaro Vanoni (1987) for corrections and statistics.

27. Dates given here are mainly as per *CR*; some of them are quite approximate.

28. Pallottino (1937, 338-44); *CR,* 58.

29. Phrygian tombs with rock-cut details of furniture and architecture also resemble those of Caere (Barker & Rasmussen 2000, 249).

30. Cristofani (1976) emphasises East Greek analogies. See also Gras (1987, 147-9); *PE,* 179-86.

31. The only possible artist's name (Colonna 1975, 184-5; Torelli 1997a, 126) is that of an Etruscan: Aranth of [servant of] Heracanasa [Hercnas], inscribed in the Jugglers tomb beside a naked man defecating, presumably an apotropaic (or simply humorous?) gesture (p. 119).

32. *CR,* 91-9; *ET,* 270-2.

33. Jannot (1988).

34. Dated to the late seventh century in *PE,* 121-3.

35. Small (1971; 1994); Cristofani (1987b).

36. Pairault Massa (2001).

37. E.g. Rallo (1989); Izzet (1998) with references.

38. Cicero, *Tusculan Disputations* (Heinemann, Loeb ed. 1927).

39. See also the Monkeys tomb (Chiusi); Szilagyi (1981) thinks the juggler held cakes (rewards).

40. See Thuillier (1985) for an exhaustive study.

41. *ET,* 265-7 (Olympics tomb); Jannot (1993); Barker & Rasmussen (2000, 246-7, 255-7); Bonfante & Bonfante (2002, 12).

42. *CR,* no. 91; *ET,* 267-9.

43. Harari (1992).

44. Seen, for example, in the work of d'Agostino (1989; d'Agostino & Cerchiai 1999), Torelli (1997a), Pairault Massa (1992; 2001).

45. Torelli (1997a, 138-9) with references.

46. Perhaps the same Spuriana who donated an ivory lion (a *tessera hospitalis?*) in the temple of Fortuna and Mater Matuta in Rome according to Torelli (1981, 165); *The Etruscans,* 554; Bonfante & Bonfante (2002, 31).

47. Torelli (1997a, 122-51) develops this thesis.

48. d'Agostino (1983) and Torelli (1997a, 123) prefer the latter view.

49. Rouveret (1988), with further references.

50. Sordi, for example, has underlined this point: *ET*, 36.

51. *CR*, no. 59; Walberg (1986); Pairault Massa (1992, 84-5); Barker & Rasmussen (2000, 216-19). Torelli (1997a, 130) regards the Biga tomb scene as a preparation of food for the deceased; Åkerström (1981) for a tentative identification of the judgement of Paris in the Olympics tomb.

52. Pairault Massa (2001).

53. Cf. Spivey (1997, 114-17).

54. Brendel (1995, 168); Pairault Massa (1992, 80-4); Spivey (1997, 75-6); d'Agostino & Cerchiai (1999, 108).

55. Cf. n. 31 (above).

56. Cataldi (1987); Brendel (1995, 271).

57. E.g. Brendel (1995, 187-91); Barker & Rasmussen (2000, 258-9).

58. Compare, for example, Rouveret (1988, 208-9); Pairault Massa (1992, 86); Torelli (1997a, 142); d'Agostino & Cerchiai (1999, 61-71).

59. Chiaramonte Treré (1987); *ET*, 112-31; *Tarquinia 1*, especially 183-212; *TE*, 27-44.

60. Chiaramonte Treré (1987, 85); Torelli 1987; *Tarquinia 1*, 203, n. 6.

61. Pelagatti (1987); Torelli (1987, 133); *Tarquinia 1*, 207. For the northward extension of the street, see Bonghi Jovino (1996, 454).

62. *Acque profonde*; Padovan (1999, 97-101); *Civita*, 27-62.

63. Romanelli (1948); Torelli (1975, 13-22); *Santuari*, 70-3; *ET*, 355-76; Bonghi Jovino (1994; 1997); *TE*, 45-51, 69-72.

64. Pelagatti (1987; 1989); Cataldi (1994); Massabò (1994); *Tarquinia 1*, 207.

65. Romanelli (1948); Pelagatti (1989); Fontaine (1994); *TE*, 73-5.

66. Romanelli (1948, 204) gives a surface area of 135 ha (= $1.35\ \text{km}^2$), compared with 121 ha by Judson & Hemphill (1981). See Mandolesi & Pacciarelli (1990, 21) on Cretoncini.

67. Heurgon (1964, 145-8); Cornell (1995, 204-8); *Architettura*, 43 (Acquarossa); Harris (1989, 379); Perkins & Walker (1990).

68. Perkins (1999, 165-70) with references.

69. *ET*, 142-72; discussion in *Tarquinia 1*, 201; *Tarquinia 2*; *TE*, 53-7.

70. Ciaghi (1993).

71. On Gravisca: Torelli (1971; 1977; 1982; 1997); Boitani & Torelli (1971; 1999); *CE*, 175-86; *ET*, 250-5; Boitani (1992); *TE*, 125-40, with references; and the monograph series now being published: e.g. Johnston & Pandolfini (2000). Frau (1982) suggests there was an artificial inner port, like a Carthaginian cothon.

72. Slaska (1985).

73. See, for example, articles in Camporeale (2001).

74. Several English editions have translated this wrongly as 'his mother was a slave in the household of Tarquinius': Cicero, *De Re Publica* (Heinemann, Loeb ed. 1928). In fact, *Tarquiniensis* should refer to the place, not a person. According to Livy (1.39.5), however, she was from Corniculum. On literary sources for the period: Pallottino (1937, 363-72); *ET*, 29-30. My chapter heading derives from Cicero's description (*Rep.* 2.19.34) of the Tarquinia to which Demaratus came: '*in urbem Etruriae florentissimam*'.

75. On Mastarna and Vulci, see for example, *TF*; Cornell (1995, 130-41).

76. *The Geography of Strabo* (Heinemann, Loeb ed., 1923).

77. Livy, *The Early History of Rome* (Penguin Books, Harmondsworth, 1960).

78. Perhaps the battle referred to by Dionysius (5.3.2; 5.14) as the Campus Naevius. Livy (1.60) states that Tarquin went into exile at Caere.

79. T.B. Macaulay, *Lays of Ancient Rome* (1842; Horatius, 1.2).

80. Torelli (1981, 183-214) for a broader discussion.

81. Torelli (1975, 30-3, 56-66) for 414 BC; Cornell (1978) is unconvinced; Colonna (1984a) proposes the Lipari campaign and makes much of the Etruscan sacrifice (*votum*) of prisoners to Apollo. Moreover, the *Orco* tomb probably belonged to a *gens* Murina, and not Spurinna as Torelli thought (Morandi & Colonna 1996; see Chapter 5).

82. Maggiani (1998, 102-5).

83. Torelli (1981); Pairault Massa (1996); *The Etruscans* 255-71, for recent discussions and references.

84. Pallottino (1937, 365-7); *ET*, 172-8; *CIE* 3,1; Torelli (1981, 185) associates the scarcity of political inscriptions with the fifth-century 'crisis'.

85. E.g. Barker & Rasmussen (2000, 167-78); Perkins (1999).

86. The epithet 'Lacus Volsiniensis' (Vitruvius 2.7.3) may refer to after 265 BC, when Velzna (probably Orvieto) was transferred to Volsinii (Bolsena): Barzanò (1998).

5. Tarquinia and Rome

1. For a commentary on sources for the fourth century BC: Pallottino (1937, 508-12, 534-42); Harris (1971); Torelli (1975, 82-92); *ET*, 29-37; Sordi (1987). Varronian dates are used here; see Cornell (1995, 399-402).

2. Sordi (1987, 162) dates this before the destruction of Veii, although Livy implies that it happened later.

3. Translation from: B.O. Foster, *Livy III* (Heinemann, London, Loeb ed., 1924). Another famous example of an Etruscan sacrifice of prisoners is that of the Phocian Greeks by Caere after the battle of Alalia (about 540 BC) according to Herodotus (1.167).

4. This colourful description might have some basis in reality, while reminiscent of the suspicion with which Livy regarded many of Rome's neighbours, notably the Samnites, associated with sinister snake-handling rites and witchcraft: Dench (1995, 159-66).

5. *Indutiae* at this time probably meant not much more than a cessation of hostilities, perhaps sometimes with a penalty prescribed for the weaker party, but did not necessarily signify a permanent resolution of the conflict in the way that a *foedus* attempted to guarantee by means of constitutional changes in the relationship between the parties: Harris (1971) with discussion.

6. Contrast, for example: Harris (1971, 45-7) for the possibility of an earlier date just after the Gallic disaster; Torelli (1981, 220) for 353 BC; Cornell (1995, 321) and Oakley (1998, 199-202) for 273 BC.

7. Torelli (1975, 67-92) for the fourth century; Cornell (1995, 231) prefers a fifth-century date.

8. Sordi (1987) is sceptical; Harris (1971, 49-61) and Cornell (1995, 355-8) less so.

9. Pallottino (1937, 538); Harris (1971, 59) with references.

10. An association with a fragmented inscription is contested by Torelli (1975, 142-6).

11. Sordi (1987, 167). Might this be connected with the *elogia* of Aulus Spurinna?

12. Romanelli (1948, 267); Torelli (1975, 162, 186).

13. *CE*, 373; Sordi (1991).

14. Harris (1971, 92-4, 141).

15. Torelli (1975, 191), with references for and against, is more persuaded of its significance than Harris (1971, 205).

16. For Monterozzi tombs of this period, see Pallottino (1937, 383-97); *ET*, 311-24; Cavagnaro Vanoni (1972; 1977; 1987; 1996); Cataldi 1994, 62; *TE*, 103-8.

17. Cavagnaro Vanoni (1997).

18. Mallegni *et al.* 1980; Bartoli *et al.* 1989-90, 257; Mallegni (1991); Becker (1993).

19. In a more recent study several age estimates are lower or less specific, casting doubt on the earlier suggestion of an average adult male and female life-span of 41 and 47, which would be quite high for this period (compare: Mallegni *et al.* 1980, 208; Bartoli *et al.* 1989-90, 256). The authors also note an apparent lack of children's burials at Monterozzi.

20. Corruccini & Pacciani (1991); Baggieri (2001); *TE*, 122.

21. *ET*, 324-40; *Scataglini 1, 2*.

22. Pallottino (1937, 454-81); Cataldi (1993b, 103-5); Bartoloni & Baglione (1987); *Scataglini 2*, 149-53; Gentili in Cavagnaro Vanoni (1996).

23. On pottery, see, for example, nn. 16, 21 above; Pianu (1980; 1982; 1988); *ET*, 342-6; Cavagnaro Vanoni & Serra Ridgway (1989); *Tarquinia 2*, 205-59; *TE*, 54-7 (all with more references).

24. For bronze-working: Bini *et al.* (1995). Goldwork: *Oro*, 306; *TE*, 111-22.

25. Stefani (1984).

26. Viterbese sites: Barbieri (1996). Settlement patterns: Perkins (1999); Barker & Rasmussen (2000, 271).

27. *ET*, 298-302; Catalli (1987; 1988); *Scataglini 2*, 169-71.

28. Pairault Massa (1988) for discussion (with references).

29. Serra Ridgway (2000, 304).

30. From a large bibliography on sarcophagi, see especially Pallottino (1937, 433-81, 518-29); Herbig (1952); *ET*, 340-2; *CE*, 320, 327, 350; Cataldi (1988; 1993b); Gentili (1994); Maggiani (1995); Cavagnaro Vanoni (1996, 355-69); *Scataglini 2*, 155-63.

31. Pallottino (1937, 543).

32. Bonfante & Bonfante (2002, 149-51), with references.

33. Martelli (1975); Blanck (1983) with references.

34. Pairault Massa (1992, 130-3).

35. Bonfante & Bonfante (2002, 149).

36. See Dench (1995) for a general discussion.

37. Bocci (1960); *CE*, 320-2 (with bibliography).

38. Prag & Neave (1997, 172-200).

39. *Santuari*, 37-8; Cagianelli (1999, 110-20).

40. Pallottino (1937, 513-29, 542-5); Cavagnaro Vanoni (1996, 371-81); *Scataglini 2*, 165-7; Pallottino (1983) (bronze plaque).

41. Pallottino (1937, 523-9, 543-56); more recently, for example, Maggiani (2000a) with references.

42. For a general bibliography for painted tombs see Chapter 4 and: *CR*; Colonna (1984b). Recent works include: Torelli (1984); Cristofani (1987c); Morandi & Colonna (1996) (Orco); Steingräber (1988) (Festoons); Morandi (1987) (Shields); Pairault Massa (1988) (Giglioli); Maggiani (1998) (Meeting); Serra Ridgway (2000) (Anina).

43. The eighteenth-century copies (see Chapter 1) of some Hellenistic tombs had added expressions of anguish to the deceased (thereby influencing interpretation by modern scholars). See Morandi (1983) for the Cardinal tomb.

44. Jannot (1997) for discussion.

45. Translation by Jackson Knight (Penguin Books, 1956), For Sisyphus, see Roncalli (1996).

46. Serra Ridgway (2000, 310-13).

47. Romanelli (1948); Pelagatti (1989); Fontaine (1994).

48. For traces of 'medieval' walls here, see Romanelli (1948, 200).

49. Pallottino (1937, 88); Cataldi (1994, 62); *TE*, 63-4.

50. Fontaine (1994).

51. Bonghi Jovino (1991, 183-6).

52. Romanelli (1948, 214-8); Stefani (1984); Cataldi (1993a).

53. Comella (1982). Traces of another shrine are recorded at Ortaccio on Monterozzi: *TE*, 20.

54. Pallottino (1937, 88-91); Romanelli (1948, 218-23).

55. Romanelli (1948); Massabò (1994, 70).

56. Romanelli (1948, 228); *Tarquinia 1*, 27-8, 208-9 (with references); Padovan (1999); and see Chapter 4.

57. Cataldi (1994) for speculation about a local boundary.

58. Pelagatti (1989, 298-9).

59. *ET*, 126-32; *Tarquinia 1*, 212-16, 224, for a synthesis.

60. Romanelli (1948, 255, fig. 42) is therefore erroneous.

61. See reconstructions in: *Santuari*, 70-2; following a slightly different proposal by Torelli (1975, 17-19); and, more recently, Bonghi Jovino (1997).

62. Goldberg (1985) for a different view; *ET*, 355-76; Cataldi (1993a); *TE*, 69-72.

63. *ET*, 357-60.

64. See, for example, Harris (1971) on the main issues; Pallottino (1937, 560).

65. Romanelli (1948, 202) thought a hypogeum on Civita to be late antique. For Etrusco-Roman tombs on Cretoncini, see Mandolesi & Pacciarelli (1990, 21).

66. Pallottino (1937, 98); Del Lungo (1999, 25) is unconvinced.

67. Torelli (1975).

68. Romanelli (1948, 257-8); Torelli (1975, 164); the idea that it was for oil is discounted by Papi (2000, 97).

69. Pallottino (1937, 92-5); *ET*, 40, 42; Del Lungo (1999, 48-50); Papi (2000, 159-62).

70. Pallottino (1937, 566-7); Papi (2000, 155-63).

71. Torelli (1975, 105-35), who notes that the presence of the *collegium* cannot be taken for granted. For a recent survey of Roman Tarquinia, see Papi (2000, 87-98).

72. Harris (1971, 284); Torelli (1969, 312-13).

73. Torelli (1975, 187).

74. Torelli (1975, 191-7). And Torelli (1997, 235) for Gravisca.

75. Torelli (1975, 150-8).

76. C. Rutilius Namatianus, *De Reditu Suo* 1.280-4 (my translation).

77. For Gravisca, see Chapter 4; also Del Lungo (1999) with references.

78. *Civita*, 7-26 (with references); Del Lungo (1999).

79. Cicerchia (1990).

Chronological Table

Year	Period/event	Tarquinia	Regional/related phenomena
3000 BC	COPPER AGE	2 chamber tombs on Monterozzi	Rinaldone culture
2200 BC	BRONZE AGE		Apennine culture
1200 BC	LATE BRONZE AGE	Protovillanovan phase	Urnfield burials in Europe
900 BC	IRON AGE	Residential clusters and burial grounds	Villanovan society
750 BC	ORIENTALISING	Urbanisation, rich burials, trade	Greek & Phoenician colonisation
580 BC	ARCHAIC	First painted tombs; Gravisca expanded	Tarquin dynasty in Rome
490 BC	CLASSICAL	Consolidation and competition	Conflict with Greeks, Celts, Romans
300-90 BC	HELLENISTIC	Scataglini cemetery	Roman expansion
281 BC?	Loss of independence, Roman conquest		
181 BC	Roman colonia founded at Gravisca		
90 BC	Tarquinia becomes a municipium, with Roman administration		
AD 161	Bath buildings sponsored by Tulli Varrones		
AD 238-44	Bath building restoration		
AD 409-11	Alaric's visigoths in the area		
AD 416	R. Namatianus observes Gravisca		
AD 504	Church at Gravisca mentioned		
ninth century	Records of four churches on Civita		
1006	Corneto a fortified town		
1307	Castellina (Civita) attacked by inhabitants of Corneto		

Bibliography

Abbreviations

Acque profonde = Bonghi Jovino, M. (ed.) 1999. *Acque profonde nel sottosuolo di Tarquinia Etrusca. Il 'progetto Tarquinia' e le cavità artificiali. Mostra fotografica e documentaria.* Tarquinia, Musis.

AC = Archeologia Classica.

AE = Barocchi, P. & Gallo, D. (eds) 1985. *L'Accademia etrusca.* Milan, Electa.

AJA = American Journal of Archaeology.

Architettura = Architettura etrusca nel Viterbese. Ricerche svedesi a San Giovenale e Acquarossa 1956-1986. Rome, De Luca (1986).

AT = Bonghi Jovino, M. & Chiaramonte Treré, C. (eds) 1987. *Tarquinia: ricerche, scavi e prospettive. Atti del Convegno Internazionale di Studi 'La Lombardia per gli Etruschi' (Milan 1986).* Milan, Edizioni ET.

BE = Bibliotheca Etrusca. Fonti letterarie e figurative tra XVIII e XIX secolo nella Bibliotheca dell'Istituto Nazionale di Archeologia e Storia dell'Arte. Rome, Istituto Poligrafico e Zecca dello Stato (1985).

BST = Bollettino della Società Tarquiniense d'Arte e Storia.

CE = Cristofani, M. (ed.) 1985. *Civiltà degli Etruschi (Firenze, Museo archeologico 1985).* Milan, Electa.

Ceramica = Martelli, M. (ed.) 1987. *La ceramica degli Etruschi. La pittura vascolare.* Novara, De Agostini.

CIE, 3,1 = Pandolfini Angeletti, M. 1982. *Corpus Inscriptionum Etruscarum, III,1. Inscriptiones in instrumento et Tarquiniis et in agro Tarquiniensi repertae.* Rome, CNR.

Civita = Del Lungo, S. (ed.) 1999. *La Civita di Tarquinia. Testimonianze di una città medievale rivale di Corneto.* Tarquinia, Regione Lazio, Comune di Tarquinia, Università Agraria.

CR = Steingräber, S. (ed.) 1984. *Catalogo ragionato della pittura etrusca.* Milan, Jaca Book.

CSE = Corpus Speculorum Etruscarum, vol. 1.1 (Great Britain).

DdA = Dialoghi di Archeologia.

DD = Pittura Etrusca. Disegni e documenti del XIX secolo dall'Archivio dell'Istituto Archeologico Germanico di Roma. Studi di Archeologia pubblicati dalla Soprintendenza Archeologica per l'Etruria meridionale, 2. Rome, De Luca (1986).

EC = Gli Etruschi e Cerveteri. (1980) Milan, Electa.

EE = Gli Etruschi e l'Europa. (1992) Milan, Fabbri editori.

EM = Camporeale, G. (ed.) 1985. *L'Etruria mineraria.* Milan, Electa.

EP = Lawrence, D.H. 1992. *Sketches of Etruscan Places.* Cambridge, Cambridge University Press.

Etruria Meridionale = Etruria Meridionale. Conoscenza, conservazione, fruizione. Atti del convegno, Viterbo, 29 novembre-1 dicembre 1985. (1988) Rome, Quasar.

ET = Bonghi Jovino, M. (ed.) 1986. *Gli Etruschi di Tarquinia.* Modena, Panini.

Bibliography

FE = Borsi, F. (ed.) 1985. *Fortuna degli Etruschi*. Milan, Electa.

Les Étrusques = Gualtier, F. & Briquel, D. (eds) 1997. *Les Étrusques. Les plus religieux des hommes (Actes du colloque internationale, Paris 1992)*. Paris, La documentation française.

MAT = *Materiali del Museo Archeologico Nazionale di Tarquinia*. Rome, Bretschneider.

MEFRA = *Mélanges de l'École Française de Rome, Antiquité*.

NS = *Atti dell'Accademia Nazionale dei Lincei. Notizie degli Scavi*.

Oro = Cristofani, M. & Martelli, M. (eds) 1983. *L'Oro degli Etruschi*. Novara, De Agostini.

ParP = *La Parola del Passato*.

PE = Rizzo, M.A. (ed.) 1989. *Pittura etrusca al Museo di Villa Giulia nelle foto di Takashi Okamura*. Rome, De Luca.

PP = Negroni Catacchio, N. (ed.) 1995. *Preistoria e protostoria in Etruria. Atti del secondo incontro di studi (Farnese 21-23 marzo 1993). Tipologia delle necropoli e rituali di deposizione. Ricerche e scavi*. Milan, Centro Studi di Preistoria e Archeologia.

Principi = *Principi etruschi tra Mediterraneo ed Europa*. (2000) Bologna, Marsiglio.

RM = *Mitteilungen des Deutschen Archäologischen Instituts. Römische Abteilungen*.

Santuari = Colonna, G. (ed.) 1985. *Santuari d'Etruria*. Milan, Electa.

Scataglini 1 = Serra Ridgway, F.R. 1996. *I corredi del Fondo Scataglini a Tarquinia*. Milan, Comune di Milano.

Scataglini 2 = Linington, R.E. & Serra Ridgway, F.R. 1997. *Lo scavo nel Fondo Scataglini a Tarquinia*. Milan, Comune di Milano.

SE = *Studi Etruschi*.

ST = *Studia Tarquiniensia, Archaeologia Perusina*, 9 (1988). Rome, Bretschneider.

Tarquinia 1 = Bonghi Jovino, M. & Chiaramonte Treré, C. (eds) 1997. *Tarquinia. Testimonianze archeologiche e ricostruzione storica. Scavi sistematici nell'abitato. Campagne 1982-88. Università degli Studi di Milano, Tarchna I*. Rome, Bretschneider.

Tarquinia 2 = Chiaramonte Treré, C. (ed.) 1999. *Tarquinia. Scavi sistematici nell'abitato. Campagne 1982-88. I materiali 1. Università degli Studi di Milano, Tarchna II*. Rome, Bretschneider.

TE = Moretti Sgubini, A.M. (ed.) 2001. *Tarquinia etrusca. Una nuova storia. Catalogo della mostra*. Rome, Bretschneider.

TF = Buranelli, F. (ed.) 1987. *La Tomba François di Vulci*. Rome, Quasar.

The Etruscans = Torelli, M. (ed.) 2000. *The Etruscans (Palazzo Grassi, Venice, exhibition volume)*. Milan, Bompiani.

TLE = Pallottino, M. (ed.) 1968. *Testimonia Linguae Etruscae*. Firenze, La Nuova Italia.

*

Åkerström, Å. 1981. Etruscan tomb painting – an art of many faces. *Opuscula Romana*, 13.1: 7-34.

Amman, P. 2001. Die Tomba del Barone. Überlegungen zu einem neuen ikonologischen Verständnis. *SE*, 64: 71-93.

Ampolo, C. 1976-77. Demarato. Osservazioni sulla mobilità sociale arcaica, *DdA*, 9-10: 333-45.

Bibliography

Arias, P.E. 1989. La pittura etrusca: problemi e metodi della ricerca archeologica. *Secondo Congresso Internazionale Etrusco (Firenze 1985), Atti, II*: 645-66. Rome, Bretschneider.

Avvolta, C. 1829. Le tombe di Tarquinia. *Annali dell'Instituto di Corrispondenza Archeologica*, 1: 91-101.

Baggieri, G. 2001. Le protesi dentarie etrusche in lega aurea. Archeometallurgia della biocompatibilità. *SE*, 64: 321-9.

Bagnasco Gianni, G. 1987. Ancora sulle epigrafi di Tarquinia. *AT*: 91-3.

—— 1996. *Oggetti iscritti di epoca orientalizzante in Etruria, Biblioteca di Studi Etruschi 30*. Florence, Olschki.

Banti, L. 1967. Disegni di tombe e monumenti etruschi fra il 1825 e il 1830: l'architetto Henri Labrouste. *SE*, 35: 575-93.

Barbieri, G. 1996. Le necropoli etrusco-romane di Poggio Giudio e Casale Merlani presso Viterbo. *Opuscula Romana*, 21: 7-51.

Barich, B., Bonadonna, F., Borgognini, S. & Parenti, R. 1968. Trovamenti eneolitici presso Tarquinia. *Origini*, 2: 173-246.

Barker, G. & Rasmussen, T. 2000. *The Etruscans*. Oxford, Blackwell.

Bartoli, F., Mallegni, F., & Vitiello, A. 1989-90. Indagini nutrizionali e odontostomatologiche per una definizione della dieta alimentare in un gruppo umano a cultura etrusca: gli inumati della necropoli dei Monterozzi di Tarquinia. *SE*, 56: 255-69.

Bartoloni, G. 1981. Nuovi dati sugli scavi comunali a Corneto-Tarquinia. *AC*, 38: 315-28.

—— 1989. *La cultura villanoviana. All'inizio della storia etrusca*. Rome, NIS.

Bartoloni, G. & Baglione, M.P. 1987. Elementi scultorei decorativi nelle tombe tarquiniesi del primo ellenismo. *AT*: 233-42.

Bartoloni, G., Buranelli, F., D'Atri, V. & De Santis, A. 1987. *Le urne a capanna rinvenute in Italia*. Rome, Bretschneider.

Bartoloni, G. & Delpino, F. 1970. Per una revisione critica della prima fase villanoviana di Tarquinia. In *Atti dell'Accademia Nazionale dei Lincei, Rendiconti*, 25: 217-61.

—— 1975. Un tipo di orciolo a lamelle metalliche. Considerazioni sulla prima fase villanoviana. *SE*, 43: 3-45.

Barzanò, A. 1998. In Tarquiniensi lacu magno Italiae duae insulae nemora circumferunt. In Aigner-Foresti, L. (ed.), *Die Integration der Etrusker und das Weiterwirken etruskischen Kulturgutes im republikanischen und kaiserzeitlichen Rom*: 215-27. Vienna, Österreichische Akademie der Wissenschaften.

Becker, M.J. 1993. Human skeletons from Tarquinia: a preliminary analysis of the 1989 Cimitero site excavations with inferences for the evaluation of Etruscan social classes. *SE*, 58: 211-48.

Bettini, C. 1987. La pittura tarquiniese: problematiche conservative e metodologie d'intervento. *AT*: 43-57.

Bietti Sestieri, A.M. 1992. *The Iron Age community of Osteria dell'Osa. A study of socio-political development in central Tyrrhenian Italy*. Cambridge, Cambridge University Press.

—— 1997. Italy in Europe in the Early Iron Age. *Proceedings of the Prehistoric Society*, 63: 371-402.

Bini, M.P., Caramella, G. & Buccioli, S. 1995. *I bronzi etruschi e romani. MAT, 13*.

Blanck, H. 1983. Le pitture del 'sarcofago del sacerdote' nel Museo Nazionale di Tarquinia. *DdA*, ser. 3,1: 79-84.

Bibliography

Blanck, H. & Weber-Lehmann, C. (eds) 1987. *Malerei der Etrusker in Zeichnungen des 19. Jahrhunderts*. Mainz am Rhein, Von Zabern.

Bocci, P. 1960. Il sarcofago tarquiniese delle Amazzoni al Museo Archeologico di Firenze. *SE*, 28: 109-25.

Boitani, F. 1992. Le ceramiche laconiche a Gravisca. In Pelagatti, P. & Stibbe, C.M. (eds), *Lakonikà. Ricerche e nuovi materiali di ceramica laconica. Bollettino d'Arte (supplement 1990)*, 64: 19-67.

Boitani, F. & Torelli, M. 1971. Gravisca (Tarquinia). Scavi nella città etrusca e romana. Campagne 1969 e 1970. *NS*, 25: 195-299.

——— 1999. Un nuovo santuario dell'*emporion* di Gravisca. In *La colonisation grecque en Méditerranée occidentale. Actes de la rencontre scientifique en hommage à Georges Vallet (Rome-Naples, 1995). Collections de l'École française de Rome, 251*: 93-101. Rome.

Bonfante, G. & Bonfante, L. 2002. *The Etruscan language. An introduction.* Manchester, Manchester University Press (2nd ed.).

Bonghi Jovino, M. 1987. Gli scavi nell'abitato di Tarquinia e la scoperta dei 'bronzi' in un preliminare inquadramento. *AT*: 59-77.

——— 1991. Osservazioni sui sistemi di costruzione a Tarquinia: tecniche locali ed impiego del 'muro a pilastri' fenicio. *AC*, 43: 171-91.

——— 1994. A proposito dei rapporti tra Sicilia, Magna Grecia e Etruria: la testimonianza archeologica dell'Ara della Regina di Tarquinia. *Atti del 33 Convegno di Studi sulla Magna Grecia, 'Magna Grecia, Etruschi, Fenici' (Taranto 1993)*: 433-69.

——— 1996. Scavi e soperte. Tarquinia. *SE*, 61: 454-6.

——— 1997. La phase archaïque de l'Ara della Regina à la lumière des recherches recentes. In *Les Étrusques*: 69-95.

Bradford, J. 1957. *Ancient landscapes. Studies in field archaeology.* London, Bell & Sons.

Brendel, O. 1995. *Etruscan art.* New Haven & London, Yale University Press (2nd ed.).

Briguet, M.F. 1988. Remarques sur les plaques de coffret de Tarquiniens du Musée du Louvre. *ST*: 7-11.

Briquel, D. 1984. *Les pélasges en Italie. Recherches sur l'histoire de la légende. École française de Rome (fascicule 252)*. Rome.

——— 1988. Une vision tarquinienne de Tarquin l'Ancient. *ST*: 13-32.

Bruni, S. 1986. *I lastroni a scala. MAT, 9*.

——— 1989. Note su un gruppo di oinochoai di bucchero con decorazione a stampo di produzione tarquiniese. *Annali, Archeologia e Storia Antica (Napoli)*, 11: 121-53.

——— 1994. Prima di Demarato. Nuovi dati sulla presenza di ceramiche greche e di tipo greco a Tarquinia durante la prima età orientalizzante. In *La presenza etrusca nella Campania meridionale, Atti delle giornate di studio, Salerno-Pontecagnano (1990)*: 293-328. Florence, Olschki.

——— 1995. Rituali funerari dell'aristocrazia tarquiniese durante la prima fase orientalizzante. In *Miscellanea in memoria di Giuliano Cremonesi*: 213-52. Pisa, Edizioni Ets.

Buranelli, F. 1983. *La necropoli villanoviana 'Le Rose' di Tarquinia.* Quaderni del centro di studio per l'archeologia etrusco-italica, 6. Rome, CNR.

Burdett, C. 1999. *Vincenzo Cardarelli and his contemporaries. Fascist politics and literary culture.* Oxford, Clarendon Press.

Bibliography

Cagianelli, C. 1999. *Bronzi a figura umana (Museo Gregoriano Etrusco, Cataloghi 5)*. Vatican City.

Camporeale, G. 1972. Buccheri a cilindretto di fabbrica tarquiniese. *SE*, 40: 115-49.

—— 2001. *Gli Etruschi fuori d'Etruria*. Verona, Arsenale editrice.

Campus, L. 1981. *Ceramica attica a figure nere. MAT, 2*.

Canciani, F. 1974. *Corpus Vasorum Antiquorum. Tarquinia, Museo Archeologico Nazionale, III*. Rome, Bretschneider.

Cassano, S.M. & Manfredini, A. 1978. Torrionaccio. Scavo di un abitato protostorico. *NS*, 32: 159-382.

Cataldi, M. 1987. La tomba dei demoni azzurri. *AT*: 37-42.

—— 1988. *I sarcofagi etruschi delle famiglie Partunu, Camna e Pulena (Museo Archeologico Nazionale di Tarquinia)*. Rome, Edizioni Procom.

—— 1993a. Terrecotte arcaiche e tardo-arcaiche da Tarquinia. In Rystedt, E., Wikander, C. & Wikander, Ö. (eds), *Deliciae Fictiles. Proceedings of the First International Conference on Central Italic Architectural Terracottas at the Swedish Institute in Rome (1990)*: 207-20. Stockholm.

—— 1993b. *Tarquinia*. Guide territoriali dell'Etruria meridionale. Rome, Quasar.

—— 1994. Nuova testimonianza di culto sulla Civita di Tarquinia. In Martelli, M. (ed.), *Tyrrhenoi Philotechnoi*: 61-8. Rome, GEI.

—— 1997. Il caso di Tarquinia. In Pelagatti, P. & Guzzo, P.G. (eds), *Antichità senza provenienza II. Atti del colloquio internazionale, 1997. Bollettino d'Arte (supplemento)*, 101-2: 85-94.

Catalli, F. 1987. *Le Monete. MAT, 10*.

—— 1988. La produzione monetaria tarquiniese. *ST*: 33-40.

Cavagnaro Vanoni, L. 1972. Sei tombe a camera nella necropoli dei Monterozzi, località Calvario. *NS*, 26: 148-94.

—— 1977. Sei tombe intatte nella necropoli dei Monterozzi in località Calvario. *NS*, 31: 157-210.

—— 1987. Tarquinia: aspetti inediti dei lavori della Fondazione Lerici nella necropoli dei Monterozzi. *AT*: 243-53.

—— 1996. *Tombe Tarquiniesi di età ellenistica (Studia Archaeologica 82)*. Rome, Bretschneider.

—— 1997. *Dromoi* non completati e l'utilizzo dello spazio nella necropoli dei Monterozzi. In *Etrusca et Italica. Scritti in ricordo di Massimo Pallottino*: 117-29. Pisa-Rome, Istituti Editoriali e Poligrafici Internazionali.

Cavagnaro Vanoni, L. & Serra Ridgway, F.R. 1989. *Vasi etruschi a figure rosse dagli scavi della Fondazione Lerici nella necropoli dei Monterozzi a Tarquinia*. Rome, Bretschneider.

Cerchiai, L. 1987. Sulle tombe 'del Tuffatore' e 'della Caccia e Pesca': proposta di lettura iconologica. *DdA*, Ser.3, 5.2: 113-23.

Chastel, A. 1959. L''Etruscan Revival' du XVe siècle. *Revue Archéologique*: 165-80.

Chiaramonte Treré, C. 1987. Altri dati dagli scavi alla Civita sugli aspetti cultuali e rituali. *AT*: 79-89.

Ciaghi, S. 1993. Appunti sulle terrecotte architettoniche dalla Civita di Tarquinia. In Rystedt, E., Wikander, C. & Wikander, Ö. (eds), *Deliciae Fictiles. Proceedings of the First International Conference on Central Italic Architectural Terracottas at the Swedish Institute in Rome (1990)*: 201-6. Stockholm.

Cicerchia, P. 1990. *Tarquinia, borgo medioevale*. Rome, Istituto Poligrafico e Zecca dello Stato.

Bibliography

Colonna, G. 1975. Firme archaiche di artefici nell'Italia centrale. *RM*, 82: 181-92.

—— 1978. Archeologia dell'età romantica in Etruria: i Campanari di Toscanella e la tomba dei Vipinana. *SE*, 46: 81-117.

—— 1984a. Apollon, les Étrusques et Lipara. *MEFRA*, 96: 557-78.

—— 1984b. Per una cronologia della pittura etrusca di età ellenistica. *DdA*, 3 ser.: 1-24.

—— 1984c. Le copie ottocentesche delle pitture etrusche e l'opera di Carlo Ruspi. In Morigi Govi, C. & Sassatelli, G. (eds), *Dalla stanza delle antichità al Museo Civico. Storia della formazione del Museo Civico archeologico di Bologna*: 375-9. Bologna, Grafis edizioni.

—— 1993. Strutture teatriformi in Etruria. In Thuillier, J-P. (ed.), *Spectacles sportifs et scéniques dans le monde étrusco-italique. Collection de l'École Française de Rome 172*: 321-47. Rome.

Comella, A. 1982. *Deposito votivo presso l'Ara della Regina. MAT, 4.*

Cornell, T.J. 1978. *Principes* of Tarquinia. *Journal of Roman Studies*, 68: 167-73.

—— 1995. *The beginnings of Rome. Italy and Rome from the Bronze Age to the Punic Wars (c. 1000-264 BC).* London, Routledge.

Corrucini, R. & Pacciani, E. 1991. Ortodonzia e occlusione dentale negli Etruschi. *SE*, 57: 189-94.

Cristofani, M. 1971. Appunti di epigrafia arcaica. *Annali della Scuola Normale Superiore di Pisa*, 3, 1.1: 295-9.

—— 1976. Storia dell'arte e acculturazione: le pitture tombali arcaiche di Tarquinia. *Prospettiva*, 7: 2-10.

—— 1983. *La scoperta degli Etruschi. Archeologia e antiquaria nel '700.* Rome, CNR.

—— 1987a. Ancora sul cosidetto specchio di Tarchon. *Prospettiva*, 51: 46-8.

—— 1987b. Il banchetto in Etruria. In *L'alimentazione nel mondo antico*: 123-32. Rome, Istituto Poligrafico e Zecca dello Stato.

—— 1987c. Pittura funeraria e celebrazione della morte: il caso della tomba dell'orco. *AT*: 191-202.

d'Agostino, B. 1983. L'immagine, la pittura e la tomba nell'Etruria arcaica. *Prospettiva*, 32: 2-11.

—— 1989. Image and society in Archaic Etruria. *Journal of Roman Studies*, 89: 1-10.

—— 1990. Military organisation and social structure in archaic Etruria. In Murray, O. & Price, S. (eds), *The Greek city from Homer to Alexander*: 59-82. Oxford, Clarendon Press.

d'Agostino, B. & Cerchiai, L. 1999. *Il mare, la morte, l'amore. Gli Etruschi, i Greci e l'immagine.* Rome, Donzelli.

Dasti, L. 1878. *Notizie storiche archeologiche di Tarquinia e Corneto.* Rome.

D'Atri, V. 1977. La necropoli delle Arcatelle: dati inediti sul villanoviano tarquiniese. *AC*, 29: 1-16.

De Angelis, D. 2001. *La ceramica decorata di stile 'villanoviano' in Etruria meridionale.* Regione Lazio, Rubbettino.

De Grummond, N.T. 1986. Rediscovery. In Bonfante, L. (ed.), *Etruscan life and afterlife. A handbook of Etruscan studies*: 18-46. Detroit, Wayne State University Press.

De La Genière, J. 1987. Rituali funebri e produzione di vasi. *AT*: 203-8.

Del Lungo, S. 1999. Insediamenti della bassa valle del Marta. *BST*, 28: 23-73.

Delpino, F. 1984. Sulla presenza di oggetti 'enotri' in Etruria: la tomba Poggio

Bibliography

Impiccato 6 di Tarquinia. In *Studi in onore di G. Maetzke*: 257-71. Rome, Bretschneider.

———— 1989. L'ellenizzazione dell'Etruria villanoviana: sui rapporti tra Grecia ed Etruria fra IX e VIII secolo A.C. *Secondo Congresso Internazionale Etrusco (Firenze 1985), Atti, I*: 105-16. Rome, Bretschneider.

———— 1991. Documenti sui primi scavi nel sepolcreto arcaico delle Arcatelle a Tarquinia. *AC*, 43: 123-51.

———— 1995. Strutture tombali nell'Etruria meridionale villanoviana. In *PP*: 217-24.

Dench, E. 1995. *From barbarians to new men. Greek, Roman, and modern perceptions of peoples of the central Apennines*. Oxford, Clarendon Press.

Dennis, G. 1878. *The cities and cemeteries of Etruria* (2nd ed.). London, John Murray.

Di Gennaro, F. 1986. *Forme di insediamento tra Tevere e Fiora tra l'età del bronzo e l'età del ferro*. Firenze, Olschki.

———— 1988. Il popolamento dell'Etruria meridionale e le caratteristiche degli insediamenti tra l'età del bronzo e l'età del ferro. *Etruria Meridionale*: 59-82.

Domanico, L. 1995. Le strutture tombali del bronzo finale in Etruria: analisi e osservazioni. In *PP*: 127-45.

Fantini, B., Bianchi, V., Catirchio, V., Conti, P. & Tedole, R. 1988. La malaria nell'Etruria meridionale. *Etruria Meridionale*: 83-6.

Ferrari, G. 1988. *I vasi attici a figure rosse del periodo arcaico. MAT, 11*.

Fletcher, I. & Stokes, J. (eds) 1984. *Degeneration and regeneration. Texts of the premodern era*. New York & London, Garland Publishing.

Fontaine, P. 1994. Tarquinia. L'enceinte et la porte nord. Contribution à l'architecture militaire étrusque. *Archäologischer Anzeiger*: 73-86.

Fornaciari, G. & Mallegni, F. 1987. Il bambino della Civita: un caso di probabile aneurisma venoso del IX secolo a.C. *AT*: 95-8.

Frau, B. 1982. *Gli antichi porti di Tarquinia*. Rome, Gruppo Archeologico Romano.

Fugazzola Delpino, M.A. 1988. Le acque interne: appunti di archeologia preistorica. *Etruria Meridionale*: 17-25.

Gentili, M.D. 1994. *I sarcofagi etruschi in terracotta di età recente*. Rome, Bretschneider.

Gianfrotta, P. 1988. Le coste, i porti, la pesca. *Etruria Meridionale*: 11-15.

Ginge, B. 1987. *Ceramiche etrusche a figure nere. MAT, 12*.

Goldberg, M.Y. 1985. The Ara della Regina: emblem of Tarquinian power. *RM*, 92: 107-25.

Gran-Aymerich, J.M.J. 1988. Le bucchero de Tarquinia et quelques vases conserves au Musée du Louvre. *ST*: 41-51.

Gras, M. 1987. Tarquinia e il mare in età arcaica. *AT*: 141-52.

Hamilton Gray, Mrs. E.C. 1841. *Tour to the sepulchres of Etruria in 1839*. London, Hatchard (2nd ed.).

Harari, M. 1992. Etruscan art: from difference to duality (and beyond). *Accordia Research Papers*, 3: 101-6.

Harris, W.H. 1971. *Rome in Etruria and Umbria*. Oxford, Clarendon Press.

———— 1989. Invisible cities: the beginnings of Etruscan urbanization. *Secondo Congresso Internazionale Etrusco (Firenze 1985), Atti, I*: 375-92. Rome, Bretschneider.

Haynes, S. 2000a. *Etruscan civilization. A cultural history*. Los Angeles, J. Paul Getty Trust.

———— 2000b. Etruria Britannica. In Ridgway, D. *et al.* (eds), *Ancient Italy in its*

Mediterranean setting. Studies in honour of Ellen Macnamara. Accordia Specialist Studies on the Mediterranean 4: 319-25. London, Accordia Research Institute.

Hencken, H. 1968a. *Tarquinia, Villanovans and early Etruscans.* American School of Prehistoric Research, Peabody Museum, Harvard University, Bulletin 23. Cambridge, Mass.

—— 1968b. *Tarquinia and Etruscan origins.* London, Thames & Hudson.

Herbig, R. 1952. *Die jüngeretruskischen Steinsarkophage.* Berlin, Verlag Gebr.Mann.

Heurgon, J. 1964. *Daily life of the Etruscans.* London, Weidenfeld & Nicolson.

Hus, A. 1976. Stendhal et les Étrusques. In *Mélanges offerts à Jacques Heurgon*: 437-69. Rome, École Française de Rome.

—— 1980. *Les Étrusques et leur destin.* Paris, Picard.

Iaia, C. 1995. Simbolismo funerario e organizzazione sociale a Tarquinia nelle fasi iniziali dell'età del ferro. In *PP*: 249-56.

—— 1999a. *Simbolismo funerario e ideologia, alle origini di una civiltà urbana. Forme rituali nelle sepolture 'villanoviane' a Tarquinia e Vulci, e nel loro entroterra.* (Grandi contesti e problemi della protostoria italiana, 3). Florence, All'Insegna del Giglio.

—— 1999b. Le Arcatelle di Tarquinia: dati ed ipotesi sull'organizzazione planimetrica della necropoli protostorica. *BST*, 28: 5-21.

Iaia, C. & Mandolesi, A. 1993. Topografia dell'insediamento dell'VIII secolo a.C. in Etruria meridionale. *Journal of Ancient Topography, III*: 17-48.

Iaia, C., Mandolesi, A. & Pacciarelli, M. 1998. Tarquinia. Scavo di un settore dell'abitato 'villanoviano' in località Poggio Cretoncini. *Atti dell'incontro di studio, preistoria e protostoria in Etruria, III*: 481-8. Florence.

Izzet, V. 1998. Holding a mirror to Etruscan gender. In Whitehouse, R.D. (ed.), *Gender and Italian archaeology. Challenging the stereotypes. Accordia Specialist Studies on Italy 7*: 209-27. London, Accordia Research Institute.

Jannot, J.-R. 1982. La tombe de la Mercareccia a Tarquinia. *Revue Belge de Philologie e d'Histoire*, 60: 100-35.

—— 1988. À propos de la tombe du lit funèbre. *ST*: 53-67.

—— 1993. Phersu, phersuna, persona. In Thuillier, J-P. (ed.), *Spectacles sportifs et scéniques dans le monde etrusco-italique. Collection de l'École Française de Rome, 172*: 281-320. Rome.

—— 1997. Charu(n) et Vanth, divinités plurielles? In *Les Étrusques*: 139-66.

Johnston, A. & Pandolfini, M. 2000. *Gravisca. Scavi nel santuario greco, 15. Le iscrizioni.* Bari, Edipuglia.

Jucker, H. 1969. Ein protokorinthischer Becher mit etruskischer Inschrift. *SE*, 37: 501-5.

Judson, S. & Hemphill, P. 1981. Sizes of settlements in southern Etruria, 6th-5th centuries BC. *SE*, 49: 193-202.

Kilian, K. 1977. Das Kriegergrab von Tarquinia. *Jahrbuch des Deutschen Archäologischen Instituts*, 92: 24-98.

Lambrechts, R. 1978. *Les miroirs étrusques et prenestins des Musées Royaux d'Art et d'Histoire à Bruxelles.* Bruxelles, Musées Royaux d'Art et d'Histoire.

Leighton, R. & Castelino, C. 1990. Thomas Dempster and ancient Etruria: a review of the autobiography and *De Etruria Regali. Papers of the British School at Rome*, 58: 337-52.

Lewis, S. 2003. Representation and reception. Athenian pottery in its Italian context. In Wilkins, J.B. & Herring, E. (eds), *Inhabiting symbols. Symbol and*

Bibliography

image in the ancient Mediterranean. Accordia Specialist Studies in the Mediterranean 5: 175-92. London, Accordia Research Institute.

Linington, R.E. 1980. La funzione dei lastroni scolpiti di Tarquinia. *MEFRA*, 92: 625-39.

—— 1982a. Tarquinia, località Calvario, recenti interventi nella zona dell'abitato protostorico. In Caporali, G.B. & Sgubini Moretti, A.M. (eds), *Archeologia della Tuscia, 1, incontro di studio 1980*: 117-23. Rome, CNR.

—— 1982b. Il villaggio protostorico nella località Calvario sui Monterozzi a Tarquinia. In *Studi in onore di F. Rittatore Vonwiller*: 245-56. Como, Malinverno.

Linington, R.E., Delpino, F. & Pallottino, M. 1978. Alle origini di Tarquinia: scoperta di un abitato villanoviano sui Monterozzi. *SE*, 46: 3-23.

Maggiani, A. 1995. Sulla cronologia dei sarcofagi etruschi in terracotta di età ellenistica. A proposito di una recente monografia. *Rivista di Archeologia*, 19: 75-91.

—— 1996. Un programma figurativo alto arcaico a Tarquinia. *Rivista di Archeologia*, 20: 5-37.

—— 1997. Réflexions sur la religion étrusque 'primitive': de l'époque villanovienne à l'époque archaïque. In *Les Étrusques*: 431-47.

—— 1998. Appunti sulle magistrature etrusche. *SE*, 62: 95-138.

—— 2000a. Republican political forms. In *The Etruscans*: 227-41.

—— 2000b. Aspetti del linguaggio figurativo tardo-orientalizzante a Tarquinia: dalla metafora al simbolo. In Prayon, F. & Röllig, W. (eds), *Akten des Koloquiums zum thema Der Orient und Etrurien zum Phänomen des 'Orientalisierens' im westlichen Mittelmeeraum (10-6 Jh.v.Ch.), Tübingen 1997*: 253-61. Pisa-Rome, Istituti editoriali e poligrafici internazionali.

Mallegni, F. 1991. Un caso di iperostosi frontale interna in uno scheletro umano di Tarquinia del III secolo a.C. *SE*, 57: 195-200.

Mallegni, F., Fornaciari, G., Tarabella, N. 1980. Studio antropologico dei resti scheletrici della necropoli dei Monterozzi (Tarquinia). *Atti della Società Toscana di Scienze Naturali, Memorie, Ser. B. (1979)*, 86: 185-221.

Mandolesi, A. 1994. Ricerche di superficie relative alla prima età del ferro nell'area di Tarquinia e nel territorio immediatamente circostante. In *La presenza etrusca nella Campania meridionale, Atti delle giornate di studio, Salerno-Pontecagnano 16-18 novembre 1990*: 329-39. Florence, Olschki.

—— 1999. *La 'Prima' Tarquinia. L'insediamento protostorico sulla Civita e nel territorio circostante.* (Grandi contesti e problemi della protostoria italiana, 2). Florence, All'Insegna del Giglio.

Mandolesi, A. & Pacciarelli, M. 1990. Poggio Cretoncini: nuove evidenze sullo sviluppo dell'abitato di Tarquinia antica. *BST*, 19: 5-26.

Marchese, L. 1944-45. Tarquinia. Tombe etrusche e romane in località Monterozzi ai Primi Archi. *NS*, 5-6: 7-22.

Markussen, E.P. 1979. *Painted tombs in Etruria: a bibliography*. Odense.

Martelli, M. 1975. Un aspetto del commercio di manufatti artistici nel IV sec.a.C.: i sarcofagi in marmo. *Prospettiva*, 3: 9-17.

—— 1981. Un askos del museo di Tarquinia e il problema delle presenze nord-ioniche in Etruria. *Prospettiva*, 27: 2-14.

—— 1985. Gli avori tardo-arcaici: botteghe e aree di diffusione. In *Il commercio etrusco arcaico. Atti dell'incontro di studio (1983)*: 207-48. Rome, CNR.

Massabò, B. 1994. Recenti scavi e ricerche sul sito urbano di Tarquinia. In Martelli, M. (ed.), *Tyrrhenoi Philotechnoi*: 69-74. Rome, GEI.

Bibliography

Micali, G. 1832. *Monumenti per servire alla storia degli antichi popoli italiani.* Florence.

Michaelis, A. 1908. *A century of archaeological discoveries.* London, John Murray.

Moltesen, M. & Weber-Lehmann, C. 1991. *Catalogue of the copies of Etruscan tomb paintings in the Ny Carlsberg Glyptotek.* Copenhagen.

Montelius, O. 1904. *La civilisation primitive en Italie depuis l'introduction des metaux (part II, plates).* Stockholm.

Morandi, A. 1983. *Le pitture della Tomba del Cardinale.* Monumenti della pittura antica scoperti in Italia, I. Rome, Istituto poligrafico e zecca dello Stato, CNR.

—— 1987. La tomba degli scudi di Tarquinia. *MEFRA*, 99: 95-110.

Morandi, M. 1995. Novità sui Velcha di Tarquinia. *AC*, 47: 267-88.

Morandi, M. & Colonna, G. 1996. La *gens* titolare della tomba tarquiniese dell'Orco. *SE*, 61: 95-102.

Musti, D. 1987. Etruria e Lazio arcaico nella tradizione (Demarato, Tarquinio, Mezenzio). *Quaderni del centro di studio per l'archeologia etrusco-italica. Etruria e Lazio arcaico. Atti dell'incontro di studio (novembre 1986)*, 15: 139-53. Rome, CNR.

Naccarato, V. 2000. *Cronaca degli scavi archeologici a Tarquinia dal 1862 al 1880. L'opera di Luigi Dasti.* Comune di Tarquinia, Quaderni della Biblioteca e dell'Archivio Storico Comunale, Tarquinia.

Naso, A. 1996a. Osservazioni sull'origine dei tumuli monumentali nell'Italia centrale. *Opuscula Romana*, 20: 69-85.

—— 1996b. *Architetture dipinte. Decorazioni parietali non figurate nelle tombe a camera dell'Etruria Meridionale (VII-V sec.a.C.).* Bibliotheca Archaeologica, 18. Rome, Bretschneider.

Oakley, S.P. 1998. *A commentary on Livy books VI-X.* Oxford, Clarendon Press.

Pacciarelli, M. 1994. Sviluppi verso l'urbanizzazione nell'Italia tirrenica protostorica. In *La presenza etrusca nella Campania meridionale, Atti delle giornate di studio, Salerno-Pontecagnano, novembre 1990*: 227-53. Florence.

—— 2000. *Dal villaggio alla città. La svolta protourbana del 1000 a.C. nell'Italia tirrenica.* (Grandi contesti e problemi della protostoria italiana, 4). Florence, All'Insegna del Giglio.

Padovan, G. 1999. Il sottosuolo percorso: le opere cunicolari della Civita di Tarquinia. *BST*, 28: 75-121.

Pairault Massa, F-H. 1988. La tombe Giglioli ou l'espoir déçu de Vel Pinie. Un tournant dans la société étrusque. *ST*: 69-100.

—— 1992. *Iconologia e politica nell'Italia antica. Roma, Lazio, Etruria dal VII al 1 secolo a.C.* Milan, Longanesi.

—— 1996. *La cité des Étrusques.* Paris, CNRS.

—— 2001. La tombe des Lionnes à Tarquinia. Emporion, cultes et société. *SE*, 64: 43-70.

Pallottino, M. 1930. Uno specchio di Tuscania e la leggenda etrusca di Tarchon. *Rendiconti della Reale Accademia Nazionale dei Lincei. Classe di scienze morali, storiche e filologiche*, 6: 49-87.

—— 1937. Tarquinia. *Monumenti Antichi dei Lincei*, 36.

—— 1983. Presentazione di due iscrizioni etrusche. *SE*, 51: 609-14.

Palmieri, A. 2001. Alle origini del bucchero. Contributo al riconoscimento di una fase sperimentale della produzione tarquiniese. *Archeologia Classica*, 52: 175-89.

Panofsky, E. 1964. The mouse that Michelangelo failed to carve. In Freeman

Bibliography

Sandler, L. (ed.), *Essays in Memory of Karl Lehmann*: 242-51. Locust Valley, New York, J.J. Augustin.

Papi, E. 2000. *L'Etruria dei Romani*. Rome, Quasar.

Pelagatti, P. 1987. Indagini recenti a Tarquinia a cura della Soprintendenza Archeologica per l'Etruria meridionale. *AT*: 33-5.

—— 1989. Ricerche territoriali e urbanistiche in Etruria meridionale. *Secondo Congresso Internazionale Etrusco (Firenze 1985), Atti, I*: 293-301. Rome, Bretschneider.

Pelfer, G. 1998. Evoluzione del paleoambiente lagunare nella pianura costiera di Tarquinia fra i fiumi Mignone e Marta. *BST*, 27: 5-36.

Perkins, P. 1999. *Etruscan settlement, society and material culture in central coastal Etruria. BAR International Series 788*. Oxford.

Perkins, P. & Walker, L. 1990. Survey of an Etruscan city at Doganella in the Albegna valley. *Papers of the British School at Rome*, 58: 1-143.

Perticarari, L. & Giuntani, A.M. 1986. *I segreti di un tombarolo*. Milan, Rusconi.

Pianu, G. 1980. *Ceramiche etrusche a figure rosse. MAT, 1.*

—— 1982. *Ceramiche etrusche sovradipinte. MAT, 3.*

—— 1988. Ceramiche etrusche sovradipinte di Tarquinia: un addendum. *ST*: 101-7.

Pierro, E. 1984. *Ceramiche ioniche non figurate e coppe attiche a figure nere. MAT, 6.*

Prag, J. & Neave, R. 1997. *Making faces using forensic and archaeological evidence*. London, British Museum Press.

Rallo, A. (ed.) 1989. *Le donne in Etruria*. Rome, Bretschneider.

Rasmussen, T. 1997. The Tarquins and 'Etruscan Rome'. In Cornell, T. & Lomas, K. (eds), *Gender and ethnicity in ancient Italy. Accordia Specialist Studies in Italy, 6*: 23-30. London, Accordia Research Institute.

Rendeli, M. 1993. *Città aperte. Ambiente e paesaggio rurale organizzato nell'Etruria meridionale costiera durante l'età orientalizzante e arcaica*. Rome, GEI.

Renfrew, C. 1986. Peer polity interaction and socio-political change. In Renfrew, C. & Cherry, J.F. (eds), *Peer polity interaction and socio-political change*: 1-18. Cambridge, Cambridge University Press.

Rhodes, D.E. 1973. *Dennis of Etruria. The life of George Dennis*. London, C. & A. Woolf.

Ricci Portoghesi, L. 1968. Sopra alcuni vasi geometrici a decorazione bicroma provenienti dalla necropoli di Tarquinia. *SE*, 36: 309-18.

Ricks, C. (ed.) 1969. *The poems of Tennyson*. London, Longman.

Ridgway, D. 1989. Jame Byres and the ancient state of Italy: unpublished documents in Edinburgh. *Secondo Congresso Internazionale Etrusco (Firenze 1985), Atti, I*: 213-29. Rome, Bretschneider.

—— 1997. Nestor's cup and the Etruscans. *Oxford Journal of Archaeology*, 16: 325-44.

Ridley, R.T. 2000. *The pope's archaeologist. The life and times of Carlo Fea*. Rome, Quasar.

Romanelli, P. 1948. Tarquinia. Scavi e ricerche nell'area della città. *NS*, ser. 8, vol. 2: 193-270.

Roncalli, F. 1996. Laris Pulenas and Sisyphus: mortals, heroes, and demons in the Etruscan underworld. *Etruscan Studies*, 3: 45-62.

—— 1997. Iconographie funéraire et topographie de l'au-delà en Étrurie. In *Les Étrusques*: 37-54.

Rouveret, A. 1988. Espace sacré/espace pictural: une hypothèse sur quelques peintures archaïques de Tarquinia. *Annali dell'Istituto Orientale, Napoli*, 10: 203-16.

Ruby, P. 1993. Tarquinia entre la Grèce et Sala Consilina. Éléments pour l'étude de la circulation des biens de prestige dans l'Italie centrale et méridionale protohistorique. *MEFRA*, 105: 779-832.

Sagar, K. 1985. *D.H. Lawrence: life into art*. Harmondsworth, Penguin Books.

Sassatelli, G. 1984. La 'Galleria della pitture etrusca' nel salone X. In Morigi Govi, C. & Sassatelli, G. (eds), *Dalla stanza delle antichità al Museo Civico. Storia della formazione del Museo Civico archeologico di Bologna*: 365-74. Bologna, Grafis edizioni.

Serra Ridgway, F.R. 2000. The tomb of the Anina family. In Ridgway, D. *et al.* (eds), *Ancient Italy in its Mediterranean setting. Studies in honour of Ellen Macnamara. Accordia Specialist Studies on the Mediterranean, 4*: 301-16. London, Accordia Research Centre.

Slaska, M. 1985. Le anfore da trasporto a Gravisca. In *Il commercio etrusco arcaico. Atti dell'incontro di studio (Roma 1983). Quaderni del centro di studio per l'archeologia etrusco-italica*: 19-21. Rome, CNR.

Small, J.P. 1971. The banquet frieze from Poggio Civitate (Murlo). *SE*, 39: 25-61.

——— 1994. Eat, drink and be merry: Etruscan banquets. In de Puma, R. & Small, J.P. (eds), *Murlo and the Etruscans*: 85-94. Wisconsin, University of Wisconsin Press.

Sordi, M. 1987. Tarquinia e Roma. *AT*: 159-69.

——— 1991. Laris Felsnas e la resistenza di Casilino. *SE*, 56: 123-5.

Spivey, N. 1987. *The Micali painter and his followers*. Oxford, Clarendon Press.

——— 1991. Greek vases in Etruria. In Rasmussen, T. & Spivey, S. (eds), *Looking at Greek Vases*: 131-50. Cambridge, Cambridge University Press.

——— 1997. *Etruscan art*. London, Thames and Hudson.

Spivey, N. & Stoddart, S. 1990. *Etruscan Italy. An archaeological history*. London, Batsford.

Springer, C. 1987. *The marble wilderness. Ruins and representation in Italian romanticism, 1775-1850*. Cambridge, Cambridge University Press.

Stefani, G. 1984. *Terrecotte figurate. MAT, 7*.

Steingräber, S. 1988. Die Tomba dei festoni in Tarquinia und die Deckenmalereien der jüngeren etruskischen Kammergräber. *Jahrbuch des Deutschen Archäologischen Instituts*, 103: 217-45.

Supino, P. 1969. La 'Margarita Cornetana', Regesto dei documenti (Miscellanea della Società Romana di Storia Patria*. Rome.

Szilagyi, J.G. 1972. Le fabbriche di ceramiche etrusco-corinzia a Tarquinia. *SE*, 40: 19-73.

——— 1981. Impletae modis saturae. *Prospettiva*, 24: 2-23.

Thuillier, J.-P. 1985. *Les jeux athlétiques dans la civilisation étrusque. École française de Rome (fascicule 256)*. Rome.

Toms, J. 1992-93. Symbolic expression in Iron Age Tarquinia: the case of the biconical urn. *Hamburger Beiträge zur Archäologie*, 19-20: 139-61.

——— 1998. The construction of gender in Early Iron Age Etruria. In Whitehouse, R.D. (ed.), *Gender and Italian archaeology. Challenging the stereotypes. Accordia Specialist Studies on Italy, 7*: 157-79. London, Accordia Research Institute.

Torelli, M. 1969. Senatori etruschi della tarda repubblica e dell'impero. *DdA*, 3: 285-363.

——— 1971. Il santuario di Hera a Gravisca. *ParP*, 136: 44-67.

Bibliography

———— 1975. *Elogia Tarquiniensia*. Florence, Sansoni.

———— 1977. Il santuario greco di Gravisca. *ParP*, 32: 398-458.

———— 1981. *Storia degli Etruschi*. Bari, Laterza.

———— 1982. Per la definizione del commercio greco-orientale: il caso di Gravisca. *ParP*, 37: 304-25.

———— 1984. Ideologia e rappresentazione nelle tombe tarquiniesi dell'Orco I e II. *DdA*, ser. 3,1: 7-17.

———— 1987. Appunti per una storia di Tarquinia. *AT*: 129-40.

———— 1988. 'Etruria principes disciplinam doceto'. Il mito normativo dello specchio di Tuscania. *ST*: 109-18.

———— 1997a. *Il rango, il rito e l'immagine. Alle origini della rappresentazione storica romana*. Milan, Electa.

———— 1997b. Les Adonies de Gravisca. Archéologie d'une fête. In *Les Étrusques*: 233-91.

Tronchetti, C. 1983. *Ceramica attica a figure nere. Grandi vasi – Anfore, Pelikai, Crateri. MAT, 5*.

Tuck, A.S. 1994. The Etruscan seated banquet in Villanovan ritual and Etruscan iconography. *AJA*, 98: 617-28.

Vickers, M. 1985-86. Imaginary Etruscans: changing perceptions of Etruria since the fifteenth century. *Hephaistos*, 7-8: 153-68.

Walberg, G. 1986. The Tomb of the Baron reconsidered. *SE*, 54: 51-9.

Weber-Lehmann, C. 1985. Spätarchäische Gelagebilder in Tarquinia. *RM*, 92: 19-44.

Weiss, R. 1988. *The Renaissance discovery of classical antiquity* (2nd ed.). Oxford, Blackwell.

Wood, J.R. 1980. The myth of Tages. *Latomus*, 39: 325-44.

———— 1981. The Etrusco-Latin *Liber Tageticus* in Lydus' *De Ostentis. Museum Philologum Londiniense*, 5: 94-125.

Zifferero, A. 1995. Rituale funerario e formazione delle aristocrazie nell'Etruria protostorica: osservazioni sui corredi femminili e infantili di Tarquinia. In *PP*: 257-65.

Index

211